Constitutionalism and the Paradox of Principles and Rules

OXFORD CONSTITUTIONAL THEORY

Series Editors

MARTIN LOUGHLIN
JOHN P MCCORMICK
NEIL WALKER

Oxford Constitutional Theory has rapidly established itself as the primary point of reference for theoretical reflections on the growing interest in constitutions and constitutional law in domestic, regional, and global contexts. The majority of the works published in the series are monographs that advance new understandings of their subject. But the series aims to provide a forum for further innovation in the field by also including well-conceived edited collections that bring a variety of perspectives and disciplinary approaches to bear on specific themes in constitutional thought and by publishing English translations of leading monographs in constitutional theory that have originally been written in languages other than English.

ALSO AVAILABLE IN THE SERIES

Constituent Power in the European Union
Markus Patberg

Religion, Law, and Democracy
Selected Writings
Ernst-Wolfgang Böckenförde
Edited by Mirjam Künkler and Tine Stein

Constituent Power and the Law
Joel Colón-Ríos

Euroconstitutionalism and its Discontents
Oliver Gerstenberg

Beyond the People
Social Imaginary and Constituent Imagination
Zoran Oklopcic

The Metaethics of Constitutional Adjudication
Bosko Tripkovic

Carl Schmitt's State and Constitutional Theory
A Critical Analysis
Benjamin A Schupmann

Law and Revolution
Legitimacy and Constitutionalism after the Arab Spring
Nimer Sultany

Unconstitutional Constitutional Amendments
The Limits of Amendment Powers
Yaniv Roznai

Constitutional and Political Theory
Selected Writings
Ernst-Wolfgang Böckenförde
Edited by Mirjam Künkler and Tine Stein

Constitutionalism
Past, Present, and Future
Dieter Grimm

Europe's Functional Constitution
A Theory of Constitutional Beyond the State
Turkuler Isiksel

Post Sovereign Constitution Making
Learning and Legitimacy
Andrew Arato

Popular Sovereignty in Early Modern Constitutional Thought
Daniel Lee

The Cultural Defense of Nations
A Liberal Theory of Majority Rights
Liav Orgad

The Cosmopolitan Constitution
Alexander Somek

The Structure of Pluralism
Victor M Muniz-Fraticelli

Constitutional Courts and Deliberative Democracy
Conrado Hübner Mendes

Fault Lines of Globalization
Legal Order and the Politics of A-Legality
Hans Lindahl

The Cosmopolitan State
H Patrick Glenn

After Public Law
Edited by Cormac Mac Amhlaigh, Claudio Michelon, Neil Walker

The Three Branches
A Comparative Model of Separation of Powers
Christoph Moellers

The Global Model of Constitutional Rights
Kai Möller

Constituting Economic and Social Rights
Katharine G Young

Constitutionalism and the Paradox of Principles and Rules

Between the Hydra and Hercules

MARCELO NEVES

OXFORD
UNIVERSITY PRESS

OXFORD
UNIVERSITY PRESS

Great Clarendon Street, Oxford, OX2 6DP,
United Kingdom

Oxford University Press is a department of the University of Oxford. It furthers the University's objective of excellence in research, scholarship, and education by publishing worldwide. Oxford is a registered trade mark of Oxford University Press in the UK and in certain other countries

First Edition published in 2021

Impression: 1

Published in the United States of America by Oxford University Press
198 Madison Avenue, New York, NY 10016, United States of America

British Library Cataloguing in Publication Data

Data available

Library of Congress Control Number: 2020952611

ISBN 978–0–19–289874–6

DOI: 10.1093/oso/9780192898746.001.0001

Printed and bound by
CPI Group (UK) Ltd, Croydon, CR0 4YY

To Renato, Bernardo, and Elvira, with gratitude

Preface

In 2003, upon returning to Brazil after several years of research and teaching activities in Europe, I came across a wide audience surrounding the debate on principles and rules, balancing and optimization, theory of principles, constitutionalization of law, and related issues. Somewhat surprised, I observed that this language was not confined to the legal and constitutional theory but it expanded on legal doctrine and judicial practice without limits.

I tried to be attentive to the discussion. I started to observe that, with some exceptions, it was again an uncritical borrowing from foreign theoretical and doctrinal constructions without the selective assessment of a legally and constitutionally proper reception. It largely consisted in trivializing principle-based models consistently developed under legal contexts that are very different from the Brazilian experience. On the one hand, invoking (moral and legal) principles was presented as a panacea to solve all the ills of Brazilian legal and constitutional practice. On the other hand, the principle-overestimating rhetoric served the removal of clear and 'complete' rules in order to cover decisions oriented towards the satisfaction of particularistic interests. Thus, both genuinely idealistic and shrewdly strategic lawyers were capable of learning how to use successfully the pomp of principles and weighing, the trivialization of which lent to any argument, even the most absurd, a bit of respectability. All this, it seems to me, occurred to the detriment of a constitutionally consistent and socially adequate legal adjudication.

This situation has not changed substantially over the last few years. The judgment of the Direct Action of Unconstitutionality (ADI) No. 4,638/DF by the Brazilian Federal Supreme Court on 2 February 2012 provides a good example: a Justice appealed to the dignity of the human person and Ronald Dworkin's authority to justify maintaining in force provisions of the Organic Law of National Judiciary (LOMAN, issued by the military authoritarian government 1964–1985) which required secret trials in any case of judgment of a judge (Complementary Law No. 35/1979, Article 27.2 and 27.6, Article 45, Article 52.6, and Articles 54 and 55); he did not consider that this plea vehemently opposed clear constitutional rules introduced by Constitutional Amendment No. 45/2004 (Brazilian Federal Constitution, Article 93.IX and 93.X), which precisely aim to remove one of the privileges of the magistrates.

The judgment of the Direct Action of Unconstitutionality (ADI) No. 1856/RJ by the Brazilian Federal Supreme Court, on 26 May 2011, offers another example, somewhat more odd and unreasonable (the case was already being solved on the basis of the constitutional rule that forbids 'all practices which ... subject animal to cruelty'—Article 225.1.VII of the Brazilian Constitution): three justices call for 'human dignity' to characterize the unconstitutionality of a State statute that allows cockfighting.

Over time I have noticed that the issue could not be dealt with only in terms of uncritical and unreflexive reception of foreign legal and constitutional theory models in Brazil because it has involved a fascination with the rhetoric of the principles and balancing on a global scale. Thus I decided to challenge the worldwide dominant models of the theory of principles, critically focusing on the problematic Brazilian case only in Chapter 4 in this book.

Nevertheless, this study is not simply proposing a 'demystification' or, to use a fashionable term, a 'deconstruction' of the legal and constitutional theory, doctrine, and practice that, under the heading of principle, balancing, optimization, and related labels, have become not only dominant but also stifling over the three last decades. Despite taking as my object of criticism the abuse of principles in legal and constitutional theory, doctrine, and practice, I take the constitutional principles seriously, pointing to their complementary relationship and tension with the rules. Along this line, I shall face theories that before and today serve as a paradigm for discussion around legal or constitutional principles and rules, discussing them critically in order to offer an alternative theoretical model.

After giving some lectures on the subject and having the initial intention to write a paper on the issue, I decided, finally, on a more comprehensive project, writing a monograph on the theme, which resulted in this book. Its first edition was published in Portuguese in Brazil (São Paulo: WMF Martins Fontes, 2013). This English edition is not a mere translation. I revised many parts of the text and added new remarks, notes, and bibliographical references to the third Brazilian edition of 2019. I aimed to update the study invoking some new literature and presenting some explanations on issues that were not properly addressed earlier.

For the preparation and publication of the Brazilian edition and this English edition, I counted on the support of some institutions and people, the mention of which serves as a record of my gratitude.

In late June and early July 2010, I worked as a visiting research fellow at the Max Planck Institute for Comparative Public Law and International Law in Heidelberg. This research stay was instrumental for the development and completion of the first edition. In that time, I could again enjoy the excellent conditions of study offered by the Institute and participate in fruitful discussions with colleagues of various nationalities. I am grateful for the invaluable support that was given to me by the Director of the Institute, Armin von Bogdandy, and his colleagues and assistants.

During the period in which I was writing the first draft, Virgílio Afonso da Silva, Regis Dudena, Thales Costa, and André Rufino do Valle proposed and sent me relevant theoretical, doctrinal, and case-law materials. To these colleagues I register here my vote of thanks. I also am grateful to Vinicius Poli, Pedro Henrique Ribeiro, Paulo Leonesi Maluf, Octaviano Padovese, and Helena Bittencourt for the revision and proofreading of the first Brazilian edition.

This English edition is the result of two research stays abroad, first as a Visiting Senior Research Fellow at the Adam Smith Foundation in the College of Social Sciences at the University of Glasgow in 2014, second as a Senior Research Scholar at Yale Law School in 2015. I wish to thank Emilios Christodoulidis, Rosa Greaves, and Marco Goldoni for the enlightening conversations during my stay in Glasgow. I am also very grateful to Robert Post, Paul Kahn, Bruce Ackerman, Daniel Markovits, William Eskridge, and Alec Stone Sweet for opening the door for me to the excellent scholarly atmosphere at Yale.

I translated myself a number of extracts from foreign theoretical and doctrinal works as well as passages from foreign case law and legislation. In the bibliographical references I have mentioned any acceptable English translations located. The footnotes to many citations also include references to the corresponding pages in the English translations available to me. In some cases I have adapted these translations where appropriate. I am very grateful to Klébert Machado and Edvaldo Moita for the linguistic revision of this English version.

In drawing up the English edition, I was again fortunate to receive the inestimable encouragement of Elvira, Bernardo, and Renato. Hence the dedication!

Contents

Abbreviations

ADI	Ação Direta de Inconstitucionalidade [Direct Action of Unconstitutionality] (Brazil)
ADPF	Arguição de Descumprimento de Preceito Fundamental [Claim of Non-Compliance with a Fundamental Precept] (Brazil)
BFC	Brazilian Federal Constitution
BVerfGE	Entscheidungen des Bundesverfassungsgerichts [Decisions of the Federal Constitutional Court; official compilation of this German Court; the numbers placed after the abbreviation refer to the volume and first page of the judgment respectively]
cf.	confer [compare]
DJ	Diário da Justiça [Law Reports; official compilation of judgments handed down by Brazil's higher federal courts]
DJe	Diário da Justiça eletrônico [electronic version of Law Reports; official compilation of judgments handed down by Brazil's higher federal courts]
ed.	editor
edn	edition
eds	editors
Engl. trans.	English translation
esp.	especially
Ext.	Extradição [Extradition] (Brazil)
ff.	following pages
HC	Habeas Corpus (Brazil)
LOMAN	Lei Orgânica da Magistratura Nacional [Organic Law of National Judiciary] (Brazil)
Mercosur	Mercado Común del Sur [Southern Common Market]
MS	Mandado de Segurança [Writ of Mandamus] (Brazil)
p.	page
pp.	pages
RE	Recurso Extraordinário [Extraordinary Appeal] (Brazil)
STF	Supremo Tribunal Federal [Federal Supreme Court] (Brazil)
STJ	Superior Tribunal de Justiça [High Court of Justice] (Brazil)
TFP	Tradition, Family and Property
TP	Tribunal Pleno [Plenary; Brazilian Federal Supreme Court]
vol.	volume
vols	volumes

Introduction

Between Herculean Rules and Hydra-like Principles

According to the mythological narrative, Hercules,[1] in his second of twelve labours performed on behalf of his cousin Eurystheus, King of Mycenae, confronted the Hydra of Lerna. Dwelling in a swamp near Lake Lerna, in Argos, the Hydra was a monstrous snake-like, multi-headed beast (sometimes described as having human heads),[2] which destroyed herds and harvests, and whose breath was lethal to those who neared her. Hercules fought the Hydra with flaming arrows or, according to a variant narrative of the legend, by cutting off her heads with a sword. The great challenge of this task stemmed from the fact that the Hydra regenerated her multiple heads every time one of them was cut off. To overcome this difficulty, Hercules resorted to his nephew Iolaus, asking him to set the nearby woods on fire and bring him firebrands to cauterize the open wounds resulting from the beheadings. Thus, after Hercules had cut off each head, Iolaus burned the Hydra's open neck stumps. The cauterization prevented the regrowth or regeneration of new heads. Finally, with the help of Iolaus, Hercules hewed down the principal head, previously thought to be immortal, and crushed it with a huge rock, under which he buried it. This way, Hercules slayed the Hydra and successfully performed his second labour.[3]

The metaphorical reference employed in the subtitle of this book, *Between the Hydra and Hercules*, designates a touchstone that shall guide this work. In my approach, I reverse the dominant perspective on principles and rules stemming from Ronald Dworkin's work. According to Dworkin, Judge Hercules, a regulative ideal, is one who is able to identify the principles suitable for solving a case, allowing for 'a single right answer' or, at the very least, the best judgment of it.[4] In this sense, it can also be said that the principles are Herculean.

[1] Hercules, in Roman mythology, corresponds to Heracles in Greek mythology.

[2] The sources vary in regard to the number of heads (from five or six to one hundred, according to Grimal, 1951, 191; Kury, 2003, 183). Venit (1989, 102 and 104) refers to nine.

[3] Cf. Grimal, 1951, 187–203 (esp. 191–2), 215, 232; Kury, 2003, 180–7, esp. 183, 192–3, 197; Venit, 1989.

[4] Dworkin, 1978, 105 ff., 279 ff.; 1986, esp. 239 ff., 380–1; 1985, 119 ff.; 2006a, 41–3, 54 ff. I return to this topic in Chapter 2 section 3.

Constitutionalism and the Paradox of Principles and Rules. Marcelo Neves, Oxford University Press. © Marcelo Neves 2021.
DOI: 10.1093/oso/9780192898746.003.0001

It is well known that Dworkin's thesis arose as a criticism of the analytical positivism posited by Hart, according to whom the legal order, defined as a system composed of primary rules of conduct and secondary rules of organization, provides the judge with room for discretion, in which the choice of one of the alternatives offered does not necessary come under any existing rules, implying the 'open texture of law'.[5] To Dworkin, cases that cannot be settled by rules ought to be decided by morally supported legal principles, which, according to this perspective, would prevent any discretionary room or power for Judge Hercules.[6]

In this book, an opposite view is offered: principles have a Hydra-like character, whereas rules are Herculean. This perspective is not related to the existence or inexistence of discretion, a theme to which I will return in the course of this work. Rather, it concerns the flexibility that principles confer to the legal system by increasing the possibilities for argumentation. According to this understanding, principles act as a stimulus to the construction of arguments capable of leading to suitable solutions to thorny legal cases, without restricting such solutions to discretionary options. Owing to their plurality, or—expressed metaphorically—their 'multi-headed' features, principles improve the argumentative process among the concerned judges, parties, and

[5] Hart, 1994, 91 ff., 124 ff., 145–7, 279 ff.; Dworkin, 1978; 16 ff., 46 ff. Although derived from another theoretical perspective, Hart's notion of the 'open texture of law' is analogous to Kelsen's conception of 'law to be applied as a frame within which several applications are possible' (Kelsen, 1960, 348–9 (Engl. trans. 1967, 350–1)). It lies outside the scope this book to engage in the 'Hart–Dworkin Debate', much less to offer a review of the extensive literature surrounding it. In this regard, see the critical review presented by Shapiro (2007). Although Shapiro (ibid., 50) maintains that 'reports of the demise' of this debate 'would be greatly exaggerated', he points out that 'the Hart–Dworkin Debate is indeed past its intellectual sell-by date'. Shapiro also presents the following thesis: 'Contrary to Dworkin's interpretation, Hart never embraced the model of rules, either explicitly or implicitly' (ibid., 30). Indeed, Shapiro recognizes that 'Hart accepts some responsibility for the confusion' (ibid., 51, note 4), quoting the following passage of Hart's Postscript: 'Much credit is due to Dworkin for having shown and illustrated [the] importance [of legal principles] and their role in legal reasoning, and certainly it was a serious mistake on my part not to have stressed their non-conclusive force' (Hart, 1994, 263). However, he emphasizes that Hart 'goes on to disavow Dworkin's interpretation of his view' (Shapiro, ibid.), quoting the continuation of this passage: 'But I certainly did not intend in my use of the word "rule" to claim that legal systems comprise only "all-or-nothing" [standards] or near-conclusive rules' (Hart, 1994, 263; the word 'standards' was added by Shapiro, who also removed 'intend'and 'to').

[6] In Dworkin's language, it is not about discretion in a weak sense but in a strong sense: 'Sometimes we use "discretion" in a weak sense, simply to say that for some reason the standards an official must apply cannot be applied mechanically but demand the use of judgment... Sometimes we use the term in a different weak sense, to say only that some official has final authority to make a decision and cannot be reviewed and reversed by any other official... I call both of these senses weak to distinguish them from a stronger sense. We use "discretion" sometimes not merely to say that an official must use judgment in applying the standards set him by authority, or that no one will review that exercise of judgment, but to say that on some issue he is simply not bound by standards set by the authority in question.' It is in this strict sense that Dworkin criticizes 'the positivists' doctrine of judicial discretion', which he defines in the following terms: 'That doctrine argues that if a case is not controlled by an established rule, the judge must decide it by exercising discretion.' But he does warn: 'The strong sense of discretion is not tantamount to license, and does not exclude criticism' (Dworkin, 1978, 31–3).

other stakeholders, opening it to manifold starting points. Observers from very diverse perspectives are motivated by principles to take an active part in the argumentative practice directed to legally ground the settlement of a juridical problem. In this regard, in today's complex society principles promote the expression of dissent on legal issues and, at the same time, serve procedural legitimation by absorbing dissent.[7]

However, principles alone do not settle the cases to which they are intended to be applied. The resolution of legal cases in a constitutional state depends upon rules. If the case is a 'routine' or an 'easy' one, it is clear that it does not entail any greater difficulties, as in this case the argumentative chain is practically reduced to the semantic determination of the meaning of provisions and the subsequent subsumption of the case under a rule. The question grows in significance when the relationship between rules and principles is considered to be relevant for the resolution of a case. In this regard, rules, although being demarcated in light of or even derived from principles, serve to domesticate the latter, enabling a definitive closure of the argumentative process surrounding the concrete interpretation and application of law. It is in this sense that rules are Herculean. Whereas principles open the process of legal and constitutional concretization,[8] instigating new argumentative problems in a Hydra-like manner, rules tend to close it, absorbing and dissipating the uncertainty that characterizes the initial stage of the procedure of norm application. The uncertainty is then qualified, and the complexity becomes relatively structured (or structurable) by virtue of the legal principles because they provide certain contours and reference points—anchored in normative expectations present in society and in those directly involved in the process—that are useful for the discussion aimed at the resolution of a case. In sequence, only rules are capable of *enabling* the transformation from the uncertainty of the starting point to the certainty drawn from the decision or ruling of a case.[9] Only rules can lead

[7] See Neves, 2000, 108 ff.

[8] In this book I shall employ the concept of *legal* or *constitutional concretization* in roughly the same sense it has been used in the German constitutional and legal theory (see esp. Hesse, 1969, 25 ff.; F. Müller, 1995, 166 ff.; 1994; 1990a; 1990b; Christensen, 1989, 87 ff.). It refers to a process that goes from abstract constitutional or legal standards to the concrete ought-decision or ought-judgment (ruling) of a case, involving the interpretation of norm texts and of facts, and finishing with the application of law to a specific case. It concludes not only with a court adjudication or decision, but also with legislative and executive interpretations (Tushnet, 2008, 79) as well as arbitration awards and legal transactions or the application of law by private acts (cf. Kelsen, 1960, 261 ff. (Engl. trans. 1967, 256 ff.)). However, legal or constitutional concretization excludes both the mere factual observance or compliance and the mere *enforcement* of a ruling applying legal or constitutional standards. I shall refer to these two factual dimensions using the phrases 'constitutional' and 'legal realization' or 'efficacy'.

[9] Of course, certainty is only reached in a case with the final ruling, which corresponds to a 'decision norm' (in the sense proposed by F. Müller, 1994, esp. 264; 1990a, esp. 48–that is, an ought-judgment of a legal case). This kind of norm is typically an 'individual norm' in Kelsen's sense (Kelsen, 1960, esp. 20,

to a reduction in complexity or to a selection capable of determining the case solution.

These remarks should not prevent us from seeing the other side of the coin. Rules alone, due to being more bound to concrete situations, are hardly proper for absorbing the high complexity of the so-called hard cases.[10] Owing to their restricted degree of flexibility and tendency to Herculean rigour, rules have to be linked to principles in order to tackle highly complex problems. In the course of the process of normative concretization, legal principles convert the unstructured complexity of the legal system's environment (values, moral representations, ideologies, efficiency models, etc.) into a complexity capable of being structured from the normative-juridical point of view, while legal rules selectively reduce the complexity that through principles has become capable of being structured, transmuting it into a legally structured complexity that makes it possible for a case to be resolved.

Rules and principles are two normative poles essential to the process of legal and constitutional concretization, nurturing each other circularly in the argumentative chain that leads up to the case decision. There is no linear hierarchy between them. On the one hand, rules depend upon being marked out or constructed from principles. On the other hand, the latter only gain practical significance if they are connected with rules providing them with density and relevance for settling a case. This is not, in anyway, a sort of harmonic relationship. It is rather a paradoxical relation, as will be shown especially in the course of the third chapter. Analogous to the relationship between the Hydra and Hercules in the mythological episode, principles and rules relate to one another in a conflicting way.

The tendency to overestimate principles at the expense of rules makes the degree of uncertainty too high and can degenerate into an uncontrollable insecurity linked with the breaking of the consistency of the legal system itself and, thus, with the destruction of its operating boundaries. Conversely, a tendency to overvalue rules to the detriment of principles makes the legal system excessively rigid to face complex social problems, in the name of a legal consistency

85, 242, 265 (Engl. trans. 1967, 19, 80, 236–7, 260–1); 1945, 37–8 and 134 ff.), but can also have general effects, such as rulings in cases concerning the abstract judicial review of legal standards (e.g. the abstract control of statutory rules). However, the uncertainty reappears at the level of enforcement, as one still has to interpret the text of the judicial decision. The problem then garners new contours, taking it beyond the scope of this book.

[10] See Dworkin, 1978, 81–130, who distinguishes them from the 'weak cases'; Aarnio, 1987, 1 ff., who contrasts them to the 'routine cases'. Carrió (1986, 55–61) distinguishes similarly between 'marginal cases' and 'typical cases'. Dworkin himself (1986, 354) qualifies the difference between hard and weak cases by taking into account the temporal and personal variables.

incompatible with the social adequacy of law. Therefore, with respect to the relation between rules and principles, one is confronted at the argumentative level with the question of overcoming or processing the paradox of legal consistency and social adequacy in each concrete case, which is, in general terms, the paradox of justice as 'a formula for contingency of the legal system'.[11]

In this introductory chapter, it is worth emphasizing that the discussion to follow will have a specific focus, being necessary to provide some background explanations. First of all, it must be noted that the term 'principle' can be both ambiguous and vague.[12] It is not uncommon to incur 'fallacies of ambiguity',[13] discussing in a nonsensical manner the same term or expression as though it was always referring to the same concept. Of course, there are terms and expressions that have such enormous seductive power in themselves that merely resorting to them serves the rhetorical purposes of those employing them, irrespective of whatever meaning is assigned to them. The term 'principle', like the expression 'constitution', has acquired this status.[14] In turn, it is obvious that every conceptual discussion implies the semantic delimitation of the corresponding terms, which makes the problem somewhat circular. It is fundamental, however, that the questions on concepts and concerning the definition of terms or expressions be treated in view of the theoretical or practical problem one intends to deal with or resolve. It is in this sense that I propose a preliminary semantic delimitation in order to specify the problem I intend to address.

In ancient philosophy, *principles* refer to starting points, foundations, or 'causes' of any process. Dating back to Anaximander and continuing through Plato, this notion of principle was comprehensively examined by Aristotle, who lists several meanings of 'principle' ('beginning'), leading up to the conclusion: 'It is a common property, then, of all "beginnings" to be the first thing from which something either exists or comes into being or becomes known.'[15] In modern philosophy, Kant, by dealing with 'reason in general', points out the ambiguity of the term 'principle': 'Every universal proposition, even if it is

[11] Luhmann, 1993, 214 ff. (Engl. trans. 2004, 211 ff.).

[12] About its various uses in the philosophical tradition, from the standpoint of existence, logical point of view and in the normative sense, see Lalande, 1968, 827–9, who quotes a suggestive passage of Condillac, 1831, 109: '*Principle* is synonymous with *beginning*, and was early used with this meaning; but then, by virtue of use, it was employed mechanically, by habit and without being assigned to it any ideas' (Lalande, 1968, 827). Condillac (1931, 109) adds: 'and we had some principles that are the beginning of nothing.' Regarding the various meanings of 'principle' in general and 'legal principle' in particular, see Carrió, 1970, 32 ff.; Atienza and Manero, 1998, 3–4.

[13] Copi, 1961, 73 ff.

[14] In regard to 'constitution', see Neves, 2009, 1–6 (Engl. trans. 2013, 5–8).

[15] Aristotle, 2003, 211, Book V, I.3.

taken from experience (by induction), can serve as the major premise in a syllogism; but it is not therefore itself a principle.'[16] Departing from this common use, Kant refers to the notion of 'principles of pure understanding in themselves', which alone are entitled to be called principles ('It is properly these that I call principles absolutely') insofar as they are purely rational (a priori).[17] They are mentioned by him when he defines reason as 'the faculty of the unity of the rules of understanding under principles'.[18] In the study of morals and ethics, in turn, Kant employs the term 'principles' to distinguish between a 'maxim' as a subjective principle of willing or action and the practical (moral) 'law' as an objective principle of the will or action, which would be valid for all rational beings, 'if reason had complete control over the desiderative faculty'.[19] In these terms, 'maxim' contains the practical *rule* according to which the subject *acts* in conformity with his own conditions, whereas the 'law' is the *objective principle* according to which every rational being *ought to act*.[20]

In modern sciences, in which the concept of 'principles' has largely lost its significance, the term has also been used to indicate the basic premises of a given field of knowledge. In the area of natural sciences, this term refers to certain empirical propositions that, by means of (suitable, useful) conventions, are precluded from experimental control, as pointed out by Poincaré.[21] In the realm of mathematics, principles were considered, in general, as premises of a demonstration and were conceptually substituted by axioms and postulates.[22]

Somehow, these varied concepts have been disseminated across several areas of theory and practice, with much imprecision and variation in meaning. By employing the term 'principle', one often intends both to denote the basic premises of some realm of knowledge or the social world in general and to invoke universal and ultimate norms. Finally, it is commonly used to refer to the ordering and unifying function performed by some norms for a given system or order, most notably the law.[23] Instead of using the vague term 'principles' to indicate such a broad conceptual family, I would rather call them, depending

[16] Kant, 1990 [$1781^A/1787^B$], vol. 1, 312 [A 300/B 356] (Engl. trans. 1998, 387–8).

[17] Kant, 1990 [$1781^A/1787^B$], vol. 1, 313 [A 301/B 357–8] (Engl. trans. 1998, 388). However, he adds: 'Nevertheless, all universal propositions in general can be called principles comparatively' (1990 [$1781^A/1787^B$], 313 [A 301/B 358] (Engl. trans. 1998, 388)).

[18] Kant, 1990 [$1781^A/1787^B$], vol. 1, 314 [A 302/B359] (Engl. trans. 1998, 389).

[19] Kant, 1965 [1785/1786], 18–19, 42 [400-1/420-1] (Engl. trans. 2012, 15–16, 33–4). The objective principle or practical law is related to the categorical imperative in Kant's work (1965 [1785], 20, 34–5, 42 [402, 414, 420–1] (Engl. trans. 2012, 17, 28, 33–4)).

[20] Kant, 1965 [1785], 42 [420–1] (Engl. trans. 2012, 33–4).

[21] Poincaré, 1905, 207–11. However, Poincaré warned that, 'if a principle ceases to be fecund, experience without directly contradicting it will nevertheless have condemned it' (209).

[22] Abbagnano, 1961, 678.

[23] Cf. Pascua, 1996, 11.

on the context, the 'premises' or 'starting points' of an argumentative process or chain, the 'postulate' of a field of knowledge, the 'basic laws' of logic, the allegedly 'fundamental' or 'presupposed norms' in the sphere of law or ethics and morality, or finally the 'binary codes' guiding the reproduction of communication systems.[24]

Employing the concept of principles in the domain of law, in the broad terms of the discussion around 'general principles of law', is not the main goal of this work either. This is rather a philosophical discussion in which the term is used to distinguish between those who claim that the general principles of law are derived from natural law and those who hold the legal positivist view on these principles.[25] This debate has its home in the context of the general theory of law in the Euro-continental tradition whenever the issue of supplying the gaps in the law is the matter under consideration, prompting the question of whether the general principles of law become valid through self-integration or hetero-integration. In this regard, the very 'Introductory Statute to the Norms of Brazilian Law' provides that the judge, besides having the competence to invoke analogy and customs, is authorized to decide in accordance with the general principles of law if the statutory law is silent on the matter of the case brought before the court.[26] The hetero-integration thesis maintains that the general principles of law are supra-positive; the self-integration thesis asserts that they belong to the respective positive order, being inducted from the set of legal norms through hermeneutic activity.[27] As there is a channel of internal reception expressly established by a statute, it seems that this question is not relevant in the Brazilian context. Strictly speaking, the so-called general principles of law, which are referred to in both statutory law and case law of several legal orders, are maxims consolidated in the Western legal tradition, especially from Roman law, with some of them constituting principles in a strict sense and others consisting of common rules. In the event that a law is silent or has gaps on a specific issue, principles are internalized in the legal system through hetero-integration in the concrete situation, or if they already belong implicitly

[24] Here I refer to binary codes in Niklas Luhnann's terms: 'Functional systems are never teleological systems. They refer each operation to a bivalent distinction—to the binary code—thus ensuring that a follow-up communication is always possible for switching to the opposing value... Binary codes are in a strict sense forms, which is to say two-sided forms that facilitate switching from one side to the other, from value to opposing value and back by distinguishing themselves as forms from other forms. For example: true/false; beloved/unloved; having property/not having property; passing exams/failing exams; exercising authority/being subject to authority, and so forth' (Luhmann, 1997, vol. 2, 749–50 (Engl. trans. 2013, 91)).

[25] See Pascua, 1996, 11 ff.

[26] 'Art. 4. If the [statutory] law is silent, the judge shall decide according to analogy, customs, and general principles of law.'

[27] See, respectively, Bobbio, 1960, 179–84; Betti, 1949, 51–2, 205 ff.

or explicitly to the legal order, it only takes self-integration for their application to the case resolution. It is clear that one might also appeal to these maxims at the constitutional level if there are gaps in the constitutional clauses, but this issue is secondary to the theme addressed in this work.

The focus of the present study is on the relation between constitutional principles and constitutional rules. On the one hand, values and moral criteria will be taken into account only insofar as they are integrated into the legal order via one of these two types of constitutional norms. On the other hand, infra-constitutional principles and rules will only be considered if their understanding, interpretation, and application shed light on or serve to the interpretation and application of constitutional principles and rules.

Moreover, even within the specific scope of the debate around the relation between constitutional principles and rules, this study does not intend to exhaust the subject or to offer an encyclopaedic review. Instead, it will concentrate critically on the legal-constitutional debate that has developed since the 1970s around constitutional principles and rules, in particular in regard to Ronald Dworkin's and Robert Alexy's works, in order, on this basis, to present an alternative model and to point out the limitations and misunderstandings of the reception of the theory of legal principles in the Brazilian constitutional jurisprudence and constitutional case-law.

In Chapter 1, I shall briefly analyse the main theoretical currents that have addressed the matter of legal principles and rules before the explosion of the theory of constitutional principles. At this point, the general theory can hardly be distinguished from the constitutional conception of principles and rules.

In Chapter 2, I will initially examine the philosophical background of the dominant model for understanding constitutional principles and rules. Thereafter, I shall analyse this model, paying special attention to two of its trends that build on the works of Dworkin and Alexy.

In Chapter 3, I will present a model for distinguishing between constitutional principles and constitutional rules, emphasizing that it concerns a legal-doctrinal difference that emerged with modern constitutionalism. In this context, principles will be defined as reflexive mechanisms in relation to rules, and the circular connection between them will become the focus of my analysis. I will also discuss the performance of principles and rules in the process of constitutional concretization as well as point out the requirement of a constitutional principle theory adequate to the complexity of contemporary society, even in the context of transconstitutionalism.

In Chapter 4, I shall review the use and abuse of principles in the Brazilian constitutional doctrine and practice. First, the problem of doctrinal fascination will be addressed, pointing out theoretical and jurisprudential mistakes. Second, I will make some critical comments on confused constitutional practices related to principles, considering some cases judged by the Brazilian Federal Supreme Court.

As a final comment, I will return to the metaphor expressed in the subtitle, in order to consider what type of judge is best prepared to face and overcome the paradox of the relation between principles and rules in each concrete case: Judge Hercules or Judge Hydra? The answer will ultimately be neither of them.

1

From Classic Distinctions Between Legal Principles and Rules

1. Norms Between Texts and Facts

When discussing the distinction between principles and rules, in terms both of the general theory of law and of constitutional doctrine, the debate turns to characterizing types of norms, even to ascertaining whether both categories are covered by the concept of norm. Therefore, the first step is to remove the confusion between norm and normative text. The terms 'norm formulation',[1] 'normative provision', and 'normative statement'[2] may also be used to distinguish the linguistic form through which a norm is expressed by positive law, particularly the written law. To this end, I will use the expressions 'normative text' in general or 'norm provision' in particular,[3] leaving 'normative statement' to refer to the linguistic expression of an interpretative or a legal-doctrinal proposition that is intended to describe or determine the semantic content of a norm.[4] (Additionally, the term 'normative statement'—rather than 'normative provision'—will sometimes be employed to refer to the assertion of a derivative legal or constitutional norm, i.e. a norm indirectly attributed to a legal or constitutional text by the officer or body in charge of its legally binding interpretation-application.) Here, it is about distinguishing between the levels of the signifier and the signified.[5] The connection between these two levels

[1] Von Wright, 1963, 93, 96–7; Aarnio, 1990, 181–2; 1997b, 19; Canotilho, 1998, 1075–6; Schauer, 1991, 62–4, who distinguishes rule from rule formulation.

[2] See Alexy, 1986, 54 ff. (Engl. trans. 2002, 21 ff.), who distinguishes between a constitutional rights norm and a constitutional rights normative statement; Canotilho, 1998, 1077–80; Guastini, 2010, 35 ff.; 1998a, 15 ff.; 1993, 17 ff.; 1992, 15 ff.

[3] On the distinction between norm and normative text, see, among many, F. Müller, 1994, esp. 147–67 and 234–40; 1995, 122 ff.; 1990a, 126 ff.; 1990b, esp. 20; Christensen, 1989, 78 ff.; Jeand'Heur, 1989, esp. 22–3; Möllers, 2015, 278 ff. (with qualifications); Grau, 2009, esp. 84–6; P.B. Carvalho, 2008, 126–31; Tarello, 1980, 101 ff., who distinguishes norms from normative documents.

[4] Aarnio, when distinguishing between interpretation in the broad sense, which refers to the various possible meanings of a normative provision ('norm formulation'), and interpretation in the strict sense, which selects one of these alternative meanings, uses the term 'interpretative statement' only in this latter sense (Aarnio, 1990, 182).

[5] The distinction between signifier and signified as two dimensions of the sign goes back to the French linguist Saussure (1922, 97–100; cf. Barthes, 1964, 103–9; Eco, 1975, 25–6). This difference

Constitutionalism and the Paradox of Principles and Rules. Marcelo Neves, Oxford University Press. © Marcelo Neves 2021.
DOI: 10.1093/oso/9780192898746.003.0002

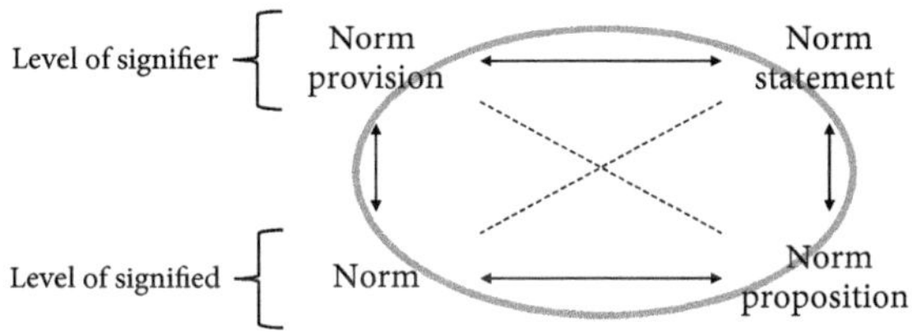

Figure 1.1 Four-element circular process of norm construction.

implies a semantic relationship of signification or, more broadly, of meaning-giving in the communication process. In the context of this work, however, this is not a relationship between two poles only (i.e. between the provision and the norm); in fact, it sets up at least a four-element circular process between a normative provision, norm, normative statement and a normative proposition (see Figure 1.1). Considering a normative provision, it is worth asking which norm(s) or normative meaning(s) may or ought to be attributed to it. The normative (or interpretive) statement assigns certain normative meaning(s) or norm(s) to the normative provision. However, again, one can ask which normative meaning(s) or norm(s) was (were) attributed to the provision by the normative (or interpretive) statement, that is, which normative (interpretive) proposition was expressed through this statement.[6] This is not a linear relation, as with meta-language and object-language.[7] Instead, it implies a reflexive circularity in the communication process of meaning-giving.

has been adopted, *mutatis mutandis*, by various theoretical models. See e.g. Lévi-Strauss, 1973 [1950], XLIX–L, referring to the discontinuity between signifier and signified, the overabundance of signifiers and the floating signifiers; Lacan, 1966, 372 and 501–2, pointing out the 'discrepancy between signified and signifier' and the closed character of the signifier's order/chain, as well as its autonomy in relation to the signified.

[6] Kelsen distinguishes between legal proposition and (prescriptive) legal norm, with the former being descriptive of the latter (Kelsen, 1960, 73–9). However, he defines the legal proposition (*Rechtssatz*) in particular or the 'ought-proposition' (*Soll-Satz*) in general as a descriptive *statement* (*beschreibende Aussage*) (cf. Kelsen, 1960, 73 and 81–3). In the present book, I correspondingly distinguish, at the level of the signifier, between normative statement (= statement of a normative proposition) and normative provision (or text of a norm). In the translation of Kelsen's book originally published in English under the title *General Theory of Law and State* and of his masterwork *Reine Rechtslehre* [*Pure Theory of Law*], the term '*Rechtssatz*' (legal proposition) was disastrously translated into the expression 'rule of law' (Kelsen, 1945, 45–7; 1960, 73–9 (Engl. trans., 1967, 71–5)).

[7] In the sense of Russell's hierarchical theory of types (Russell, 1994 [1908], 75–80; 1956 [1940], 62 ff.). See also Tarski, 1935; Carnap, 1948, 3–4; Barthes, 1964, 130–2. Criticizing this kind of distinction, Hofstadter (1979, 21 ff.) argues that the theory of types would ban 'the strange loops' and paradoxes within language, leading to a hierarchy between object language and meta-language. Although Hofstadter's criticism of Russell's theory of types is controversial in the realm of formal artificial language, such as mathematics and formal logic, his ideas on 'strange loops' and 'tangled hierarchies' makes sense when applied to ordinary language, even if it is a specialized language, such as law, humanities and social sciences. I will return to this issue later (see below p. 93).

Besides the signifier and the signified, the referents are relevant at the semantic level, which are not the ultimate raw material of the experience (whose existence is only assumed in the communicative process), but instead are facts and objects constructed in the language, or rather in the communication process. Thus, one is confronted, on the one hand, with the relationship between *legal norm text* (signifier) and *legal norm* (signified), and on the other hand, with the relationship between *legal norm* and *legal fact* (referent). In turn, the legal fact is defined mainly in terms of the *norm scope*, that is the abstract description of the fact(s) capable of bringing about the respective concrete legal consequence(s).[8] It is further worth distinguishing the legal fact defined in terms of the norm scope from the *fact situation* or *fact pattern* [*Sachverhalt*][9] as the set of circumstances counted as relevant (and thus communicatively constructed) to the application of the norm, whose selective qualification according to the norm scope leads to the construction or definition of the legal fact, which is followed by the legal consequence. The fact pattern is not an underlying raw datum, the pure material of the experience, but something that has already entered the legal realm, that is it has already been processed by the legal language or communication.[10]

[8] I employ here the phrase 'legal facts' in the sense of 'juridical' or 'juristic facts' ('*fait juridique*', '*fatto giuridico*', '*hecho juridico*', '*facto jurídico*'), according to its traditional use in continental jurisprudence, as it is accurately defined and exemplified by Hage (2005, 225): 'Juristic facts are facts to which the law attaches consequences. Examples of juristic facts are sale, theft, death and lapse of time. Possible legal consequences of these examples include the coming into existence of the vendor's right to be paid, the liability of the thief to be punished, inheritance and preclusion of criminal proceedings, respectively.' In turn, I employ 'norm scope' to refer to the 'norm condition(s)' ('protasis of a norm', '*Tatbestand*'), i.e. the part of a norm that defines abstractly the 'juristic fact'—a usage which also derives from this same tradition, in particular German legal culture. The other part, 'norm conclusion' ('apodosis of a norm', '*Rechtsfolge*'), establishes the abstract definition of the 'legal consequence' of a given norm (see e.g. Hage, 2005, 87–8, specifically about the rule condition and the rule conclusion as parts of a rule; Alexy, 1986, 83–4 (Engl. transl. 2002, 53–4; in this translation, '*Tatbestand*' was usually translated as 'scope of rights'; cf. ibid. 272 ff., Engl. trans. 196 ff.)).

[9] I have to admit here that it is often difficult to translate expressions between different legal cultures, since there is often ambiguity between terms used within the same legal culture. Concerning the distinction between *Tatbestand* (here translated as 'norm condition') and *Sachvehalt* (here translated as 'fact pattern'), the following passage of a German legal dictionary shows the ambiguity: '*Sachverhalt* is the specific factual event in the reality of life. The legally relevant *Sachverhalt* is the object of the legal application. In the legal application, the (concrete) effects brought about by *Sachverhalt* are checked on the basis of the respective abstract legal norms. In the procedural law, *Sachverhalt* is often referred to as *Tatbestand* (e.g. § 313 I No. 5 ZPO [German Code of Civil Procedure]), although the legal methodology understands the latter as the sum of the abstract conditions for an abstract legal effect' (Köbler, 2003, 403). Elsewhere in the same dictionary (ibid. 456), it is stated that in the procedural law (quoting the above-mentioned provision of the ZPO), *Tatbestand* is the 'concise description' of a *Sachverhalt*, but here it refers to the concrete situation.

[10] Pontes de Miranda, 1974, vol. I, 21; 1974, vol. V, 231. Against the naturalistic perspective of Pontes de Miranda, I understand the fact situation or fact pattern as a legal construct, placing it at the level of the referents of the legal language or communication, but distinguishing it from the legal fact, which is also located at the level of the referents, but additionally has legally binding effects.

The question of principles and rules lies on the level of the norm (signified) between the planes of the normative text (signifier) and legal fact (referent). However, of course, the problems concerning the norm provisions and the factual referents play a key role in relation to the norm. In this respect, it is worth considering the problem of ambiguity (in the connotation) and vagueness (in the denotation) of normative texts.[11] In this context, ambiguity means that the provisions, particularly the constitutional ones, are not univocal: they can be assigned more than one meaning at least prima facie. This implies the possibility that more than one norm can be 'extracted' from the same normative provision, or, more precisely, attributed to it. In turn, vagueness relates to inaccuracy in determining the precise referents of the norm, that is uncertainty concerning the limits of the field of legal facts and their legal consequences defined in the normative provision and, thus, in the norm. Even when the ambiguity is cleared (the meaning of the legal provision was determined and therefore the norm to be applied was defined), problems of vagueness may still arise, given the difficulty of determining which facts fall into the respective norm. Thus, for example, even if the meaning of 'political pluralism' it is clearly defined under the terms of Article 1.V of the Brazilian Federal Constitution, the difficulty in determining the factual situations in which an extremist party should be considered a threat or danger to the political pluralism persists. Therefore, an 'interpretation of the facts'[12] is required in order to overcome the vagueness in relation to the concrete case, so that the norm can be applied.

To overcome the ambiguity of legal provisions, the *interpretation of* the relevant *texts* is fundamental. To overcome the vagueness and apply the norm to a particular case, one needs to go beyond it, developing a comprehensive selective process of concretization of the norm.[13] It should be clarified, however, that the legal norm does not become concrete and individual with the

[11] In the logical sense, the connotation corresponds to the semantic dimension of sense (meaning), and the denotation concerns the semantic dimension of reference (cf. von Wright, 1963, 93–4; Copi, 1961, 107 ff.). Specifically on the (connotative) ambiguity and (denotative) vagueness of legal language, see Carrió, 1986, 28 ff.; Koch, 1977, 41 ff.; Warat, 1984, 76–9; 1979, 96–100. Moving in the opposite direction, Dworkin (1978, 133 ff.) proposes a re-reading of the notion of 'vague constitutional provisions' based on the distinction between 'concept' and 'conception'. Endicott (2000) offers a comprehensive treatment of vagueness in law requiring a re-reading of the notion of rule of law (185 ff.). I see no reason to affirm that, unlike ambiguity, vagueness 'is a necessary feature of law' (Endicott, 2000, 2) or for asserting that, unlike an ambiguous term, the choice of a vague term 'should, in the absence of contrary evidence, be assumed to have been conscious' (Ely, 1980, 199, note 66). Ambiguity and the vagueness, which do not imply arbitrariness, are intrinsic to the legal and constitutional language in the modern society as a highly complex society, and go far beyond the purposes or conscious choices of the involved actors, rather being related to complex social structures and processes (see Neves, 2000, 155 ff.).

[12] Ivainer, 1988.

[13] In this regard, see above note 8 of the Introduction. The interpretation concerns only the text (cf., e.g., F. Müller, 1995, 272–3).

completion of its concretization, since concretization allows only for the subsumption of the case under the legal norm through a concrete ought-decision or ought-judgment, by the ruling of a given case.[14] The concretization thus involves the interpretation of both the text of the norm and the legal facts relevant to the case. In a broader sense, it encompasses, in the terminology of Friedrich Müller, the articulation both of the 'normative programme' ('primarily linguistic data') and the 'field of normative operation' ('primarily real data') as components of the 'norm-structure'.[15] The process of moving from prima facie ambiguity (connotative imprecision) of the normative provision to overcoming its vagueness (denotative imprecision), in a proper review, does not require 'considering all factors' of context, but rather selectively determining whether the legal facts relevant to the case fall under the norm scope.[16]

The awareness of this selective process has led to the understanding, which has become commonplace, that 'the legal norm itself is only produced in the course of solving the case',[17] even by stating that the judge is 'the only legislator'[18] and correspondingly characterizing law-making and constitution-making as

[14] See above note 9 of the Introduction.

[15] F. Müller, 1995, esp. 41 ff.; 1994, esp. 232–4; 1990b, esp. 20; 1975, esp. 38–9.

[16] Aarnio distinguishes between a prima facie analysis and an all-things-considered analysis of an expression, a distinction which he also uses in relation to the applicability of norms (1990, 185 ff.; 1997, 179–80). Before, Peczenick (1989, 250–1) defined the 'all-things-considered law as interpreted law', asserting that 'the all-things-considered law is an optimal product of an interpretation'. The use of the phrase 'all-things-considered' in this legal context goes back to the moral philosophy developed by Searle, 1978, in a review of Ross's concept of prima facie duty (Ross, 1930, 19 ff.). However, Searle was mindful in regard to the concept of prima facie obligations: 'we do well in philosophy to abandon the terminology of prima facie obligations and duties as it embodies confusion' (1978, 84); and also to the limits of 'all-things-considered': 'But in the hard cases one may simply not be able to decide what to do on rational grounds alone. Reflection on the relative weights of our obligations (and commitments and duties and other sorts of reasons) may not be sufficient to provide answer to "What ought we to do, all things considered?"' (1978, 85). Indeed, going beyond morality and regarding law in contexts of high complexity, it is notable that there is a necessary selective attitude towards contextual factors in any decision-making process established by norms, or, in other words—invoking here Schauer (1998a, 239)—'rules have some degree of resistance to some decision-maker's determination of what now appears to her to be the best all-things-considered decision'. In this sense, Schauer says: 'A decision-maker not constrained by rules has the power, the authority, the jurisdiction to take everything into account. Conversely, the rule-constrained decision-maker loses at least some of that jurisdiction' (Schauer, 1991, 159). Instead of just covering the rules, one might broaden the scope of this assertion to include the norms in general. However, Schauer starts from other assumptions and gives other consequences to this assertion, strictly defining the rules 'as tools for the *allocation of power*' (ibid.). It should also be noted that other factors, in addition to norms, prevent all things to be taken into consideration. Hence, I have to clarify that, when using the term 'prima facie', I am not employing it in the strict sense of the philosophical tradition that opposes it to 'all-things-considered', but simply to refer to the meaning of normative provision or even to the norm as presented in the beginning of the concretization process, before the existence of a selective determination of the (complete) rule that serves as a definitive criterion to the case solution.

[17] F. Müller, 1994, 273. See Christensen, 1989, 89; in a similar but more careful direction, Grau, 1996, 60–1; 2009, 86–9.

[18] F. Müller, 1990b, 127, note 16. Similar wording had already been expressed by Cardozo, who referred to the 'judge as a legislator' (1991 [1921], 102 ff.), emphasizing 'The law which is the resulting product is not found, but made. The process, being legislative, demands the legislator's wisdom' (115).

procedures for issuing legal text and establishing constitutional text.[19] Though fascinating, it seems to me that these formulations can be misleading. If we say that a norm is only produced in the process of concretization, the question persists as to whether the judges and other officials responsible for concretizing the norms would be bound to these in settling each case. One can fall into a decisionist realism if these models are not treated with due care and, I would say, with certain restrictions.

The relationship between those who produce the normative text and those who interpret and apply it in particular cases, or, more simply put, between legislators (including the constitutional ones) and judges, involves a double contingency.[20] In principle, the problem of double contingency is present in the observation of the reciprocal relationship between ego and alter in the interaction. But the issue of double contingency in terms of Luhmann's systems theory is not restricted to the interaction, in which the poles alter and ego refer to (but should not be confused with) persons.[21] Alter and ego may also refer to social systems[22] and therefore to their dimensions (subsystems)—here, the legislation (or legislator), primarily political, and the judicature (or judiciary), primarily legal.

Double contingency means that ego reckons the possibility of alter's actions being different from what ego would expect and vice-versa. Although there can be no such thing as 'pure double contingency'—because of the conditioning of interaction[23] and the 'absorption of uncertainty' by means of 'stabilizing expectations'[24]—'[a]ny attempt to calculate the other will inevitably fail'.[25] This entails the mutual assumption of 'degrees of freedom'[26] (an alter's action may be entirely different from those expected by ego and vice-versa), which converts behaviour into action: 'Behaviour becomes action if it is found free to be determined differently'.[27] Hence, double contingency involves a combination

Cardozo added: 'There is in truth nothing revolutionary or even novel in this view of the judicial function' (116).

[19] Cf. F. Müller, 1994, 264 and 270.

[20] Luhmann, 1987a, 148 ff. (Engl. trans. 1995, 103 ff.); 1987b, 32 ff. (Engl. trans. 2014, 26 ff.); 2002, 315 ff. According to Luhmann (1987a, 148 (Engl. trans. 1995, 103 and 522–3, note 1); 2002, 317), the concept of double contingency dates back to Talcott Parsons and the group of researchers associated with him. See Parsons et al., 1951, 16; Parsons, 1968, 436.

[21] 'We would like to call psychic systems that are observed by other psychic systems or by social systems *persons*' (Luhmann, 1987a, 155 (Engl. trans. 1995, 109)).

[22] Luhmann, 1987a, 152 and 155 (Engl. trans. 1995, 106 and 108).

[23] Cf. Luhmann, 1987a, 168 and 185–6 (Engl. trans. 1995, 118 and 133).

[24] Luhmann, 1987a, 158 (Engl. trans. 1995, 110).

[25] Luhmann, 1987a, 156 (Engl. trans. 1995, 109).

[26] Luhmann, 1987a, 186 (Engl. trans. 1995, 133).

[27] Luhamnn, 1987a, 169 (Engl. trans. 1995, 120).

of non-identity and identity: 'ego experiences alter as alter ego. But along with the *nonidentity of perspectives*, ego also experiences the *identity of this experience* on *both* sides.'[28]

In the relationship between legislation and adjudication or, more broadly, between norm-making and norm concretization, a double contingency is initially established, as in any communicative process. When referring to the legislator (not in the subjective or personal, but in the institutional sense), the interpreter-applicator assigns a meaning to the respective normative text. This does not mean that such assignment implies that the latter can replace the former as producer of the corresponding norm. The situation points to the limitation in giving structure to the double contingency and determining the content of a communication (what did alter mean to say?). The message of the legislator or constituent (alter) carries information content that needs to be understood by the judge (ego), who may misunderstand it. This alterity is analogously present in all social processes, even the simplest everyday interactions: 'I say that you said this when you spoke on that occasion.' In this case, ego is not saying that it is the author of the speech. Ego assigns a meaning to the alter's speech, as it understood the informative content of the message. This relation of information, message, and understanding, inherent to any communication,[29] also operates at the macro scale of social systems. In our context, this means that attributing content to a normative text (or a literary text) does not mean that the legal interpreter (or the reader) is the author of the respective norm (or book). In this sense, we might distinguish two levels: the institutional *production* (including the unorganized one, in the case of legal customs) of a norm and the hermeneutic *construction* of the norm in the concretization process. A prima facie meaning-giving by the law-making body is assumed, which is completed or transformed by a definitive meaning-giving at the end of the concretizing process. But the alterity remains: the hermeneutic construction (in the broad sense of the term) starts with the institutional production of the norm and is socially controlled during the processing of double contingency, being, therefore, subject to criticism as improper or inadequate to the present conditions.[30]

These observations serve us to clarify that the problem of the distinction between principles and rules (especially constitutional ones) lies on the plane of the argumentation developed in the concretizing process, where one intends

[28] Luhmann, 1987a, 172 (Engl. trans. 1995, 121–2).

[29] Luhmann, 1983a, 137 (Engl. trans. 1987, 18—in this translation, 'Mitteilung' was inappropriately translated into 'communication', which rather refers to the three elements of the communication process); 1987a, 193 ff. (Engl. trans. 1995, 139 ff.—in this translation, 'Mitteilung' was translated into 'utterance', but I prefer the term 'message', which implies the act of messaging); 2002, 292 ff.

[30] For a similar account (although based on other theoretical assumptions and with other implications), see Betti, 1955, 816 ff.; Gadamer, 1990, 330 ff.

to determine the content of the norm to be applied. This presupposes the issue of selective processing of double contingency and, in particular, the confrontation with the ambiguity and vagueness of legal provisions, involving the connection between prima facie and definitive norm meanings and also the interpretation of the legal facts relevant to the cases to be decided.

2. Imprecision, Discretion, and Generality as Criteria for Distinguishing Between Principles and Rules

The debate on the distinction between constitutional principles and rules has largely been confined to the classic topic of the general principles of law. This perspective allows for a multitude of definition criteria, for instance, that principles mean 'different fundamental ideas'[31] or simply 'the foundation of the legal order',[32] they play a heuristic function,[33] they are important to the legal system,[34] and they perform a unifying function for the legal system[35] (and many others).[36] In this context, the claim also arises for enumerating principles into catalogues (catalogues of topoi).[37] A detailed exposition of these several patterns of criteria for distinguishing between principles and rules and for enumerating principles goes beyond the framework of the present study, as mentioned in the introduction. It means that the classic debate on the so-called general principles of law should not be confused with the issue of the relationship between constitutional principles and rules. However, some aspects of the classical discussion on principles have persistently resurfaced in addressing this issue so that they deserve further commentary.

In this context, it has become a common approach to distinguish between theses of weak demarcation (quantitative difference), strong demarcation (qualitative difference), and confusion or overlap between principles and rules.[38] The models that I want to address briefly in this section are placed under the discussions of the weak demarcation thesis.

[31] Engisch, 1983 [1956], 165–6, dealing with the contradictions between principles.

[32] Betti, 1949, 212, referring to the general principles of law. In a similar sense, Bandeira de Mello (2003, 817) defines principle as 'a nuclear requirement of a system, its true foundation'.

[33] Jakab, 2006, 60–1.

[34] Peczenik, 1971, 30; 1989, 74. See also Jakab, 2006, 57, 65.

[35] Canaris, 1983, 46–7, dealing with the general principles of law.

[36] For a brief review of several criteria for distinguishing between principles and rules, see Alexy, 1986, 72–5 (Engl. trans. 2010, 45–7); 1985, 14–15.

[37] See e.g. Struck, 1971, 20–34; Eckhoff and Sundby, 1988, 98–9.

[38] Alexy, 1979, 64–5; 1986, 74–5 (Engl. trans. 2002, 47); Aarnio, 1990, 180 ff., concluding that, 'all things considered' (see above note 16 of this chapter), i.e. 'following interpretation', there would be

First, I shall consider models that point out the greater imprecision of principles in comparison to rules. These models are very often tied to the question of the degree of discretion the norm offers those interpreting and applying it.[39] In this regard, some initial clarifications are required.

The issue of imprecision should not be confused with the issue of discretion in the strict sense. Semantic imprecision, in the forms of ambiguity (connotative) and vagueness (denotative), starting primarily from the meaning of the text and its field of reference, implies cognitive uncertainty regarding the norm to be applied.[40] This issue is closely linked to those of complexity, contingency,[41] and diversity of interpretative expectations about normative texts and relevant norms.[42] In less complex societies, the norms are presented as obvious[43] in such a way that the question of imprecision of normative texts is not relevant. The problem of semantic imprecision in applying norms arises whenever a number of normative expectations are in conflict, not only in relation to law-making and constitution-making but also with respect to the normative understanding of statutory and constitutional texts. This also includes the diversity of interpretations of the relevant case as different understandings of the underlying facts emerge.

Discretion in the strict sense should not be confused with the inherent semantic imprecision of normative texts and the denotative uncertainty regarding the norm to be applied to each case; instead, it is concerned with the fact that the norm itself presents alternatives to the official(s) in charge of its legal concretization.[44] While discussion of the types of discretionary acts goes

no distinction between rules and principles, which would only make sense in the prima facie analysis (192). I will return to this point later on.

[39] Cf. e.g. Eckhoff and Sundby, 1988, 108.

[40] Here I employ 'imprecision' in a very broad sense in order to embrace both vagueness and ambiguity as sources of indeterminacy or uncertainty of law, it is neither in the strictly technical sense referred to by Endicott ('vagueness in the technical sense of apparent susceptibility to the tolerance principle') nor according to his broad application of the term as a synonym of vagueness (Endicott, 2000, 33 ff.).

[41] Complexity understood in the sense 'that there are always more possibilities than can be actualized'; contingency understood as the condition in which 'the indicated possibilities of further experience can turn out differently from what was expected' (Luhmann, 1987b, 31 (Engl. trans. 2014, 25)), thus implying uncertainty in terms of expectations.

[42] It must be clear, however, that issues of complexity and contingency in the communicative process go beyond the semantic (connotative and denotative) imprecision of texts, provisions or statements.

[43] Ultimately, in archaic forms of society, one does not distinguish between norm and action, there being therefore no institutionalized procedure for legal adjudication or application (see Weber, 1985 [1922], 445–6 (Engl. trans. 1968, vol. 2, 760–1); Schluchter, 1979, 146; Habermas, 1982a, vol. 1, 349 and 351; vol. 2, 261–2 (Engl. trans. 1984/1987, vol. 1, 257–8; vol. 2, 175–6); 1982b, 135; Luhmann, 1993, 257 (Engl. trans. 2004, 243–4); 1987b, 150 (Engl. trans. 2014, 117–18)).

[44] This distinction between discretion in the strict sense and imprecision corresponds somehow to the difference between 'intentional indefiniteness of the law-applying act' and 'unintended indefiniteness of the law-applying act', as formulated by Kelsen (1960, 347–8 (Engl. trans. 1967, 349–50)).

beyond the scope of this chapter (the topic is thoroughly examined within administrative law),[45] one can generally distinguish two typical forms of discretion (in the strict and rigorous sense): the first, in relation to the act itself, is when performing it becomes subject to political conditions regarding the administrative margin of appreciation to be assessed by the official(s) in question; and second, concerning the content of the act, is when, given the applicability of a norm to a particular situation, the official(s) may choose one of the alternatives offered by the norm in the material, personal, temporal, or territorial dimension. However, the choice between the alternatives that the norm leaves at the discretion of the competent authority is not to be confused with the semantic imprecision (ambiguity or vagueness) of the norm to be applied. It is worth clarifying that determining whether a norm opens up a space for discretion (in the strict sense) to the official(s) in charge of applying the norm requires that occasional problems of semantic imprecision are solved, in order to establish whether there is discretionary competence; that is whether the norm offers optional applications *a*, *b*, or *c*, for example, or merely prescribes application *a*. Even if one begins with a model that admits only of a single right decisional or interpretive answer, it can be one that which determines the discretionary nature of the authority granted by the norm.

Taking these aspects into consideration, one may conclude that the quantitative discussion that delineates the distinction between rules and principles refers to the problem of the semantic imprecision of normative texts, in so far as this leads to cognitive uncertainty regarding the norm to be applied. It is for this reason that principles are often thought to be more imprecise than rules.[46] This position does not seem sustainable, however: both at the ordinary law and at the constitutional level, we find semantically imprecise rules that are thus highly dependent on the context of application.

Consider, for example, the legal rule expressed in Article 94.II of the Brazilian Criminal Code, which refers to 'good public and private behaviour'

However, I assume neither the concept of 'intentionality' nor the 'cognition/will', 'subjective/objective', or 'political/scientific' dichotomy in Kelsen's terms that 'the law to be applied constitutes only a frame within which several applications are possible' (1960, 348 ff. (Engl. trans. 1967, 350 ff.)). Legal concretization is understood here as a social process of communication, which implies overcoming the classical epistemological dichotomy 'subjective/objective' in the name of the difference 'system/environment' (cf. Luhmann, 1987a, 25–6 (Engl. trans. 1995, 9)).

[45] See, among others, Bandeira de Mello, 2006, 9 ff.

[46] Guastini, 1992, 145–6, with some qualifications; Betti, 1949, 207–8, referring to the general principles of law; Eckhoff and Sundby, 1988, 108, asserting the vagueness of the directives, which, in their view, do not identify with the principles, but have much in common with these (107).

as a requirement for rehabilitation.[47] How can we define 'good behaviour' without considering the social context and the values of the judges? It is clear that in matters relating to non-dominant forms of affective relationships, for example, the assessment of good public and private behaviour is likely to vary widely between, say, a feminist judge or a judge associated with an institution combating homophobia, on the one hand, and a judge linked to 'Opus Dei' or 'Tradition, Family and Property' (TFP), on the other hand. Likewise, in cases where alcohol use is a relevant consideration (for example, when attempting to justify criminal rehabilitation), judgments as to what constitutes 'good behaviour' can vary substantially between a judge who is fond of drink and one who is a teetotaller (a variation that is no doubt even greater depending on the social and geographical context, whether it is metropolitan, cosmopolitan, urban, provincial, or rural).

There are also constitutional rules whose language and wording lead to semantic imprecision and, therefore, to a cognitive uncertainty about which norm to apply. Note the rule expressed in Article 55.II of the Brazilian Federal Constitution, which establishes that '[a] Deputy or Senator shall lose his office ... if his conduct is declared incompatible with parliamentary decorum'. Although paragraph 1 of this Article establishes a semantic delimitation of what is incompatible with the parliamentary decorum, by pointing out the 'abuse of the prerogatives ensured to a congressman or the gaining of undue advantages', such hypotheses are mere examples, with the definition of other 'cases' being left on the under-constitutional plane (there is an express reference to the National Congress bylaws). Though a typical provision of a constitutional rule, it clearly reveals a high degree of vagueness, which exceeds the imprecision of some constitutional principles.

In relation to the imprecision concerning the above-mentioned criminal rule, the delimitation of meaning depends mainly on the personal, material, temporal, and spatial context of the judicial act. In the case of the Constitution, the context is more complex, depending both on Congressional bylaws and statutory law and on the concrete act of imposition of sanctions by the Chamber of Deputies or the Federal Senate. Of course, this highest contextual dependence is hardly a 'semantic aphasia'—in which words lose their meaning and become mere signifiers, whose meaning depends on the axiological variable invoked in

[47] 'Art 94—Rehabilitation may be requested after two (2) years from the date the penalty was in any way extinguished, or its enforcement ended, including the period of probation and release on parole, unless in case of a supervening revocation order, provided that the convict: ... II—has expressed in such time effective and steady *good public and private behaviour* ...' (wording by Law No. 7,209, 11 July 1984—emphasis added).

the context of the legal application[48]—and much less so a 'floating signifier'.[49] There is a historical sedimentation of meaning, grounded especially on established precedents, that is an argument-based 'redundancy'—in the terms of the systems theory—is built.[50] But the foregoing examples already show that, at least prima facie, the rules can be markedly imprecise.

In turn, nothing prevents provisions related to constitutional principles from having some degree of semantic precision, at least when compared with constitutional and legal rules similar to those alluded to above. Consider, for example, the principle of free enterprise, expressed in Article 1.IV of the Brazilian Federal Constitution, which is presented as one of the fundamental principles of the Republic. It seems to me that it has a much lesser degree of imprecision than that of the above-mentioned rules. A possible difficulty in applying this principle is primarily associated not with a problem concerning the semantic delimitation in view of the ambiguity and vagueness of its provision. Instead, it is concerned with its relationship to other constitutional principles and rules: what is the normative force of this principle as compared to other competing principles? What are the constitutional rules whose effects prevent this principle from being applicable to the case?

Even in cases involving goal-concerning principles (such as that expressed in Article 3.III of the Brazilian Federal Constitution, which includes among the fundamental objectives of the 'Federative Republic of Brazil' 'to eradicate poverty and substandard living conditions and to reduce social and regional inequalities'), we are not necessarily dealing with semantic imprecision.[51] Although varying somewhat according to the context, definitions of poverty are, nonetheless, relatively consistent, sharing quantitative criteria developed by international organizations and the academic community. Reducing social and regional inequalities is not something that inherently involves semantic vagueness. In these cases, the difficulty of applying the norm is not primarily a matter of legal conditions, that is the relationship of this goal-concerning principle with other constitutional principles and rules. Instead, it arises from the

48 Warat, 1972, 178–9.

49 See above note 5 of this chapter.

50 See Luhmann, 1986c, 34 ff. I will return to this subject in Chapter 3, sections 2 and 3.

51 Of course, one could say that this constitutional provision also contains a rule (or rules). Indeed, in certain extreme situations, it can be directly assigned a rule (or rules) in view of the manifest omission against its (their) purposes, leading to political proceedings against the competent authority. But those situations are very exceptional or unlikely. It seems to me that, prima facie, it must be characterized, in general, as a constitutional provision of a principle (or principles), since its concretization and realization depend on political measures from which rules derive. Furthermore, the constitutional review of such measures or their omissions usually depends on rules constructed from these principles and indirectly attributed to the constitutional text.

factual conditions for its implementation. In the Brazilian constitutional experience, this situation is a typical episode of symbolic constitutionalization[52] and does not raise any special problem of semantic imprecision. This principle is, beyond any doubt, a much more precise norm (or less imprecise) than the above-mentioned rules about decorum and good behaviour.

Yet principles not *directly* attributable to the constitutional text or a constitutional provision ('derivative principles'),[53] but with normative force in the constitutional system, may have a higher degree of precision (or lower level of imprecision) than certain constitutional and statutory rules such as, for example, the so-called principle of maximum effectiveness developed (albeit controversially) in Brazilian Constitutional case-law.[54] In relation to this principle, semantic imprecision is not the primary issue but rather the question of the legal and factual conditions of its concretization and realization.

These remarks serve to demonstrate that a quantitative (or qualitative) criterion regarding the semantic imprecision of normative provisions cannot be taken as the decisive criterion for distinguishing between constitutional principles and rules. Of course, one can verify a tendency towards a greater degree of imprecision among principles but defining principles as more imprecise norms than rules is wrong. At the constitutional level, especially in the Brazilian experience, this criterion is entirely unsustainable. The legal and factual limitations in maintaining and implementing constitutional principles are often confused with issues of semantic imprecision concerning the normative provisions and with questions (arising therefrom) related to the cognitive uncertainty regarding the applicable law. This misconception must be rejected. Although it may be possible to observe a trend, only through a comparative analysis of each case it is possible to ascertain the degree of difficulty arising from the imprecision of a normative provision or semantic uncertainty in determining the

[52] Neves, 1998.

[53] It seems to me that the formulation of Alexy (1986, 57–63 (Engl. trans. 2002, 33–8)), by introducing the notion of 'derivative constitutional rights norms' as norms 'attributed' to the constitutional text (in the original: '*zugeordnete Grundrechtsnorm*'), in order to distinguish them from constitutional rights norms that 'are directly expressed' by provisions of the constitution, is misleading. Strictly speaking, every constitutional norm can be directly or indirectly attributed to constitutional provisions or, in general, the text of the constitution (and where there is no written constitutional document, the statements which play the role of constitutional provisions, or the sparse set of texts that acts as the functional equivalent to the constitutional document). The so-called attributed fundamental rights norms [in the simplified English translation: 'derivative constitutional rights norms'] might be characterized for being *mediately or indirectly* attributed to constitutional provisions or the constitutional text. But this is a matter of degree, analogous to the (semantic) distinction between implicit and explicit dimensions of language, as well as the (pragmatic) division between the so-called interpretivism and non-interpretivism, to use a distinction proposed by Ely (1980, 1 ff.).

[54] Canotilho, 1998, 1097. See similarly Barroso, 1996, 218–44; 2010, 306; Barroso and Barcellos, 2005, 303. In the Brazilian case-law, cf. ADI 2596/PA, judgment 19/03/2003, TP, DJ 02/05/2003.

applicable norm, being substantially irrelevant if we are dealing with a constitutional rule or a constitutional principle.

If these observations are valid for semantic imprecision, they are even more relevant on the issue of discretion in the strictly technical sense. Having clarified above that these two issues are not to be confused and keeping in mind that norms establishing alternatives to the exercise of the discretionary power can be precise, it is worth considering that rules are a much more appropriate standard for the purposes of establishing discretion for the relevant official. Constitutional rules establishing the jurisdiction of the supreme political bodies, the National Congress and the President, are largely discretionary concerning the exercise of the act, thereby establishing a facultative power. The exercise of this power depends largely on criteria of convenience and opportunity, in other words political discretion. This is particularly evident in the case of the rules providing that statutory law may grant amnesty by the Congress (Article 48.VIII BFC) and that the President may appoint and dismiss Ministers of State at his or her discretion (Article 84.I BFC). Although not involving arbitrary power, such rules expressly grant a large degree of freedom to the respective officials, something to which principles are not well suited. Indeed, principles (but also rules) may be semantically too imprecise and therefore offer discretionary spaces in a weak (or not strict) sense, as in the principle of human dignity (Article 1.III BFC). Nonetheless, they do not lend themselves to providing options for discretion in a strictly technical sense, be it to establish a mere facultative power or to provide various alternatives to the officials charged with interpreting and applying the constitutional law. It is a duty for public authorities to act in defence of human dignity, individual freedom, equality, etc. This is not something optional nor does it offer alternatives within each of these principles. The fact that there are legal conditions (other constitutional principles and also rules) and factual ones that can provide different contours to the field of application of these principles does not imply discretion: once these conditions are defined, the respective principle ought to be applied within the limits set out by the prevailing conditions in the context of the case.

Another distinguishing criterion based on quantitative characteristics of the normative types (and therefore included in the so-called weak demarcation thesis) is the degree of generality. In this sense, principles are defined as more general norms than rules.[55] Some clarification is necessary before proceeding to an analysis of this conception.

[55] MacCormick, 1974, 22; 1995 [1978], 152–3, 232; Raz, 1972, 838; Bergel, 1999, 91; Guastini, 1992, 146–7; Betti, 1949, 207.

It seems appropriate first to distinguish the generality from abstraction. In this regard, the following excerpt from Norberto Bobbio is remarkable for its clarity: 'we advise speaking of *general norms* when we are facing norms that address a class of people, and *abstract norms* when we are facing norms regulating an action-type (or class of actions)'.[56] In this sense, one can say that the generality concerns the pragmatic dimension of the addressees of the norm, referring to its personal sphere of validity. Abstraction, in turn, concerns the semantic dimension of the referents of the norm, relating to its material sphere of validity and involving the question of defining the legal facts and cases that are subsumable under the norm. Both principles and rules are general and abstract norms. The issue here is determining the degree of generality and abstraction. This involves the question of establishing the reach of the class of people addressed by the norm (generality) and the scope of the class of facts, actions, or cases regulated by it (abstraction).

However, in the context of the debate on constitutional principles and rules, the term 'generality' is intended to refer to both the personal and the material sphere of validity, that is the generality and abstraction in the sense stated above, and perhaps more related to the latter than the former. I will discuss this issue considering the two meanings of the term.

In stating that principles are more general norms than rules, we sometimes start from the deductive models analogous to axioms or postulates. In such a model it is common to consider principles as self-evident norms of reason, independent of empirical verification.[57] In other cases, the thesis of greater generality is based on an inductive model in which the principles emerge from the systematic generalization or abstraction of existing rules.[58] In relation to the constitutional principles and rules, both theses are irrelevant since they are norms constructed within the legal order in so far as they are directly or indirectly attributed to the constitutional text produced by a constituent act or constitutional amendment (or, in cases where there is no constitutional document, the sparse set of texts that acts

[56] Bobbio, 1958, 231.

[57] Del Vecchio, 1921, 17 ff. and 61. However, Del Vecchio moved away from the idea that from the general principles the contingent empirical elements of the legal order could be automatically deduced and, vice versa, that from the latter could be directly induced the former (20).

[58] Crisafulli, 1939, 20–1; 1952, 38–9. See Pascua, 1996, 15; Jakab, 2006, 59. Critical of the models of deduction and induction, see Betti, 1949, esp. 206–7, according to whom the principles carry a plus when compared to the existing rules.

as a functional equivalent of a constitutional document, including case-law standards).

The thesis of generality is unsustainable. Alexy rightly points out the case of the legality of crimes and punishments precept,[59] which is also expressly stated in the Brazilian Federal Constitution (Article 5.XXXIX). Although it must be considered a rule to the extent that it serves as a definitive criterion for deciding a case, it has a high degree of generality when compared to certain constitutional principles. Many other examples can be added, especially if we address this question without confusing it with the difficulties of interpretation associated with imprecision. If we consider that certain principles have only a sectorial relevance,[60] such as the constitutional principles relating to the tax system or the public administration, it can be stated that, within their personal sphere of application, they are less general and, regarding the material sphere of application, they are less abstract than many constitutional rules unrestricted to a specific sector of actors and activities. For instance, Article 146.III.c of the Brazilian Federal Constitution sets forth that a supplementary law 'shall establish general rules concerning tax legislation', especially with regard to 'adequate tax treatment for the cooperative acts of cooperative associations'. Therefore, it links a rule of jurisdiction to a specific principle, that of the appropriate tax treatment of cooperative activity, which will be articulated with other constitutional principles and rules. But would this principle be more abstract and general than the rule contained in Article 5.XLV of the Constitution, which determines, definitively, that 'no punishment shall go beyond the person of the convicted'? Here, there is no doubt that the generality of this rule, at least in the personal sphere of validity, is much greater than the aforementioned principle, since the provision directly refers to any person, not only to Brazilian citizens. Also, in the material sphere of validity, it seems possible to assert a higher abstraction of this rule when compared to that constitutional taxation principle, because the former, despite being specific to criminal law, regulates a much broader class of cases and actions. The same situation appears in relation to the rule contained in Article 12.2

[59] Alexy, 1986, 92–3 (Engl. trans., 2002, 61). Of course, in this regard, it may be objected that it is a principle or, in the terminology of Larenz (1983, 461; 1969, 465–6), one of the 'principles in the form of legal propositions'. Nevertheless, one may consider this norm a rule to the extent that it is able to serve as a definitive and immediate criterion for making a decision to settle a case subsumed under it. As we shall see in Chapter 3.1, this norm might also be defined atypically as a hybrid.

[60] They may be linked to a 'small complex of rules' (Eckhoff and Sundby, 1988, 101, referring, in their terms, to 'directives', which correspond to the 'principles' in the dominant legal and constitutional terminology—cf. above note 46 of this chapter). See Canaris, 1983, 47–8.

of the Constitution, which prohibits 'any distinction between native-born and naturalized Brazilians, except as provided in this Constitution', and the principle of judicial independence, which unfolds in the rules expressly warranting it in Article 95 ('life tenure', 'irremovability', and 'irreducibility of pay' of the judges) but is not to be confused with these rules. Of course, the rule regarding nationality is more general than this principle (which particularly addresses magistrates and particularly regulates the judicial function), since the former refers to *all* citizens, and is more abstract, because it relates to *any* discrimination between them (save the constitutional exceptions).

It is quite common to address imprecision issues as a matter of generality.[61] That can lead to confusion when considering the rules and principles mentioned as examples. But even if the thesis of generality is understood in terms of imprecision, the distinction between principles and rules based on these criteria does not hold up, according to the arguments presented above. It can be affirmed, indeed, that the principles tend to be more general and vaguer than rules. In this respect, Alexy maintains that 'one reason that the principles usually show a greater degree of generality lies in the fact that they still do not relate to the boundaries of the possibilities of the factual and normative world'.[62] It is, however, important to insist that this characteristic does not possess any essential relationship but only a contingent one, although it may be considered a trend, with principles' greater generality and imprecision in regard to rules.[63] Of course, compared to the rules that are built on principles and which provide them with practical support, principles will always be more general, even if they are domain-specific, as in the case of the relationship between the rules that guarantee life tenure and the principle of judicial independence. This, nevertheless, does not invalidate the main thesis: the degree of generality (as well as the degree of imprecision) is not an adequate criterion for distinguishing between constitutional principles and constitutional rules.

[61] The lack of this distinction, for example, is to be found out in Alexy, who, by pointing out the generality of the rule of criminal legality, affirms that its disposition 'may give rise to a whole host of problems of interpretation' (1986, 92 (Engl. trans., 2002, 61)). In turn, Jakab (2006, 58) states that 'the highest degree of generality leaves more room for interpretation', confusing the concepts of imprecision, generality, and discretion.

[62] Alexy, 1979, 81.

[63] Similarly, Esser (1956, 51–2), while proposing the distinction between principles and 'norms' on the basis of the 'determinability of the cases of application', rejects the criterion of the degree of generality or abstraction. It should also be added that, in Esser's formulation, this is not about the criterion of semantic precision or imprecision, but about a structural difference.

3. Reference to Goals and Values as a Criterion for Distinguishing Between Principle and Rules

Another strand in demarcating the differences between principles and rules points out, either in qualitative or quantitative terms, the reference to purposes and values as a distinctive feature of principles in contrast to rules. This broad stream of thought also includes the reference to the 'idea of law'[64] or an 'ideal state of affairs'[65] as a typical characteristic of the principles, but ultimately these conceptions are also teleological. Although there is some affinity between the criterion based on purposes and the one based on values, I shall analyse the corresponding conceptual models separately, given the peculiarities of each of them.

However, before entering into a proper analysis of the topic, I would like to make some critical remarks about an inappropriate use of Georg Henrik von Wright's works found in the recent juridical discussion about principles and rules.

Laporta, based on his own reading of a masterwork of Georg Henrik von Wright,[66] introduces a distinction between 'a logic of ought-to-do' ['a logic of the *Tunsollen*'] and 'a logic of ought-to-be' ['a logic of the *Seinsollen*'], as a way of associating rules with the first and principles with the second, linking these to the notion of norms concerning 'ideal states of affairs' and the idea of 'practical necessity' in Von Wright's sense.[67] This distinction was adopted by Aarnio to define principles as ' "ought to be" norms', which refer to ideal states of affairs, distinguishing them from rules as ' "ought to do" norms', which refer directly to actions.[68] Hage introduces an analogous distinction, not to distinguish between principles and rules but between norms and goals.[69] In his understanding, principles as norms are distinct from goals,[70] although these 'can easily be "translated" into corresponding norms' and, therefore, into principles.[71] Ávila (who also mistakenly attributes this model to Hage) speaks of 'ought-to-be-norms' (principles) and 'ought-to-do-norms' (rules), arguing that the former 'define a sort of practical necessity' in von Wright's the sense; that is they 'create the duty of adopting the behaviour required to realize the

64 Larenz, 1983, 218, 405; 1969, 394, 460.
65 See the next paragraphs.
66 Von Wright, 1963, 13 ff.
67 Laporta, 1999, esp. 280 ff.
68 Aarnio, 1997, 181–3, quoting the then unpublished work of Laporta; Aarnio, 2011, 124.
69 Hage, 1997, 67.
70 Hage, 1997, 99–100.
71 Hage, 1997, 67.

state of affairs' or 'describe an ideal state of affairs that will be accomplished only if some behaviour is adopted'.[72] Borrowing von Wright's model to distinguish rules and principles in this way, however, seems objectionable. First, the notion of 'necessity' for reaching an end is instead associated with technical and pragmatic rules (hypothetical imperatives in Kant's sense),[73] not with norms, let alone principles. The technical and pragmatic rules establish a 'must' (*Müssen*, what one needs to do in order to reach an end) rather than an 'ought' (*Sollen*, what is due within the space of possibilities or the 'freedom' of the agent without that success in itself being the determinant factor). Regarding technical rules, it is relevant here, prescinding from a priori metaphysical assumptions, to quote the following passage from Kant:

> There is no question here whether the end is rational and good, but only what one must do in order to attain it. The prescriptions for the physician thoroughly to cure his man, and for a poisoner reliably to kill him, are of equal worth, in so far as each serves to effect its purpose perfectly.[74]

Von Wright himself relates the notion of 'practical necessity' to the 'technical ought' ('*technisches Sollen*') as follows:

> We are here, I say, faced with another 'ought'–as usual as the deontic or normative ought of moral or legal norms. I will call it a *technical* ought... The technical ought expresses a requirement, a practical necessity, and is often–and perhaps better–expressed by the word *must* [*muβ*].[75]

He adds: 'it is closely associated with what Kant called "hypothetical imperative"'.[76] He warns then: 'The technical ought should not be confused with the ought of genuine norms. There is a strong tendency to do so.'[77] It is therefore profoundly mistaken to use this passage of von Wright to associate the principles with the notion of 'practical necessity'. Secondly, von Wright defines the rules that are more closely related with being than with doing as 'ideal rules'.[78] Although he claims it

[72] Ávila, 2003, 64 (Engl. trans. 2007, 35).
[73] Kant, 1965 [1785/1786], 34 ff. [414 ff.] (Engl. trans. 2012, 28 ff.).
[74] Kant, 1965 [1785/1786], 35 [415] (Engl. trans. 2012, 29).
[75] Von Wright, 1994a, 36. Kant also asserted that 'all imperatives are expressed by an *ought*' (Kant, 1965, [1785/1786], 33 [413] (Engl. trans. 2012, 27)), but one might distinguish in his work a strong *ought* of the moral and legal norms from a weak *ought* of the technical or pragmatic rules, which rather express, as already said, a *must* or *have to*.
[76] Von Wright, 1994a, 36.
[77] Ibid.
[78] Von Wright, 1963, 14.

would be 'a mistake to think of the ideal rules as norms concerning means to ends', arguing that they establish not a causal, but a 'conceptual' relation, he notes that 'there is a certain similarity between ideal rules and technical norms'.[79] According to von Wright, ideal rules 'are similar to rules of a game' and have to be distinguished from 'moral principles'.[80] Ideal rules hold 'a position between technical norms about means to an end and rules which determine a pattern or standard'.[81] It is at least arguable, therefore, to associate von Wright's concept of 'ideal rule' with the notion of principles as norms, as proposed by Laporta.[82]

Let us return now to our central argument.

There are numerous authors who point out the teleological or predominantly purposive character of principles as compared with rules.[83] From this perspective, for example, Humberto Ávila states that 'rules are immediate descriptive norms', whose 'content directly regards actions', their 'up-front quality' being 'the definition of behaviours', whereas 'principles are immediate finalistic norms', 'whose up-front quality is exactly the definition of a legally relevant purpose'.[84] It seems to me that such a model, based on a long tradition, does not provide a precise criterion for distinguishing between constitutional principles and constitutional rules.

First, it is necessary to make explicit from which philosophical or theoretical stream of thought one is arguing when proposing a classification based on the reference to purposes. Three models may be roughly presented: those based on the Aristotelian notion of final causes, those based on the conception of an ideal teleology dating back to Hegel, and those guided by Weber's concept of purposive or instrumental rationality.

In Aristotelian metaphysics, the notion of final cause concerns the end for whose attainment anything exists or is done, being related to the 'good', 'for this is the end of every generative or motive process'.[85] The concept is not restricted to human action but also encompasses animal behaviour and structure, the plant world, and, finally, nature in general.[86] Even when referring to the 'good' as the final cause of human action, Aristotle does not address the issue in terms of contemporary axiological preferences but as an *ontological*

[79] Von Wright, 1963, 14–15.
[80] Von Wright, 1963, 15–16.
[81] Von Wright, 1963, 16.
[82] Laporta, 1999, esp. 280–1.
[83] In addition to the references made in the previous paragraph, see, among many, MacCormick, 1974, 222; 1995 [1978], esp. 263–4, linking the notion of principles to that of policies.
[84] Ávila, 2003, 63–4 (Engl. trans. 2007, 34–5).
[85] Aristotle, 2003, 17, Book I, III.1–2. See Aristotle, 2005, esp. 131–3, Book II, Chapter III (194b–195a).
[86] Aristotle, 2005, 169–79, Book II, Chapter VIII (198b 10–199b 32).

necessity of the being. If a process or a being deviates from its final cause, it corrupts itself, losing its intrinsic and essential characteristics: it becomes degraded, deformed.

If we consider legal principles in terms of Aristotelian teleology, we are urged to adopt a markedly ontological and metaphysical model concerning principles. Constitutional principles, however, are contingent constructs of a legal order. It does not make sense, for example, to state that the programmatic principle contained in the sole paragraph of Article 4 of the Brazilian Federal Constitution—by establishing that the Federative Republic of Brazil shall seek the integration of the peoples of Latin America, 'viewing the formation of a Latin-American community of nations'—is directed towards a final cause in Aristotle's sense. This is a policy goal incorporated into the Constitution in the form of programmatic or purposive principle.

Similar considerations are appropriate in relation to teleological approaches of law dating back to Hegel. Unlike the realist ontology of Aristotle regarding ends, the Hegelian teleological model is idealistic.[87] As such, the historical process is understood as the dialectical development of the spirit from lower to higher forms, until it reaches an 'absolute' final form.[88] Thereby 'universal history' is defined as 'the *actualization of the universal spirit*' or as the history of 'immersion of the world spirit in itself'.[89] It was based on this understanding of history that the teleological perspectives regarding legal principles were developed from Hegel's work. This is about, so to speak, following the path towards an ideal state at the highest level of the 'world spirit'. Yet, Hegel's construct is not an axiological model in terms of preferences assumed by the respective collectivity but rather a rationally determined development. And if we consider the identity of the rational and the real according to Hegel, it involves an evolution determined by reality.

I do not think a model of this kind can serve to explain the theory of constitutional principles without adopting an idealist historicism, which begins from meta-positive principles guiding the development of positive law. Constitutional principles are contingent; they are achievements, inventions, or constructs of the modern constitutional state. If we consider, for example, the principle of equality, as expressed in the head provision of Article 5 of the Brazilian Federal Constitution, it would be clearly mistaken to claim that it presents itself as a legal principle because it directly

[87] Of course, it is an objective idealism, within which the famous assertion is pivotal: 'What is rational is actual; and what is actual is rational' (Hegel, 1986 [1821], 24 (Engl. trans. 1991, 20)).
[88] Luhmann, 1997, vol. 1, 422–3 (Engl. trans. 2012, 256–7).
[89] Hegel, 1986 [1821], 435–6 (§ 273) and 504 (§ 342) (Engl. trans. 1991, 308, 372).

refers to purposes to be achieved. This is a norm, a counterfactual determination, which may be more or less socially effective (which is true for any and all norms, including rules). In this sense, when distinguishing between the equality principle (isonomy) as a requirement for the concrete adjudication and enforcement of norms and the so-called substantive equality as the political-legal target for the equality of social conditions, Fabio Comparato is right in warning: 'Therefore, one should not intend to erase or conceal the fact of social inequalities among human beings with the application of the principle of equality.'[90] In fact, the principle of equality acts as a norm designed to immunize the law against differences which, while being relevant and legitimate in other social spheres, are not relevant in the context of rights. In other words, this is a counterfactual determination to counteract the pressures these differences exert on law. This means that, for example, greater wealth or power, higher educational level, closer affective or familial relationship, by themselves, do not entitle anyone to succeed in a lawsuit against another less wealthy, less powerful, less educated individual, or against someone who is merely strange or socially distant.[91] Of course, thus understood, the normative force of the principle of equality does not imply the pursuit of an ideal state but rather it relates to the counterfactual feature of all legal orders and respective norms.

Models that address an ideal situation in a teleological way, even without being linked with the Hegelian tradition, are not suitable for understanding the programmatic purposive principles contained in the constitution. Achieving the contingent principle-based goals of a constitutional order, such as the granting of political asylum (Article 4.X BFC), depends on the real conditions or factual and legal possibilities, always within the limits of their relationship with other constitutional norms (principles and rules). What, then, would be the ideal state of affairs in the relationship between competing principles (e.g. the principle of 'the social values of labour' *versus* the principle of 'free enterprise' in Article 1.IV, 'solidarity' *versus* 'free competition' in Articles 3.I and 170.IV, 'freedom of expression' *versus* 'inviolability of privacy' in Articles 5.IV and 5.X of the Brazilian Federal Constitution)? Striving to reach an ideal state of affairs in line with a principle may involve the total abandonment of another.

[90] Comparato, 1993, 77–8. See Neves, 2000, 128 ff. This also applies to the improperly called principle of factual equality, which rather follows from the principle of the social state (Alexy, 1986, 380–9 (Engl. trans., 2002, 278–85), referring to Article 20(1) Basic Law of Germany) or the programmatic principle attributable to Article 3.III of the Brazilian Federal Constitution (reduction of social inequalities).

[91] Here we are faced with the issue of complex equality posed by Walzer (1983, 33 ff.), to which I shall return in Chapter 3.5.

For this reason, an idealistic teleologism seems inappropriate to demarcate the distinction between legal or constitutional principles and rules.

Of course, one can follow a purposive model of principles invoking Max Weber's concept of 'instrumental rationality' (*Zweckrationalität*). In this perspective, principles are related to social action 'determined by expectations as to the behaviour of objects in the environment and of other human beings; these expectations are used as "conditions" or "means" for the attainment of the actor's own rationally pursued and calculated ends'.[92] Here it is about seeking the means to achieve rational ends, that is according to the interests of the agent, either in an instrumental form in the strict sense (the means are objects) or in a strategic way (the means are the action of another).[93] Although the Weberian concept of purposive or instrumental rationality refers to the actions of individuals, not to norms, it can be considered from the perspective of the structures that guide the necessary or appropriate behaviour towards achieving a certain end. In this case, however, purposive rationality (which is primarily a rationality of *means* suitable for certain purposes)[94] would be much more related to the rules that establish the means and conditions for achieving certain purposes intended to satisfy specific interests.[95] If Weber's terminology is used, one would have to discuss instead whether principles are tied to value-rationality, which is 'determined by a conscious belief in the value for its own sake of some ethical, aesthetic, religious, or other form of behaviour, independently of its prospects of success'.[96] I will return to this topic later, when dealing with models that distinguish principles and rules based on reference to values.

It seems to me that the reference of constitutional norms to goals can be analysed more precisely if we consider the distinction between purpose-specific programmes, primarily political, and conditional programmes, primarily legal. The former concerns the establishment of purposes and the determination of means to achieving them, specifying means–end relationships. The

[92] Weber, 1985 [1922], 12 (Engl. trans. 1968, vol. 1, 24). Weber adds: 'Action is instrumentally rational *(zweckrational)* when the end, the means, and the secondary results are all rationally taken into account and weighed. This involves rational consideration of alternative means to the end, of the relations of the end to the secondary consequences, and finally of the relative importance of different possible ends' (1985 [1922], 13 (Engl. trans. 1968, vol. 1, 26)).

[93] In his reconstruction of Weber's theory, Habermas (1982a, vol. 1, 384 ff. (Engl. trans. 1984, vol. 1, 284 ff.)) distinguishes instrumental and strategic action as two types of purposive action (orientated to success) in contrast to communicative action (orientated to inter-subjective understanding).

[94] Considering specifically the passage cited above in note 92, von Wright (1994b, 123–4) argues that the purposive rationality, in Weber's terms, is not the *mere* rationality of means, consisting 'essentially of the rational choice and employment of means to the purposes of an actor'. However, it is undeniable that the Weberian concept of purposive or instrumental *rationality* emphasizes the *rational means*, an understanding that is suggested in the very formulation of von Wright.

[95] In this sense, it has affinity with the Kantian notion of technical rules (see above p. 28).

[96] Weber, 1985 [1922], 12 (Engl. trans. 1968, vol. 1, 24–5).

latter involves the determination of the conditions that can lead to a particular effect, establishing if-then links.[97] The purposive-specific programmes, allocated primarily in the political system, correspond to *policies*. These can be incorporated into the legal system, becoming the content of legal *norms*. Thus, they become 'conditioned', in other words they become the content of conditional programmes.[98] Therefore, the primary question that arises is no longer whether a purpose can be reached (prospectively), but whether the public or private agent acted (or failed to act) in pursuit of the purposes normatively established (retrospectively).[99] This is typically a kind of 're-entry' in Spencer Brown's sense.[100] Something that was outside enters the system but gains a new meaning (primarily legal), distinct from that which was originally its primary meaning (political).

Purpose-specific programmes or policies enter the legal system through principles and rules. From one side, they enter it through the so-called programmatic principles as constitutional norms,[101] that is via purposive constitutional principles. From the other side, they enter it through legal rules concerning public policies and planning. In other words, by setting the targets to be achieved by the political-administrative planning, the public authority often provides it a legal form through rules. Thus, for example, while projects aimed at restoring a dilapidated urban neighbourhood can be legally regulated, it is not fitting to speak of principles in this case.

It is true that the rules containing policies are usually at a sub-constitutional level and, apart from referring to purposes, they tend to regulate the means in detail, unlike purposive constitutional principles. However, rules primarily related to purposes can be found in the constitution and, moreover, may not specify the means to reach the goals but only impose on public officials or citizens a duty to act in order to achieve the established purposes. This category seems to include Article 7 of the Temporary Constitutional Provisions Act: 'Brazil shall strive for the creation of an international court of human rights.' This normative provision expressly points to an end, but it does not contain any principle (of course, it is rooted in constitutional principles). Somehow, the goal laid down in this provision was achieved with the creation of the Rome Statute of the International Criminal Court, its ratification

[97] See Luhmann, 1973, 88 ff.; 1981, 140–3 and 275 ff.; 1983b [1969], 130 ff.; 1987b, 227–34; (Engl. trans. 2014, 174–9), 1993, 195 ff. (Engl. trans. 2004, 196 ff.).

[98] Luhmann speaks of 'reconditioning' or 'supplementary conditioning' of purposive-specific programmes (1993, 232 (Engl. trans., 2004, 224)).

[99] See Luhmann, 1993, 202 (Engl. trans. 201–2).

[100] Spencer Brown, 1971, 56–7 and 69 ff.

[101] J.A. Silva, 2008, 135 ff.

by Brazil and its corresponding domestic enactment by Decree No. 4,388, 25 September 2002. Hence, it can be affirmed that the rules primarily related to purposes *tend* to be exhaustible, to be definitively implemented with the achievement of their goals, while purposive principles tend to be inexhaustible, not definitively implemented just for having achieved their ends. However, this is a gradual distinction and there are exceptions. Nothing, for example, prevents the purposive principle of eradicating poverty, expressed in Article 3.III of the Brazilian Federal Constitution, from being achieved one day due to radical changes in the socioeconomic conditions of the country, as it has somewhat occurred in Scandinavian countries (yet one has to be aware of the possibility of reversions). In turn, legal rules of urban planning can establish the goal of preserving historical sites as a duty of public officials.

In short, the thesis of the distinction between constitutional principles and rules based on the criterion of reference to purposes seems to be unsustainable: first, because there are principles that do not contain purpose-specific programmes or are simply not goal-orientated (e.g. the principles of human dignity, equality, freedom); second, because there are also rules that incorporate purposive programming, referring primarily to goals, even at the constitutional level.

Analogous to the concepts based on the mode of reference to purposes, one also intends to distinguish between principles and rules through the criterion of reference to values. According to this view, principles have a greater value-content than rules, or refer directly and explicitly to values, while rules are only indirectly or implicitly linked to values.[102] As this is also an ambiguous term, we must determine its specific meaning in this context in order to be able to analyse this type of criteria. If one conceives of values as ideal goods, the same criticisms developed above in regard to the models based on teleological criteria are applicable.[103] Other meanings of the term 'values' are possible, however: values as beliefs, as preferences, or as the more abstract referents of the expectations that structure a social system.

If 'value' is defined as a belief in the Weber's sense mentioned above, as a conscious belief in the inherent value belonging to a particular behaviour regardless of its outcome (which could, in principle, contrast value with interest), any attempt to distinguish between constitutional principles and rules based

[102] Canaris, 1983, 50 and 52, rather distinguishing principle (explicit and direct valuation) from concept (implicit and indirect valuation); MacCormick, 1974, 25; 1995 [1978], 234, asserting that the values embedded in law 'are characteristically expressed in statements of the principles of a given legal system'; Betti, 1949, 211–12, referring to the 'excess of axiological content' of the general principles of law.

[103] It is common to identify the teleological with the axiological (see e.g. Canaris, 1983, 41–6).

on the form of reference to values becomes untenable. Deeply held beliefs are spelled out, for instance, in the rules contained in the Brazilian Criminal Code, especially in Title VI of the Special Part, which deals with 'crimes against sexual dignity',[104] such as the provision establishing confinement of two to five years for anyone who runs a 'house of prostitution' (Article 229). This normative provision and other clauses of Title VI exhibit a strong value appeal, directly expressing to a certain extent socially shared beliefs. This also applies to certain constitutional rules, as for example those pertaining to marriage, divorce, and the family unit (Article 226 BCF). In contrast, it is also true that sometimes constitutional principles match strategic interests of the State–such as Latin American integration (sole paragraph of Article 4 BFC), the reduction of regional inequalities (Article 3.III BFC) and even national development (Article 3.II BFC), rather than values as absolute principles maintained regardless of the results.

Another alternative is to define a value as a preference of an individual or of a group or collectivity, which places us, respectively, before individual or political ethics in the sense proposed by Habermas.[105] What matters here is the notion of ethical-political value (of a collectivity). In this case, the question is: what is 'good for us'? It is about the ethical issue concerning the particular form of life that is considered good for 'a historical community'.[106] Habermas distinguishes this problem from the moral issue, which is related to (deontological) principles with a claim to universality.[107] Although this distinction is questionable under Habermas's model of ethical and moral discourses counterfactually oriented towards consensus,[108] we may distinguish attitudes that say that something is good for my group (e.g. 'do not eat pork', for certain religious communities) and positions that claim that a certain duty applies to everyone (if I say that you should not murder, I do not mean, as a rule, only I should not murder those in my group, but any human being).[109] This does not necessarily imply consensus or an orientation towards mutual understanding in the collectivity, much less in a universal sense, but instead it

[104] In the wording provided by Law No. 2,015, of 2009. In the initial drafting, the expression was 'crime against morals'.

[105] Habermas, 1992, 198–9 (Engl. trans. 1996, 160–1).

[106] Note that later, in another theoretical context (within the debate on genetic engineering and cloning), Habermas refers to an 'ethics of the human species' (2001, 27, 49 and 70 ff. [2003, 11, 25, 37 ff.]), namely, an '*ethical self-understanding of the species*, which is shared by all *moral persons*' (74 (Engl. trans. 40)) and on which morality itself would be seated.

[107] Habermas, 1992, 200 (Engl. trans. 1996, 161–2).

[108] See, critically, Neves, 2000, 100 ff.; 2011, where I emphasize the problem of dissent.

[109] So 'moralistic' attitudes, here understood as those in which persons and groups overextend their claims concerning what and how every human being ought to do and act, lead to intolerance towards the *others* and, ultimately, to their exclusion or destruction.

instigates dissent. The legal system, however, through procedures open to a diversity of values (and moral representations: 'principles'), can select those that will be legitimately incorporated as the content of legal norms. Yet, as argued above with respect to the teleological model of values and the pattern of values as beliefs, there is nothing to justify a difference between constitutional principles and rules based on how values as collective preferences (and the dominant moral representations) are incorporated into the legal system or referred to by it. There is a strong value content and direct reference to values as preferences, both in the above-cited rules on criminal offences against sexual dignity and in the aforementioned constitutional rules relating to the family. There is also a direct link to 'moral principles' (those with a claim to universality and, therefore, deontological, but which are often confused in this debate with the axiological preferences);[110] for example, in the constitutional rules that prohibit the death penalty (Article 5.XLVII.a BFC) and torture (Article 5.III BFC). In contrast, sometimes constitutional principles correspond primarily, though not exclusively, to the strategic interests of the State, as for instance, in addition to those already mentioned, those that prescribe the promotion of a balanced development of the country by the national financial system (Article 192 BFC) and, I would add, the efficiency of public administration (head provision of Article 37 BFC).

Finally, we must assess whether the model for distinguishing between principles and rules based on the criterion of value pertinence finds support in the notion of values as the most abstract referents of the set of expectations underpinning a social system. This notion of values derives from Luhmann, who distinguishes four levels of abstraction to which behavioural expectations are concerned: 'a concrete person', 'a specific role', 'specific programmes (purposes, norms)', and 'specific values'.[111] In the legal system, the person is considered as a subject of concrete rights and duties which endow her or him with legal uniqueness. The roles imply a plexus of expectations regarding a set of behaviours and tasks that are independent from personal traits. In law, they are related to, for example, public offices and their functions, the status of a party in a contract or the party in court proceedings (plaintiff or defendant), and parental power (over their children). Programmes, which relate to purposes and norms, establish certain conditions in order that certain actions or action effects are expected. As mentioned above, they are purposive (primarily political), concerning the means–ends relationship, or conditional

[110] See e.g. Betti, 1949, 211.

[111] Luhmann, 1987b, 85–93 (Engl. trans. 2014, 66–73).

(primarily legal), pertaining to the if-then scheme. In law, the programmes are presented primarily as norms. Luhmann refers to programmes as rules, but in this context, they are not to be confused with legal rules, as they include the purposive programmes of politics.[112] The key aspect is that programmes feature a concrete specification of their application conditions. In contrast, values are very abstract, with a high chance of finding consensus (e.g. peace, hygiene, wisdom), but are virtually incapable of being implemented or accomplished by themselves, especially due to the contradictions between them. Only on the abstract plane of values, which 'has very indeterminate complexity with regard to permitted action', a 'justification for action is not achieved': 'It is particularly for this reason that concretely structured programmes are necessary in order to make correct action expectable and available for decision.'[113] In terms of law, this means that the values that guide the legal system in a given context have practical significance only if they are selectively incorporated into legal norms, transforming an indeterminate complexity (referring to values) in determinate (programmed) complexity.

Alexy suggests that his distinction between principles and rules would present 'a certain kinship' with the difference between values and programmes proposed by Luhmann (this may be the result of the use of the term 'rule' by Luhmann, when dealing with programmes).[114] This approach seems untenable. Values, in Luhmann's understanding, do not serve to justify actions or decisions. The legal system programmes are basically norms, including both principles and rules. Norms establish a conditional if-then relation. In this respect, although starting from other theoretical assumptions, it is opportune to affirm that, unlike values, principles 'comprise already the bipartition—characteristic of legal propositions—into legal antecedents and legal consequents'.[115] While the values do not have an if-then conditional structure, principles are already conditionally structured. Nonetheless, it should be added that the values do not enter the legal system only by means of principles but also directly through rules, as we have shown above with several examples relating to constitutional and statutory provisions. The difference in the selective programming of value contents seem to be this: principles, which are typically structured by a more elastic relationship between 'if' and 'then', that is between antecedent and consequent, tend to involve a more flexible and open posture when incorporating values in the course of the concretization process; the rules, which are

[112] Luhmann, 1987b, 88 (Engl. trans. 2014, 68–9).
[113] Luhmann, 1987b, 88–9 (Engl. trans. 2014, 69).
[114] Alexy, 1979, 82, note 96.
[115] Canaris, 1983, 51.

structured by a less elastic if-then connection, tend to imply a narrower and less open attitude towards the incorporation of values during the concretization process.

Considering the above, I conclude that constitutional principles and rules cannot strictly speaking be distinguished by the teleological or value-related character of the former in contrast to the latter, nor by the way that these types of norms refer to values. There are both principles and rules that refer immediately, directly, and explicitly to values and purposes, just as there are principles that are not characterized by this way of referring to them.

2

Through the Still Dominant Models of Division Between Constitutional Principles and Rules

1. Moral-Philosophical Background of the Turn in the Theory of Legal Principles

In the mid-1970s, H.L.A. Hart had already pointed out the transformation of the Anglo-American legal theory and political philosophy in the sense of denying the utilitarianism and the positivist thesis of separation between morality and law, highlighting John Rawls's and Robert Nozick's theories of justice[1] as starting points for this change of perspective and Ronald Dworkin's theory of principles as a pioneering approach of this turn in the legal field.[2] This reorientation was not limited to the Anglo-American world, having repercussions in the legal systems of Euro-continental tradition too. In Germany, the involvement of Jürgen Habermas with legal philosophy and legal and constitutional theory stands out, proceeding, so to speak, to 'take seriously the law',[3] unlike his predecessors in the Frankfurt School, Adorno and Horkheimer.[4] It was in this broader context of transformation that Ronald Dworkin's and Robert Alexy's models of principles developed with far-reaching international reception. The difference between legal principles and rules, as proposed by these authors, can be understood better if we consider an analogous distinction within the philosophy of justice or morality.

[1] Rawls, 1971; Nozick, 1990 [1974].

[2] Hart, 1976, 541 ff.; cf. Alexy, 1979, 59.

[3] Habermas, 1982a, vol. 1, 332–65; vol. 2, 522–47 (Engl. trans. 1984/1987, vol. 1, 243–71; vol. 2, 356–73); 1982b; 260–7; 1987; 1988; 1992 (Engl. trans. 1996).

[4] In the classic and paradigmatic *Dialectic of Enlightenment*, for example, Adorno and Horkheimer (1969 [1947]) did not consider law. In a way, this attitude is linked to a purely instrumental conception of law taken as a secondary phenomenon in the framework of a 'totalized purposive rationality' (Habermas, 1982a, vol. 2, 490 (Engl. trans. 1987, 333)), in terms of a certain Marxist tradition. In contrast, Walter Benjamin (1965, 45) considered the law in its relation to the violence, regarding the former as the only way through which the latter can be rendered valid.

Constitutionalism and the Paradox of Principles and Rules. Marcelo Neves, Oxford University Press. © Marcelo Neves 2021.
DOI: 10.1093/oso/9780192898746.003.0003

As a starting point, I am interested here in Rawls's theory of justice. It is based on the hypothetical idea of an 'original position' in which all members of the community are considered to be 'behind a veil of ignorance', not allowed to know the respective positions they would occupy in society and, therefore, being unbound from their particular and concrete interests.[5] This leads to the rational construction of the two principles of justice: (1) equality in the allocation of basic rights and duties, also formulated as the principle of 'equal liberty'; (2) economic and social inequalities are justified only if they conform to the rational expectation that they will bring 'compensating benefits for everyone, and in particular for the least advantaged members of society', and are 'attached to positions and offices open to all under conditions of fair equality of opportunity' (subordinate to the first principle).[6] Rawls's justice model clearly implies a defence of pluralism. Therefore, it is sensitive to the diversity of values of modern society, which should be treated fairly by the procedures of the constitutional state.[7] However, despite its reference to the historical context, it is a hypothetical construct.[8]

Against the dominant interpretation of Rawls's theory of justice, Rorty[9] argues that this 'is thoroughly historicist and antiuniversalist',[10] 'represents a reaction against the Kantian idea of "morality" as having an ahistorical essence',[11] and 'no longer seems committed to a philosophical account of the human self, but only to a historico-sociological description of the way we live now'.[12] Rorty does not distinguish the unequivocal historical conditionality and applicability of Rawls's construction (but this is also found in Kant's moral philosophy) from its hypothetical, abstract, and non-historical character in its own formulation. Although one can assume that Rawls's theory refers to 'a historically appropriate form of legal consciousness' and, therefore, that its principles cannot 'claim any culturally invariant validity',[13] one should not disregard the emphasis that Rawls earlier put on the 'purely hypothetical' character of the

[5] Rawls, 1971, esp. 11 ff., 136 ff.; 1993, 22–8.

[6] Rawls, 1971, esp. 14–15, 60 ff., 243 ff., 302–3; 1993, 5 ff. In this regard, see critically Höffe, 1977, esp. 16–17, 20 ff., who refers to the tautological character of the principles of justice in Rawls: 'The character of fairness of the conclusions, i.e. the principles of justice, only reproduce the character of fairness of the premises, i.e. the starting conditions' (35). See also J.P. Müller, 1993, 44 ff.; Hart, 1973, presenting objections to 'the argument for the priority of liberty' (551 ff.); also addressing this issue, Alexy, 1997.

[7] Indeed, Rawls refers normatively to the 'fact of reasonable pluralism', not empirically to the 'fact of pluralism as such' (1993, 36–7).

[8] On the nonhistorical character of Rawls's theory of justice see Barber, 1977, esp. 245 ff.; J.P. Müller, 1993, 47 ff.

[9] Rorty, 1991, 179 ff.

[10] Rorty, 1991, 180.

[11] Rorty, 1991, 186, note 29.

[12] Rorty, 1991, 185. Of course, he refers to the 'American way of life'.

[13] Höffe, 1977, 31.

'original position'[14] nor his later conception that the 'initial agreement' is 'hypothetical and nonhistorical'.[15]

Although aprioristic, Rawls's theory influenced the empirical model of ontogenetic development (of the individual), as conceived by Lawrence Kohlberg starting from Jean Piaget's psychology of the cognitive and moral development.[16] Kohlberg proposed a model of development of moral judgment in three levels: pre-conventional, conventional, and *post-conventional* or *principled*. These three levels are defined according to three types of relationship of the self with society's rules and expectations: at the pre-conventional level, 'rules and social expectations are something external to the self'; at the conventional level, the self is identified with or has internalized the rules of others, especially those of authorities; at the post-conventional level, the person differentiates 'his self from the rules and expectations of others and defines his values in terms of self-chosen principles'.[17] Three types of social perspective correspond to these three levels of moral development, respectively: the concrete individual, the member-of-society, and the prior-to-society perspective.[18] The three levels of moral development are divided into six stages with corresponding social perspectives, so that two pre-conventional, two conventional, and two post-conventional stages are shaped.[19]

The sixth and final stage in the development of moral consciousness (the second of the post-conventional level), according to Kohlberg, is the stage of universal ethical *principles*. Morally right means 'following self-chosen ethical principles', so that 'particular laws and social agreements are usually valid because they rest on such principles'. If laws violate these principles, one ought to act according to the latter. These are 'universal principles of justice: the equality of human rights and respect for the dignity of human beings as individual persons'. The reason for doing right is therefore the belief in 'the validity

[14] Rawls, 1971, 12–21.

[15] Rawls, 1993, 271–5. In this regard, Rawls argues: 'Thus, it is evident why the social contract must be regarded as hypothetical and nonhistorical. The explanation is that the agreement in the original position represents the outcome of a rational process of deliberation under ideal and nonhistorical conditions that express certain reasonable constraints' (1993, 273).

[16] Kohlberg, 1976, 1981. Piaget (1995 [1932], esp. 12–13 (Engl. trans. 1965, 26–8)) pointed out the non-linear aspects of the four stages ('individual and motor', 'egocentric', 'incipient cooperation', and 'codification of rules') of the moral judgment of the child.

[17] Kohlberg, 1976, 33.

[18] Kohlberg, 1976, esp. 32–3. See also Günther, 1988, 162–4 (Engl. trans. 1993, 125–7). Despite a critical attitude to Piaget, Kohlberg formulated his three levels parallel to Piaget's three stages of cognitive development: 'sensorimotor intelligence', 'period of preparation and organization of concrete operations' ('subperiod of preoperatory representations' and 'subperiod of concrete operations'), and 'period of formal operations' (Piaget, 1972, 55–66 (Engl. trans. 1973, 49–61)).

[19] Kohlberg, 1976, esp. 34–5 (Table 2.1); 1981. See also Günther, 1988, 164 ff. (Engl. trans. 1993, 127 ff.); Habermas, 1983, esp. 130–43 (Engl. trans. 1990, 119–33); 1982b, esp. 71 ff.

of universal moral principles, and a sense of personal commitment to them'. At this stage, the social perspective is 'of a moral point of view from which social arrangements derive' and on which social agreements, norms, and values are based. This perspective belongs to 'any rational individual' who recognizes 'the nature of morality or the fact that persons are ends in themselves and must be treated as such' ('basic moral premise').[20] This stage, the highest, corresponds to the universalistic paradigm of justice constructed by Rawls.[21]

In the framework of the theory of communicative action and discourse theory, Habermas reconstructs the model of ontogenetic development (of the individual), as formulated by Piaget and developed by Kohlberg, carrying it into the realm of phylogenetic evolution (of society).[22] Still in relation to ontogenetic evolution, Habermas speaks of a 'deinstitutionalized' morality at the post-conventional level.[23] Through the discourse, the validity claims in relation to the objective, the social, and the subjective worlds, that is the claims, respectively, to truth, rightness, and truthfulness, implicitly supported in the everyday life practice having the shared 'lifeworld as background',[24] become critically questionable and liable to be contested *in light of principles*. From the point of view of the social world, this means that the requirement of a universal justification of normative validity as a pattern of conduct (autonomy) oppose the heteronomy as a 'dependence on existing norms'.[25] Regarding the authority, it means that the ideal validity opposes the social validity. In the fifth stage (the first of the post-conventional level) of ontogenetic development, the structure of behavioural expectations presents itself as 'rules for testing norms', that is, as *principles* (*norms of norms*). Thus, the notion of justice is expressed through *principles with a claim to universal validity*, according to the prior-to-society perspective. In the sixth stage (the second of the post-conventional level) of ontogenetic development, the structure of expectations is presented as 'rules for testing principles: a procedure for justifying norms'. Therefore, the perspective is procedural (ideal role-taking); justice is conceived as an 'orientation toward procedures for justifying norms'. This stage involves a higher degree of reflexivity in relation to the fifth stage, given that the principles are discussed in the ambience of discourse-rational procedures. But in turn, these procedures

[20] Kohlberg, 1976, 35 (Table 2.1); 1981, 412. See also Günther, 1988, 165, 167 (Engl. trans. 1993, 128, 130); Habermas, 1983, 135, 139 (Engl. trans. 1990, 124–5, 129); 1982b, 71–3, 75.

[21] Habermas (1983, 130 (Engl. trans. 1990, 119)) emphasizes the affiliation of Kohlberg to Rawls's theory of justice.

[22] Habermas, 1983, 127 ff. (Engl. trans. 1990, 116 ff.); 1982b, 13 ff., 63–91, 133 ff., 232–3; 1982a, vol. 2, esp. 259 ff. (Engl. trans. 1987, 173 ff.); 1991, 49–99.

[23] Habermas, 1982a, vol. 2, 261 (Engl. trans. 1987, 174).

[24] See e.g. Habermas, 1983, 146 ff. (Engl. trans. 1990, 135 ff.).

[25] Habermas, 1983, 173–4 (Engl. trans. 1990, 161–2).

are based on *universal principles* that are understood as essential conditions of possibility of rational discourse.[26]

Despite his reservations, Habermas argues the existence of homologies and draws a parallel between the ontogenetic development (of the individual) model and the phylogenetic development (of society) model, establishing analogies in 'sequences of basic concepts and logical structures'.[27] In his view, modern society is at the post-conventional level of development of moral consciousness. Under the law, the legal norms are no longer based directly on the principles of metajuristic nature, but specifically on legal principles. These, in turn, become procedurally reflexive and therefore critically questionable; they thus require rational justification under the terms of procedures.[28] Although Habermas distinguishes the positive law, which corresponds to the post-conventional moral level, from morality and ethics, he does not attribute a lack of 'foundation' to this type of law—in contrast to Weber's conception of formal rationality. In Weber, the formal rationality of modern law corresponds to the purposive rationality prevalent in modern society.[29] The formal law is presented as an instrument of capitalism: 'What it requires is law which can be counted upon, like a machine'.[30] In this sense, positivity means that the law is permanently constructed and revisable by decision according to purposive-rational requirements.

Habermas critiques this model, arguing that 'the principle of enactment and the principle of justification reciprocally require one another'.[31] Besides positivity, legalism, and formality as three formal properties of modern law, he points out its universality, which involves the need of justification in the framework of a post-conventional morality, founded on universal principles.[32] By losing its sacred foundations, the law, on the one hand, assumes the role of instrument of power and market, but it, on the other hand, requires a justification in terms of a procedural—both ethical and moral—rationality. While differentiating itself from the concrete ethical life of the group and a substantive morality, law requires a rational justification not only within the limits of the legal discourse concerning consistency but also from ethical and moral

[26] Habermas, 1983, 172 ff. (Engl. trans. 1990, 160 ff.).

[27] Habermas, 1982b, 17 ff. See ibid., 97 ff., 133 ff.; 1982a, vol. 2, esp. 259 ff. (Engl. trans. 1987, 173 ff.); Eder, 1980.

[28] See Habermas, 1982a, vol. 1, 351 (Engl. trans. 1984, 258–9), based on Schluchter, 1979, 146.

[29] See Weber, 1985 [1922], 124 ff., 198, 503–13 (Engl. trans. 1968, vol. 1, 215 ff., 336–7; vol. 2, 880–95).

[30] Weber, 1985 [1922], 817; 1924, 293 (Engl. trans. 1961, 252).

[31] Habermas, 1982a, vol. 2, 266 (Engl. trans. 1987, 178). On the development of his argumentation, critically 'reconstructing' Weber's theoretical model, see Habermas., 1982a, vol. 1, 332 ff. (Engl. trans. 1984, 243 ff.). Cf. also Habermas, 1992, 97 (Engl. trans. 1996, 72).

[32] See Habermas, 1982a, vol. 1, 351 ff. (Engl. trans. 1984, 259 ff.); 1982b, 264 ff.

discourses. Procedural legitimacy implies, then, that legal principles can be criticized in light of a comprehensive discursive rationality, involving legal (on consistency), pragmatic (on seeking the appropriate means to achieving determined goals), ethical-political (on values), and moral (on justice) questions, as well as questions concerning the formation of fair compromise.[33]

In fact, this model of development of moral consciousness in the evolutionary sense of an orientation by principles with priority over both the particular values of a collectivity and the rules in force in society (prior-to-society perspective)—devised by Kohlberg, based on Piaget, and inspired by Rawls's theory of justice, and also 'reconstructed' by Habermas in his model of phylogenetic development (of society)—does not have a direct relationship with the turn that took place from 1960 to 1970 in the theory of legal principles. Nonetheless, there is a common context that allows us to verify a homology regarding the moral distinction between universal principles and particular values or conventional rules and the difference between legal principles and rules developed from Dworkin. Moreover, this stream of the theory of legal principles supports a close relationship between legal principles and moral principles.

2. All-or-Nothing versus Dimension of Weight (Ronald Dworkin)

The theory of law and constitution, along with the constitutional doctrine, grew to reflect a fascination with the model developed by Ronald Dworkin on the difference between rules and principles since the 1960s and reconstructed by Robert Alexy from 1970.[34] A full or comprehensive analysis of the models constructed by these legal scholars is beyond the purpose of this work. I shall provide here a brief account of the main features of their understandings of the distinction between principles and rules to clarify their similarities and differences regarding the model to be presented in Chapter 3.

Dworkin, whose legal theory presupposes a dialogue with John Rawls's theory of justice,[35] takes as a starting point of the development of his concept

[33] Habermas, 1992, 196–207 (Engl. trans. 1996, 158–68). See Neves, 2000, 96–8.

[34] Note that the article in which Dworkin presented for the first time his thesis under the title 'The Model of Rules' was originally published in 1967 and republished in 1977 under the title 'The Model of Rules I' (Dworkin, 1978, 23–72). In turn, Robert Alexy's starting point was his article entitled 'On the Concept of Legal Principle' (*Zum Begriff. des Rechtsprinzips*), published in 1979 (Alexy, 1979). Alexy's model will be addressed in section 3 of this chapter.

[35] See Dworkin, 1978, 150–83.

of principle the criticism of Hart's notion of 'open texture of law', according to which situations not regulated by rules would fall within the discretion (in a strong sense) of the judge.[36] The positivist argument would lead to the thesis 'that when a judge runs out of rules he has discretion, in the sense that he is not bound by any standards from the authority of law, as to say that the legal standards judges cite other than rules are not binding on them'.[37] Dworkin is peremptory: 'He [the positivist] also concludes that they are extra-legal standards which each judge selects according to his own lights in the exercise of his discretion, which is false.'[38] So, in a diametrically opposite direction to the thesis of discretion, Dworkin mainly introduces the concept of principles as norms or standards pertaining to the legal system. Principles bind judges in that zone where rules are not enough to settle a case.

In this context, Dworkin distinguishes three guiding standards for judges within the legal system: rules, principles, and policies. Rules are standards that 'are applicable in an all-or-nothing fashion',[39] that is in the logic form of an exclusive disjunction. In this sense, a rule is valid or invalid and should be taken as a criterion of settling the case or be rejected. Therefore, in the relationship between two rules in conflict with each other, only one can be valid and thus serve as the legal standard for the decision of the case.[40] From this perspective, all exceptions to a rule belong to its complete statement and are theoretically enumerable: 'In theory, at least, the exceptions could all be listed, and the more of them that are, the more complete is the statement of the rule.'[41] Stated completely (expressed all their exceptions), rules involve an automatic relationship between the occurrence of legal conditions and legal consequences.[42] In sum, dealing with rules implies the 'validity–invalidity' binary difference, the 'rule-exception' including distinction and, finally, the 'if-then' automatic conditional relationship.

The principles, unlike rules, have, according to Dworkin, 'the dimension of weight or importance'.[43] When there is an interweaving of principles, we must define which is the most relevant to the solution of the case. That is why two colliding principles can be simultaneously valid. Dworkin argues that

36 See p. 2 above.

37 Dworkin, 1978, 34.

38 Dworkin, 1978, 39.

39 Dworkin, 1978, 24.

40 Dworkin, 1978, 27.

41 Dworkin, 1978, 25.

42 Ibid.

43 Dworkin, 1978, 26. This does not mean that, from a functional point of view, there are not rules that are more important than others in regulating behaviours within a particular game or normative order (Dworkin, 1978, 27).

opposing principles do not, strictly speaking, constitute exceptions to each other. He argues accordingly that the 'counter-instances' are not, even theoretically, enumerable; they cannot be captured 'by a more extended statement of the principle'.[44] Furthermore, the principles are not intended 'to set out conditions that make its application necessary' because, rather, they state reasons that argue 'in one direction', not requiring a 'particular decision'.[45] In short, the principles imply analogical weight differences; they do not contain exceptions susceptible to enumeration in all-embracing statements and do not establish an automatic conditional 'if-then' relation.

In regard to their distinction from the rules, Dworkin often uses the term 'principles' to also encompass policies as standards for legal responses. But he also distinguishes between both. 'Policy' is defined as 'that kind of standard that sets out a goal to be reached, generally an improvement in some economic, political or social feature of the community (though some goals are negative, in that they stipulate that some present feature is to be protected from adverse change)'. 'Principle' means 'a standard that is to be observed, not because it will advance or ensure an economic, political, or social situation deemed desirable, but because it is a requirement of justice or fairness or some other dimension of morality'.[46] This distinction is important for the arguments that I will present later, but for now, I am interested in the principles in the strict sense: principles first as a requirement of morality.

As is well known, the dimension of weight (implying a possible weighing) is removed by Dworkin when dealing with the fundamental principles of justice (equal concern and personal responsibility) or dignity (self-respect and authenticity).[47] The principles of this kind can never be outweighed by other principles. Even he does not see any morally worthy possibility of collisions or conflicts between them:

> We need to find attractive interpretations of the two principles that seem right in themselves—that seem to capture what self-respect and authenticity really do require—and that do not conflict with, but rather reinforce, each

[44] Dworkin, 1978, 25. In a work supposedly concluded in 1971 but unpublished until recently, Luhmann (2013, 275, 281), despite his entirely different presuppositions and consequences, presented a similar definition of principles 'as rules with exceptions to be adopted case by case in the decision making process of law application', referring to them 'when rules are understood so that they, *in a number of open cases*, admit its opposite as an exception' (emphasis added).

[45] Dworkin, 1978, 26.

[46] Dworkin, 1978, 22. Dworkin explains, however, that his intention was not to reduce the law to 'a fixed number of standards' (1978, 76; 2006a, 234).

[47] See e.g. Dworkin, 2011, 3, 260–4.

other. We need to treat our principles as simultaneous equations to be solved together.[48]

Moreover, he does not admit any conflict between equality and liberty.[49] One would have to recognize in such cases a sort of pre-established harmony between these kinds of moral principles.

Related to this question is the idea of right as a 'trump'. According to Dworkin a constitutional right that he calls fundamental, moral, or political 'is a *trump* over the kind of trade-off argument that normally justifies political action'.[50] Without falling into a sterile polemic here about what right as a 'trump' ultimately means,[51] it is worth noting that Dworkin does not want explicitly to 'overstate this point', as he takes into consideration the problem of competing fundamental rights in holding that 'we must acknowledge that the Government has a reason for limiting rights if it plausibly believes that a competing right is more important'.[52] So he admits that '"balancing" is appropriate when the government must choose between competing claims of right'.[53] In addition to the question of competing fundamental rights, Dworkin does not exclude other exceptions, even regarding considerations of public or collective interests, to his idea of right as a 'trump', the idea that fundamental rights cannot be 'repealed' by the government. He admits, for instance, that the right to free speech may be overridden by the government 'when necessary ... to prevent a catastrophe, or even to obtain a clear and major public benefit'.[54] Finally, among other sorts of grounds capable of being 'consistently' 'used to limit the definition of a particular right', he refers to situations in which the government 'might show that if the right were so defined, then the cost to society would not be simply incremental, but would be of a degree far beyond the cost paid to grant the original right, a degree great enough to justify whatever assault

[48] Ibid., 262–3.

[49] Dworkin, 2000, 121, 134. One has to notice, however, that 'liberty' is understood by Dworkin not as a synonym of 'freedom', but as 'the right to do what you want with the resources that are rightfully yours' (Dworkin, 2006b, 69).

[50] Dworkin, 2006b, 31. Cf. Dworkin, 1978, 191 ff. This conception traces back to Rawls's liberal notion of 'priority of right' (Rawls, 1971, 31–2, 40 ff.; 1993, 173 ff.).

[51] A debate that goes in this direction is that between Klatt and Meister (2012a, 15 ff.), on one side, and V.A. Silva (2011, 280, ff., from a critical perspective on Waldron, 1994, 815 ff.), on the other side, when they discuss what 'rights as trumps' means. This confusing debate seems to result from a 'fallacy of ambiguity' (Copy, 1961, 73 ff.) about a phrase to which each one attributes a different concept. Costa Neto (2015) offers a critical review of this debate.

[52] Dworkin, 1978, 191, 194.

[53] Dworkin, 1978, 199.

[54] Dworkin, 1978, 191.

on dignity or equality might be involved'.[55] After taking into consideration all the caveats presented with this and other kinds of grounds for overriding fundamental or moral rights, it seems to be misleading to insist that Dworkin's ideas of (fundamental) right as a 'trumps' and the corresponding principles as not being subject to weighing refer to something absolute, entirely incompatible with balancing.[56] However, one can observe that these ideas of Dworkin are very weak, inconsistent, and confusing in the framework of his copious writings.

The question that arises in relation to Dworkin's theory of principles (in the narrow sense) refers to the possibility that this is another natural law model: legal principles would be deducted from universal moral requirements. It seems to me that this argument is unfounded. Indeed, Dworkin's work does not exclude the presence of elements of a rational natural law a priori, such as the idea that the right to equal concern and respect is 'a natural right'[57] and the belief that 'there are objective truths about value'.[58] However, legal principles are based on 'the community's constitutional morality', understood as 'the political morality presupposed by laws and institutions of the community',[59] and their origin, albeit not residing 'in a particular decision of some legislature or court' or in a rule of recognition, lies 'in a sense of appropriateness developed in the profession and the public over time'.[60] That is, according to Dworkin, the legal principles rely on the morality of a *particular political community* and arise and change in the course of the *historical process*. Moreover, although Dworkin states that, while serving to define the rights people have, 'all the principles of political morality that have currency in the community in question, at least, are legal principles',[61] it does not mean that a reference to the community's morality is enough for a principle to deserve legal-constitutional validity. It is necessary that the originally moral principle pass the test of consistency,[62] involving the 'superhuman intellectual power and patience'[63] of the

55 Dworkin, 1978, 200. On these passages Costa Neto (2015, 161–2) brings a similar argument to the one presented here.

56 One might read the Klatt and Meister's 'weak trump model' as an attempt to reconstruct Dworkin's idea of 'right as a trump' in light of Alexy's principle theory and balancing schema (Klatt and Meister, 2012a, 23 ff.). Indeed, one would have to be aware that not all constitutional rights are 'trumps' against the government according to Dworkin (such as the 'constitutional right to vote for a congressman every two years'), but only 'fundamental' rights (Dworkin, 1978, 191).

57 Dworkin, 1978, 182.

58 Dworkin, 2011, 7.

59 Dworkin, 1978, 126.

60 Dworkin, 1978, 40.

61 Dworkin, 1978, 344.

62 See Páscua, 1996, 28.

63 Dworkin, 1986, 239.

Judge Hercules: 'Individuals have a right to the consistent enforcement of the principles upon which their institutions rely. It is this institutional right, as defined by the community's constitutional morality, that Hercules must defend against any inconsistent opinion however popular.'[64] Therefore, it can be said that in Dworkin's model, legal principles have their origin in the principles of the community's morality (or in morally anchored practices of judges and legal practitioners), but they must withstand a kind of test of constitutional consistency or coherence in order not to dissipate amidst conflicts within the community's morality.[65] This is not an immediate induction or incorporation into the practice of judges and courts but rather a process of 'discovery' and control of constitutional consistency. Yet, in the context of Dworkin's theory, there is not a clear boundary between morality and law, since his notion of principles serves, in effect, to weaken or dilute the borders.

On these theoretical assumptions concerning principles, Dworkin asserts, as already anticipated in the Introduction to this book, that Hercules, a judge guided by principles and able to identify them in the controversies around rights, makes it feasible to reach 'a single right answer' or, at least, the 'best answer' to complex legal questions.[66] Although this is a regulative ideal,[67] the ability of Judge Hercules to make the single right decision or to offer the best judgment relates to a model of principles as means to overcome any discretion in the so-called hard cases. And although the understanding of whether a case is 'hard' or 'easy' varies temporally and personally[68] and, therefore, what can be defined as *the single right* decision or *the best* judgment also diversifies according to the context,[69] Judge Hercules has the ability to adapt the principles to the context in Dworkin's model. This is related to 'law as integrity',[70] which requires Judge Hercules and makes him able to interpret legal texts 'in their best moral light' and to hold the " 'best-lights" analysis' of legal cases.[71]

It is not intended here to denigrate or underestimate Dworkin's contribution to the legal theory, the theory of constitution and the constitutional doctrine in general, and to the theory of principles in particular, which has had enormous influence and reception in many countries, belonging both to common law

[64] Dworkin, 1978, 126.
[65] Ibid.
[66] Dworkin, 1978, esp. 279; 1985, 119 ff.; 1986, esp. 239; 2006a, 41–3. See pp. 1–2 above.
[67] As Habermas points out by addressing Dworkin's thesis, while in turn referring to 'the fallibility of actual decision making' (1992, 263, 277 (Engl. trans. 1996, 215, 226)).
[68] Dworkin, 1986, 354.
[69] See Dworkin, 1986, 239–40.
[70] Dworkin, 1986, 176 ff.
[71] See critically Shapiro, 2011, esp. 33, 304–5, 308, 310, 312, 325, 327, 329–30.

and civil law traditions.[72] Notwithstanding, it seems to me that the moralistic conception of Dworkin is susceptible to fundamental criticism.

First, it is worth restating what I have already advanced in the Introduction regarding the question of discretion. The thesis that the principles are used to cover or remove the space of discretion, of which the judge would avail himself to decide free from legal standards according to the 'positivist' model of rules, is an illusion about principles. This thesis, which is closely linked with that of 'a single right answer' or 'the best answer', is based on the argument that, by admitting discretion, it must be recognized that there are no rights and obligations before the court decision. But it appears that the question, seen in terms of Dworkin's model, masks the problem of complexity and contingency. This is not, as I advanced earlier,[73] to state that principles necessarily imply a greater degree of discretion as compared with rules. The problem does not lie in discretion but in the selective way of structuring complexity. The constituent or legislative law-making already entails a strong selective reduction or structuring of normative expectations of what the rights and duties prevailing in society are. This selection by the constitution-making or law-making procedures does not exhaust the selection process. The interpretation of constitutional and legal texts and the corresponding normative concretization for the case solution involve a new selection regarding the various normative and also cognitive expectations that have developed to determine the rights and duties as established in the constitution and laws. Therefore, it is not correct to consider that the interpreters 'in the strict sense' (the bodies responsible for interpreting and applying the law) are *only* intermediaries of the interpreters 'in a broad sense' (including the whole public sphere), as Häberle intended.[74] They act selectively to exclude certain normative expectations around constitutional or legal rights and duties and to include others as norms attributable to the respective normative texts. In the process of constitutional concretization, principles, on the one hand, have the greatest ability to structure selectively the unstructured complexity of the legal system environment in which various colliding normative expectations are intended to be presented in the public sphere as constitutionally supported. But, on the other hand, they enrich the potentials and alternatives of the argumentative process from the internal point of view of the legal system. By means of constitutional principles, the law grows more flexible to allowing an increased adequacy of the legal argumentation to

[72] In an opposite view see Haba, 2001; 1996, 301 ff.
[73] See Chapter 1 section 1 above.
[74] Häberle, 1980, 90. See critically Neves, 2000, 154–5.

address the complexity of society. In turn, for the non-routine cases, although rules have little flexibility directly to address the disorder of the law environment, in which the most contradictory expectations regarding constitutional rights and duties are present, they reduce the complexity of the principles, allowing the transition from an initial state of uncertainty to the certainty at the end of the case settlement.

This is neither a matter of discretion (or of imprecision as the cognitive uncertainty resulting from the vagueness or ambiguity of expressions) nor of 'a single right answer'. It is just a problem of how to control the contingency by decisions that are legally consistent and complexly adequate to society, implying a permanent paradox in the pursuit of justice in the legal system.[75] Of course, in the public sphere, there are actors morally oriented towards a universal audience (those seeking the rationally correct decision for all), while others are oriented in a particular way of upholding the values of their group, just as there are those who work from a strategic perspective of satisfying their interests, and we should not exclude those who assume expressive, cathartic postures[76] in order to influence the constitutional concretization or to protest against it. To state that only the first posture is morally legitimate in the public sphere is somewhat 'unfair' in an overly complex society and in a public sphere characterized by structural dissent. But the regulative ideal of Dworkin, Judge Hercules, a monological,[77] solipsistic, and, I would say, simplistic 'judge', is not the most appropriate 'subject' to acknowledge his own limits.[78]

These considerations lead us to the relation of the legal principles with the political morality of the community or, more precisely, the community's morality. It is true that Dworkin, as I have noted, acknowledges that 'the community's morality is incoherent', characterized by conflicts.[79] But then this is a purely factual concept of morality existing in a particular community. When he refers, however, to the community's morality as the political morality presupposed by the laws and institutions of the community, he asserts a

[75] This question leads to the concept of justice as 'a formula for contingency' (Luhmann, 1993, 214 ff. (Engl. trans. 2004, 211 ff.)), to which I will return in the 'Final Comment'.

[76] Expressive action is characterized by the confusion between the act and the satisfaction of the need, constituting 'a vehicle of catharsis' (Gusfield, 1986, 179; see Neves, 1998, 27–8).

[77] Michelman, 1986, 76. See, in the same sense, Habermas, 1992, 272 ff. (Engl. trans. 1996, 222 ff.). And the conception of 'the chain novel' (Dworkin, 1986, 228 ff.) only suggests a temporal succession of the monologues.

[78] In turn, Shapiro (2011, 312) argues: 'The main problem is that Dworkin's meta-interpretive theory is overly demanding, by which I mean that it requires meta-interpreters to engage in highly abstract and intricate thought processes in order to determine the correct method for reading legal texts.' He contends that 'the law aims to obviate' this sort of engagement (ibid., 307; see also Shapiro, 2007, 46).

[79] 'if we wish to use the concept of a community morality in political theory, we must acknowledge conflicts within that morality as well' (Dworkin, 1978, 126).

normative concept dependent on Judge Hercules. This ideal judge would have the ability to determine which principles of morality consistently serve as supports for the institutions and laws and have to be distinguished as legal principles.[80] Also in this regard, the question arises from an idealistic normativism incompatible with the form of reproduction of an over-complex society and a pluralistic public sphere marked by dissent. The very notion of community or community morality is problematic because the concept of community implies shared values or common moral representations that are rather appropriate to pre-modern social formations.[81] In modern society, the observation points multiply increasingly so that it is unseemly that one insists on a regulative ideal capable of uncovering the consensus underlying the community's morality. What instead has to be discussed and sought after are the normative processes and structures that are appropriate to absorb the structural dissent present in the public sphere about the determination of the constitutional rights and duties legitimately. The paradoxical articulation of principles and rules in the argumentative chain of constitutional concretization has an important role in this context.

Finally, it is opportune to offer a brief note about Dworkin's distinction between rules and principles from the point of view of the logical structure. As for the argument that the rules are applied in an 'all-or-nothing' manner and, at least in theory, susceptible of being completely set out with all their exceptions, Robert Alexy's criticism is proper.[82] A system of rules in which all exceptions are enumerable is too simple: 'In theory', perhaps we can imagine this kind of enumeration in the rules of a game, such as baseball or football. In the legal systems of a complex society it is not plausible to speak of enumerable exceptions, not even in theory, as Alexy highlights: 'One can never be sure that in some new case a new exception should not be created.'[83] On the one hand, the general prohibition of 'limiting rules by the incorporation of exceptions' does not seem to be something suitable to the legal orders of the contemporary constitutional state.[84] On the other hand, it is problematic to try to save the criterion of

[80] Dworkin, 1978, 126.

[81] In this sense, the distinction between ('old', traditional) community and ('new', modern) society was developed from Tönnies (1979, esp. 3–6, 34, 73, 106 ff.) to Weber (1985 esp. 21–3 (Engl. trans. 1968, vol. 1, 40–3)). See Neves, 1992, 11 ff. In other words and with other implications, Shapiro (2011, 326 ff.) comes to the same conclusion in attributing to Dworkin an 'organic conception of society' and stressing: 'Dworkinian meta-interpretation, however, is a process that demands a shared background of values, beliefs, and interests. For only in a community unified in its conception of political morality will Dworkinian meta-interpreters converge on the same interpretive methodologies' (ibid., 326–7; see also 329–30).

[82] Alexy, 1979, 68 ff.; 1985, 15 ff.; 1986, 88–9 (Engl. trans. 2002, 57–8].

[83] Alexy, 1986, 89 (Engl. trans. 2002, 58). See Alexy, 1979, 68; 1985, 16–17.

[84] Alexy, 1979, 69; 1986, 89 (Engl. trans. 2002, 58).

'all-or-nothing', resorting to general reservation clauses such as '"and if something else is not legally prescribed according to a principle" or "and if reasons to be considered from the point of view of law do not require something different"'.[85] Alexy also clarifies that the strategy of introducing general reservation clauses to principles such as the clause 'if another principle with contrary results does not have precedence' makes the principles also applicable 'in an all-or-nothing fashion'.[86] Albeit removing, with these arguments, such a criterion for distinguishing between rules and principles, Alexy admits, referring to the case of vagueness, that 'only when interpretation is set up, the all-or-nothing feature becomes effective'.[87] But, in this regard, it should be added that, except in cases of mere compliance or routine application (no disputes or questions that lead to argumentation), any rule is only applicable in an 'all-or-nothing fashion' at the end of concretizing process, when all (possible) exceptions relevant to the case settlement have already been considered (or excluded), making it possible to subsume the case under the rule by the concrete ought-judgment (the ruling in a case). Yet this is also true for the model that identifies the rules as norms characterized by the binary distinction between fulfilment and non-fulfilment, as proposed by Alexy. I will return to this issue below.

Dworkin's thesis that principles have a dimension of weight, non-existent in rules, which are valid or invalid, also deserves clarification and some reservations. The clarification concerns the fact that principles may be incompatible with a particular legal order and therefore do not belong to this order or, if they arise within it, they should be declared invalid owing to the validity of the constitutional principles and rules incompatible with them.[88] Alexy refers to the principle of racial segregation as not belonging to the German constitutional law,[89] an example that is also applicable for the Brazilian constitutional law. The balancing or weighing between principles presupposes the validity of both. In addition to this clarification, it is worth acknowledging a reservation about Dworkin's model in so far as he states the thesis that only principles have the dimension of weight. Two rules taken prima facie, that is, before the concretizing process, can collide with each other in solving a particular case, in such a way that the dimension of weight may earn special significance in order to determine which should prevail in the concrete situation, without affecting the validity of the relevant rules.[90] It is also worthy of consideration that in the

85 Alexy, 1979, 70.
86 Alexy, 1979, 71. See Alexy, 1985, 18.
87 Ibid.
88 Alexy, 1986, 93–4 (Engl. trans. 2002, 61–2).
89 Ibid.
90 See Peczenik, 1989, 249–50; Ávila, 2003, 44–5 (Engl. trans. 2007, 21).

relationship between rule and exception, the determination of the prevalence of one of the alternatives depends on the attribution of weight.[91] Although adopting another line of argument and without drawing the conclusions I want to draw, Alexy asserts that if 'the rule is not applicable without some balancing test, then it is an incomplete rule', so that 'constitutional adjudication must fall back on the level of principle'.[92] The question that arises from this—taking as a starting point that it is not about mere compliance or about a routine case, which does not still require an argumentative questioning or controversy—concerns the possibility of a rule being complete (or expressed in a complete statement) before the end of the concretizing process, as well as the need for a falling back on the level of principles when a rule depends on weighing. In light of this issue, it is now appropriate to move on to Robert Alexy's model.

3. Definitive Reasons versus Optimization Requirements (Robert Alexy)

Alexy proposes reformulating Dworkin's theory of the principles, based on reconstructing the jurisprudence prevailing in the German Federal Constitutional Court in the 1970s. Although this model is related to *a* reconstruction of *a* legal experience of *a* particular country in a specific period of its constitutional development, its reception has crossed so many borders that Alexy's principles theory has been claimed to feature a character of 'universality' or 'universal' rationality, as if it were immediately valid for any legal system of the constitutional state. Regardless of a restriction on this naïve claim to universality,[93] I shall provide herein a brief analysis of the model, given its wide impact.

As already advanced, Alexy criticizes the view that the rules are applied in an all-or-nothing fashion on the grounds that, in modern legal systems, the exceptions to a rule cannot be exhaustively enumerated, even in theory. New exceptions can arise with each new case. He reformulates the 'all-or-nothing' model to maintain the view that '*rules* are norms which are always either fulfilled or not'.[94] That is why, in a real conflict between rules, that is when it is not possible to introduce an exception that eliminates the contradiction between

[91] See Ávila, 2003, 45–6 (Engl. trans. 2007, 22).
[92] Alexy, 1986, 121 (Engl. trans. 2002, 83).
[93] But see p. 86 below.
[94] Alexy, 1986, 76 (Engl. trans. 2002, 48); 2000, 32 (Engl. trans. 2000, 295: 'rules are norms that can only be either complied with or not'). See also Alexy, 1979, 80.

them, one of the rules must be declared invalid.[95] The criteria for conflict resolution may be the most diverse, including the substantive importance of each rule, but the decision on the dispute is a decision on the validity of the norm.[96]

By contrast, Alexy defines the principles as '*optimization requirements*, characterized by the fact that they can be satisfied to varying degrees, and that the appropriate degree of satisfaction depends not only on what is factually possible but also on what is the legally possible', considering that the 'scope of the legally possible is determined by opposing principles and rules'.[97] Due to criticism, this formulation became more precise later on when the principles were defined as 'requirements to be optimized' ('objects of balancing'), whereas the 'optimization requirement' was placed on a meta-level,[98] that is on the level of the 'requirement of balancing'. In this debate, the original formulation prevails in the sense that '*principles* are norms which require that something be realized to the greatest extent possible given the legal and factual possibilities', different from valid rules, which 'contain *fixed points* in the field of the factually and legally possible', implying a requirement to do 'exactly' what their respective contents prescribe, 'neither more nor less'.[99] The collision or competition between principles, unlike the binary character of the distinctions 'validity/invalidity' and 'fulfilment/non-fulfilment' of rules, implies a matter of determining which principle has the greater weight in a concrete case, that is, which principle outweighs the other 'in certain circumstances', without arising therefrom a premise that 'the outweighed principle is invalid'.[100]

Put in these terms, Alexy's theory of principles is closely associated with the requirement or 'principle' (*Grundsatz*) of proportionality,[101] especially

[95] Alexy, 1979, 72; 1986, 77–8 (Engl. trans. 2002, 49).

[96] Alexy, 1986, 78 (Engl. trans. 2002, 49–50).

[97] Alexy, 1986, 75–6 (Engl. trans. 2002, 47–8). See also Alexy, 1985, 19–20; 2000, 32 (Engl. trans. 2000, 295).

[98] Alexy, 2000, 38–9 (Engl. trans. 2000, 300–1: 'commands to optimize and commands to be optimized'), reacting to criticism of Aarnio, 1990, 187, and Sieckmann, 1990, 63–7.

[99] Alexy, 1986, 75–6 (Engl. trans. 2002, 47–8). See also Alexy, 2000, 32 (Engl. trans. 2000, 295). In this sense, Alexy refers to principles as a type of 'ideal Ought' and to rules as a kind of 'real Ought' (1979, 79–82; 1986, 120 (Engl. trans. 2002, 82)), more carefully here, considering the misunderstandings that might arise from the distinction between these terms; see Sieckmann, 1990, 67 ff.

[100] Alexy, 1986, 79 (Engl. trans. 2002, 50). Following Alexy, Sieckmann (1990, 18–19) distinguished rules from principles by the difference between application by subsuming and application by balancing, respectively. See also Borowski, 1998, 309–1; Alexy, 2003a. For criticism based on Kelsen's positivism ('law to be applied as a frame'), see Jestaedt, 2007, 272 ff. (Engl. trans. 2012, 169 ff.). For this debate in terms of Alexy's principles theory (starting from Dworkin), see Borowski, 2007, 70 ff.

[101] Here there is a problem of translation, as we can see in the following footnote: 'The *Principle* of proportionality [Verhälnismäßigkeits*grundsatz*] is not actually a principle in the sense defined here. Suitability, necessity, and proportionality in the narrow sense (balancing) are not balanced against other things. They cannot take precedence in one situation or be outweighed in another. Instead, the question is whether the sub-*principles* [Teil*grundsätze*] are satisfied or not, and their non-satisfaction leads to illegality. Thus these sub-*principles* [Teilgrund*sätze*] are actually *rules*' (Alexy, 1986, 100, note 84 (Engl. trans. 2002, 66–7, note 84); emphasis added). With this reservation, I will follow the English translation

proportionality in the narrow sense, but not only that.[102] The first and second 'sub-principles of proportionality', namely the requirements of suitability and necessity ('use of the least intrusive means'), 'follow from the nature of principles as optimization requirements relative to *what is factually* possible', while the '*principle of proportionality in its narrow sense*, that is, the requirement of balancing, derives from its relation to the *legally* possible', or more precisely, it 'follows from the fact that principles are optimization requirements relative to what is legally possible'.[103] In this regard, Alexy argues that 'the principle of proportionality in its narrow sense can be deduced from the character of constitutional rights norms as principles'.[104] But he clarifies that the balancing is not limited to the dimension of principles. In analysing the case of *Lebach*,[105] he maintains that 'the result of every correct balancing of constitutional rights can be formulated in terms of a derivative constitutional rights norm in the form of a rule under which the case can be subsumed'.[106] This means admitting

of Alexy's main work maintaining the expression 'principle of proportionality' when quoting it or—if that is the case—his other translated writings, but I will use 'requirement of proportionality' or 'proportionality requirement' when not quoting them.

[102] Alexy, 1986, 100–4 (Engl. trans. 2002, 66–9); 2000, 35–6 (Engl. trans. 2000, 297–8); 2002, 397 ff. Proportionality, formulated in these terms, relates to a conceptual debate already solidified in Germany at the time Alexy developed his thesis. In this regard, see, in the extensive literature, Lerche, 1961; Häberle, 1962; Schlink, 1976; Hirschberg, 1981; Haverkate, 1983. Later, see Leisner, 1997; Lerche, 1997 (considering 'the constitution as a source of optimization requirements'); Schlink, 2001; Clérico, 2001; Klatt and Meister, 2012a. On the 'migration' of proportionality from the German public law to other legal orders (domestic, supranational, and international), see Barak, 2012a, 181 ff.

[103] Alexy, 1986, 100–1 (Engl. trans. 2002, 66–7). Alexy refers to the proportionality in the narrow sense as the 'genuine [*eigentliches*] balancing requirement' (1986, 100 (Engl. trans. 2002, 66, where '*eigentliches*' was not translated)). This relates to the fact that in the German constitutional debate the term '*Abwägung*' ('balancing' or 'weighing') has been used to embrace the two others proportionality requirements–suitability and necessity (see, for instance, Schlink, 1976). Moreover, it is worth noting that the 'genuine' balancing itself does not occur only within the application framework of proportionality in the narrow sense (see V.A. Silva, 2009, 178–9).

[104] Alexy, 1986, 101 (Engl. trans. 2002, 67). More broadly, Alexy (1986, 100 (Engl. trans. 2002, 66)), while considering it 'rather obscure', invokes a decision of the German Federal Constitutional Court which stated that the requirement of proportionality emerges 'basically from the nature of constitutional rights themselves' (BVerfGE 19, 342, [348–9]; BVerfGE 65, 1 [44]). See also Alexy, 2002, 397.

[105] BVerfGE 35, 202. It is here about a collision between the protection of personality and the freedom of media reporting, in which the first took precedence over the second, considering that the media report on a murder perpetrated many years ago could illegitimately endanger the resocialization of the convict, about to be released from prison (see next footnote). Cf. Alexy, 1986, 84–7 (Engl. trans. 2002, 54–6)).

[106] Alexy, 1986, 87 (Engl. trans. 2002, 56). He exemplifies with his formulation of the rule resulting from the balancing in *Lebach*, describing four structural sub-*conditions* (*Tatbestandsmekmale*) (*Fs*) for its legal consequence (*Q*): 'a repeated (F_1) media report, no longer required by the interest in current information (F_2), concerning a serious criminal offense (F_3), which endangers the resocialization of the offender (F_4) is constitutionally prohibited (Q)' (1986, 86 (Engl. trans. 2002, 56)). He adds: 'Thus even if all directly established constitutional rights norms were principles, which, as will be shown is not the case, there would still be constitutional rights norms which are principles and those which are rules' (1986, 87 (Engl. trans. 2002, 56)).

an intermediate normative layer between the principle that took precedence under the circumstances of the case and the concrete ought-decision.

Another fundamental distinction between principles and rules concerns the prima facie and definitive character of these types of norms. Because principles 'lack the resources to determine their own extent in light of competing principles and what is factually possible', they 'are thus not *definitive* but only prima facie *requirements*'. In contrast, since rules contain 'a decision about what is to happen within the realm of the legally and factually possible', they have a definitive character to settle the case if this decision does not run up 'against legal and factual impossibility, which can lead to the rules invalidity'.[107] Alexy adds that a rule will lose its definitive character for a case decision when it is possible to incorporate an exception into the rule for this decision to be made. But the prima facie character a rule acquires by losing its strict definitive character for the case is very different from the prima facie character of a principle, because while this 'is trumped when some competing principle is of greater weight in the case to be decided', 'a rule is not automatically trumped when the competing principle is of greater weight than its own underlying principle on the facts of the case'. For a rule to be trumped under these conditions, it is necessary that other (formal) principles are trumped, such as the one that requires the fulfilment of the rules passed by a legitimate rule-making authority and the principle that forbids behaviours which deviate from an established practice without reason.[108] And strengthening the prima facie character of principles by introducing a 'burden of argumentation' in their favour does not mean that principles obtain the same prima facie character as rules, whose prima facie character rests on the existence of decisions made by relevant authorities or on established practices and therefore is 'something quite different and much stronger'.[109]

Based on these assumptions, Alexy comes to a distinction between rules and principles that is the most consistent, in its outcome, with the present work: 'Principles are always *prima facie reasons* and rules are *definitive reasons*, so long as no exception is to be read into them.'[110] In this sense, rules and principles work directly as reasons for norms, either universal (abstract-general) or individual (concrete legal ought-judgment) norms, and only indirectly reasons

[107] Alexy, 1986, 88 (Engl. trans. 2002, 57); see 1979, 79.
[108] Alexy, 1986, 89 (Engl. trans. 2002, 58).
[109] Alexy, 1986, 89–90 (Engl. trans. 2002, 58–9).
[110] Alexy, 1986, 90 (Engl. trans. 2002, 59).

for actions.[111] Alexy goes further to say that not only rules can work as *direct* reasons for a concrete ought-judgment, but also principles, which therefore would not act only as direct reasons for rules. He points out cases in which a rule would act as reason to another rule and cases where a principle would operate as reason for a concrete ought-judgment.[112] However, he qualifies that position, considering that, taken separately, the principles state just prima facie rights and asserting as follows:

> Decisions about rights presuppose the identification of definitive rights. The route from the principle, that is, the prima facie right, to the definitive right runs by way of the relation of preference. But establishing a preference relation is, according to the Law of Competing Principles, to create a rule. We can therefore say that whenever a principle turns out to be the dominant reason for a concrete ought-judgment, then that principle is a reason for a rule, which in turn is the definitive reason for the judgment. Principles in themselves are never definitive reasons.[113]

With this passage, Alexy admits that principles can only be direct reasons for rules and, through these, indirect reasons for concrete legal ought-judgments. By contrast, although rules can be deduced from other rules, and albeit meta-rules do exist, rules may always act as immediate reasons for a legal ought-judgment, even if it is related to a concrete judicial review or if it settles a controversy in the scope of an abstract control of norms.

Finally, it should be noted that Alexy, a German, does not adopt the distinction of Dworkin, an American, regarding principles (relating to individual rights) and *policies* (concerning collective interests). He admits that principles can cover both individual rights and collective interests, pointing out that collisions also emerge between both, without being possible prima facie to determine the prevalence of the former over the latter and vice-versa.[114]

Critiques of Alexy's model were manifold. This book is not intended to provide a proper overview of them. However, before introducing some brief

[111] Alexy, 1986, 91 (Engl. trans. 2002, 59), formulating unlike Raz (1999, 15), who defines norms as reasons for actions. For Raz (1972, 841), also principles, in some cases, operate 'as the sole ground for action in particular cases', i.e. without the mediation of rules.

[112] Alexy, 1986, 91 (Engl. trans. 2002, 59–60).

[113] Alexy, 1986, 92 (Engl. trans. 2002, 60), supporting the assertion of Esser (1956, 51–2) that 'a principle, according to the continental notion, is not itself a "directive" ["Weisung"] but the reason, criterion and justification for a directive'.

[114] Alexy, 1986, 99 (Engl. trans. 2002, 66).

restrictions to this model, it seems appropriate to consider four critical positions that Alexy directly confronted.[115]

Let us begin with the position of Klaus Günther,[116] who states that 'Alexy's description of the reactions in cases of conflict does however make it highly probable that the distinction between rules and principles has less to do with the structure of norms than with the application of norms in concrete situations' and maintains that the difference between principles and rules does not concern the concept of norm, but is a matter of 'presuppositions of conversation' or 'presuppositions of action on which norms are applied'.[117] In this sense, a norm will be treated as a rule if it is applied without considering the 'changed features of the situation', or treated as a principle if 'we apply it on considering all the (actual and legal) circumstances of a situation'.[118] According to Günther, these 'different kinds of treatment result from the fact that deliberations on appropriateness are precluded by virtue of institutional restrictions in the case of applying a rule and are permitted in the case of applying principles'.[119]

In Alexy's view, the core of Günther's criticism is the thesis that, irrespective of the institutional framework, 'the requirement that a norm be applied relative to the actual and normative (legal) possibilities in a situation can however be directed at *every* norm'.[120] Alexy responds to this criticism by arguing that there is a difference between the 'consideration of all circumstances' and optimization. For Alexy, 'the consideration of all circumstances is also possible using norms that can either be fulfilled or not, whereas optimization requires that one be able to adhere to a norm to a greater or lesser extend'. From this perspective, he argues that the optimization idea (and therefore the difference between principles and rules) is important to help distinguish between the weight dimension and the validity of a norm.[121] Finally, he acknowledges Günther's warning about the fact that there are cases where it is difficult to determine whether the norm must be treated as a principle or as a rule,[122] but maintains that this is a matter of interpretation and therefore does not affect the difference itself, which would be anchored at the level of normative structure: 'The

[115] To later criticisms and corresponding replies that I cannot delve into here see Klatt (ed.), 2012; Pavlakos (ed.), 2007; Sieckmann (ed.), 2007.

[116] Günther, 1988, 268 ff. (Engl. trans. 1993, 212 ff.). See in reply Alexy, 2000, 36–8 (Engl. trans. 2000, 299–300).

[117] Günther, 1988, 269–70, 273 (Engl. trans. 1993, 214, 217).

[118] Günther, 1988, 270 (Engl. trans. 1993, 214).

[119] Ibid.

[120] Günther, 1988, 272 (Engl. trans. 1993, 216). Cf. Alexy, 2000, 37 (Engl. trans. 2000, 299).

[121] Alexy, 2000, 37 (Engl. trans. 2000, 299).

[122] Günther, 1988, 272 (Engl. trans. 1993, 216).

very question whether a norm is a rule or a principle presupposes that norms *qua* principles be possible entities.'[123]

To the criticism that it would not be appropriate to distinguish between rules and principles by characterizing the latter as 'optimization requirements' considering that such requirements could not be satisfied or fulfilled gradually,[124] Alexy responds with a more precise definition of the principles as 'requirements to be optimized', which would thus be 'objects of balancing or weighing', that is would be found at the level of the object of optimization, not at the 'meta-level' where this is required.[125] Yet, as he says there is a necessary relationship between the 'optimization requirement' and 'requirements to be optimized' (the principles), he maintains his previous terminology, reserving the more rigorous distinction to the contexts in which it is essential to the analysis.[126]

In the same context, he does not adopt the complicated thesis proposed by Sieckmann, according to which the principles are 'reiterated validity obligations'.[127] This model aims to address the issue of the foundation and the binding character of validity requirements (*OVn*—the norm *n* ought to be valid) by making reference to their endless reiteration, according to the following formula: *OVOVn*.[128] Alexy avoids this formulation because it seems to him 'as though the reiteration thesis only describes in a relatively complicated way the notion that principles stand somewhere between definitive validity and non-obligation'.[129] But according to Alexy, this thesis would not add anything to his view that principles are requirements to be optimized, to which optimization requirements are to be applied.[130]

123 Alexy, 2000, 38 (Engl. trans. 2000, 300).

124 Sieckmann, 1990, 63–7, defining the optimization requirement as a rule (65); Aarnio, 1990, 187; 1997, 181.

125 Alexy, 2000, 38–9 (Engl. trans. 2000, 300–1). In this sense, Sieckmann (2006, 129–32) speaks of 'optimality as a criterion of weighing' and 'optimizing weighing" (distinguishing this from the 'comparative weighing').

126 Alexy, 2000, 39 (Engl. trans. 2000, 300–1). He refers to the following excerpt from Peczenik (1989, 78): 'The difference between those two ways of speaking thus concerns the question whether the command to weigh, necessarily accompanying a principle, is "inside" or "outside" of the meaning of this principle. This difference has no material consequences in moral or legal philosophy.' But it seems to me that the distinction has an analytical value to the understanding of the concepts, although the two levels refer to each other.

127 Sieckmann, 1997, 51 ff.; 1994a, 209 ff.; 1994b, esp. 170–1; 2000, 72 ff. See in reply, Alexy, 2000, 39–43 (Engl. trans. 2000, 301–4). See also Sieckmann, 2006, 82, 84–103, treating principles as normative arguments; 2009, 19 ff., referring to normative arguments and defining principles 'as fundamental premises of a normative argument' (24).

128 Sieckmann, 1997, 352; 2000, 75–6; 2006, esp. 88 ff. See Alexy, 2000, 42 (Engl. trans. 2000, 303).

129 Alexy, 2000, 42 (Engl. trans. 2000, 303, here without 'only'). 'In the end, nothing is claimed other than that the argumentative power of principles is to be found somewhere between definitive validity and non-obligation' (ibid., 43 (Engl. trans. 303)). For a rebuttal to Alexy's criticism, see Sieckmann, 2006, 99.

130 Alexy, 2000, 43 (Engl. trans. 2000, 304).

According to Atienza and Manero, only 'principles' regarding '*policies or program norms*' constitute optimization requirements but not the '*principles in the strict* sense', concerning especially the 'highest values of a legal order' or rights declared constitutionally, which would have the character of rule.[131] This is peremptorily rejected by Alexy.[132] Somehow, this criticism had already been answered in the initial formulation of Alexy's theory of principles, as mentioned above: if a general reservation clause is introduced ('and there is no countervailing principle of higher weight in the case at hand'), the principles would also be norms structured in an all-or-nothing fashion. By assigning the structural character of a rule (in Alexy's sense) to the norm that they construct from the equality provision contained in Article 14 of the Spanish Constitution,[133] Atienza and Manero precisely introduce a general reservation clause in the terms formulated by Alexy.[134]

Finally, it is worth considering the criticism made by Habermas to the optimizing model of weighing proposed by Alexy.[135] Habermas starts from the understanding that principles as 'higher-level norms, in the light of which other norms can be justified, have a deontological sense, whereas the values are teleological'.[136] Based on this premise, he criticizes the model of principles as optimization requirements because it would be rather more appropriate to a model of weighing values. These, as preferences shared inter-subjectively, are liable to purpose-oriented weighing, implying tensions and competition for primacy. Principles as norms would be valid or invalid, not admitting 'weighings' and contradictions among themselves, for they must rather belong to a coherent connection of meaning, in other words a 'system'. They do not determine what is preferred or what is good for us (or me) as the values, but what any person ought to do. In this sense, Habermas emphasizes:

> Norms and values therefore differ, first, in their references to obligatory rule-following versus teleological action; second, in the binary versus graduated coding of their validity claims; third, in their absolute versus relative bindingness; and fourth, in the coherence criteria that systems of norms and systems of values must respectively satisfy. The fact that norms and values

[131] Atienza and Manero, 1998, 4–5, 9–11, 25, 43. They add, however, other elements of the concept of rule (9–10, note 1), which makes it stricter than that proposed by Alexy (fulfilment *or* non-fulfilment as a peculiarity of the rules); but, to the point in this context, i.e. the criticism of Alexy's notion of principles, this question is not relevant (see Alexy, 2000, 44, note 38).

[132] Alexy, 2000, 43–6.

[133] Atienza and Manero, 1998, 9–11.

[134] Alexy, 2000, 44–5.

[135] Habermas, 1992, 310 ff. (Engl. trans. 1996: 254 ff.); 1996, 1529 ff. See Alexy, 2000, 46–52.

[136] Habermas, 1992, 310–11 (Engl. trans. 1996, 255).

differ in these logical properties yields significant differences for their application as well.[137]

From this perspective, although the legal principles relate to a particular circle of addressees within the limits of a specific legal order, this factual restriction of the sphere of validity should not weaken their deontological character since they determine what their addressees ought to do, not least because the teleological contents entering the law, particularly those axiological orientations of the legislator, are 'domesticated' by the system of rights 'through the strict *priority* of normative points of view'.[138] Finally, Habermas argues that a judgment cannot be *justified* by a weighing of goods but can only *result* from this weighing, and he maintains that only a model free from optimization or weighing can define a decision as correct or incorrect. Otherwise, the decision would be a value judgment more or less suitable for a form of life articulated around a concrete order of values.[139]

Alexy responds to Habermas's criticism analysing a collision between constitutional rights that was settled by the German Federal Constitutional Court, namely between freedom of expression and the general right to personality in a case in which a satirical magazine called a hemiplegic reserve officer a 'natural born killer' and, in a later edition, a 'cripple'. The use of the term 'natural born killer' was not considered a serious enough offence to the personality right as to give rise to a limitation of the 'freedom of expression' as a competing principle. But the decision, considering the gravity of the offence to the personality right in the use of the second expression, ruled for the payment of compensation by the magazine. In the first context, the freedom of expression had preference over the right to personality; in the second, the latter prevailed over the former.[140] Alexy then argues that these weighings constitute reasons and that the decision, irrespective of being right on all points, has a claim to rightness.[141]

Beyond the 'conceptual-constructive' objection, Habermas presents a 'substantive' objection, referring not to the collision of rights but the collision between individual rights and collective goods, asserting that in the weighing and optimization model 'individual rights can be sacrificed at times to collective goals'.[142] From Habermas's perspective, on the contrary, there would be a strict

137 Habermas, 1992, 311 (Engl. trans. 1996, 255).
138 Habermas, 1992, 312 (Engl. trans. 1996, 256).
139 Habermas, 1996, 1531–2.
140 Alexy, 2000, 48–50, analysing the case *TITANIC* (BVerfGE 86, 1).
141 Alexy, 2000, 50.
142 Habermas, 1996, 1531. See Alexy, 2000, 50.

primacy of basic rights over collective goods, according to a view analogous to Dworkin's. Against this objection, Alexy argues that if there was a strict priority of all individual rights over collective goods, there could neither be a restriction of the property right in favour of environmental protection nor a limitation of the freedom of profession in favour of consumer protection, scientific freedom would be unlimited in relation to animal experiments, any consideration of aspects of general prevention in prescribing penalties would be prohibited, and so on.[143] Habermas's counterargument is the assertion that the rights only cede before collective goods if these are justified in light of principles, that is, if they are, in the final instance, considered from the point of view of individual rights that may be associated with them.[144] Alexy rejects this argument that collective goods can only take precedence if they are traced back to individual rights, alleging that in this way, the very problem of limitation of individual rights by collective goods would lose its practical meaning in the argumentative chain of law.[145] In this context, he emphasizes that the problem of collision can neither be solved with the absolute primacy of individual rights over the collective goods nor by the understanding that the limitation of the former by the latter is part of the formation or regulation of the former, adducing that if so, individual rights would not need protection against the collective goods.[146] However, Alexy argues, finally, that to the formal theory of principles a substantial theory of individual rights must be added, of which the 'idea of a prima facie primacy' of the latter in relation to collective goods is 'an essential element'.[147]

This is not the place for a comprehensive critical assessment of Alexy's theoretical principles model, much less for considering the objections of the leading critics with whom he engaged in dialogue. But before presenting the model I wish to outline, it seems appropriate to provide a brief preliminary critical analysis of some aspects of his theory of principles, advancing divergences that will become clearer in the course of the next chapter.

Initially, it is worth noting that only from a theoretical point of view it is relevant to distinguish between Dworkin's formulation that rules are applied in an 'all-or-nothing fashion'—and therefore do not have a weight dimension as principles do—and Alexy's definition that rules are satisfied (fulfilled) or not satisfied (not fulfilled), whereas the principles are more or less satisfied according to the factual and legal possibilities. The difference is primarily

143 Alexy, 2000, 50–1.
144 Habermas, 1992, 315–16 (Engl. trans. 1996, 259–60).
145 See Alexy, 2000, 51.
146 Alexy, 2000, 51–2.
147 Alexy, 2000, 52.

restricted to determining whether, at least theoretically, all exceptions to a rule can be listed and can be part of the full statement of this rule (Dworkin), or if exceptions are not exhaustively enumerable, even in theory, and are not part of the rule, but are only able to restrict its definitive meaning in a particular case (Alexy). Having established the exceptions that are relevant or verifying the lack of them, there is no difference in saying that the rules as definitive reasons are applied in an 'all-or-nothing fashion' and saying that they are necessarily satisfied or not satisfied. The binary split is present in both formulations.

This is why the criticism of Dworkin's work due to the fact that he denies a weight dimension in rules also applies in a certain way to Alexy's. Although a rule in its definitive and complete formulation, as an immediate reason for a concrete ought-judgment, can only be applied in a binary fashion, it is prima facie liable to embrace a dimension of weight and, therefore, to undergo weighing criteria in a concrete case. No doubt this is related to the existence of exceptions, but not only to this. In this regard, Alexy leaves a gap when he admits the possibility, cited above, that a rule cannot be applied without balancing, asserting that in this case it is incomplete as a rule. However, he adds: 'To the extent that it is incomplete in this sense, constitutional adjudication must fall back on the level of principles with all its uncertainty.'[148] Nonetheless, a question remains concerning the problem of defining when a rule becomes complete and if two incomplete rules may not compete with each other without necessarily falling back on the level of principles.

Of course, in the case of mere everyday compliance and simple routine bureaucratic application of the law, it is still not relevant to distinguish between prima facie and the definitive character of a rule. The completeness of the rule is assumed. For example, the determination by a competent authority—within the public administration bureaucratic routine—that a civil servant at seventy-five years of age shall compulsorily retire in accordance with Article 40.1.II of the Brazilian Federal Constitution presupposes a constitutional rule applicable in an 'all-or-nothing fashion', to be fulfilled or not fulfilled, with the specific conditions of the case being irrelevant.

But if disputes arise regarding the rule to be applied in the process of constitutional concretization, the distinction between prima facie and definitive character of the invoked rules is pertinent. The full statement of the rule can only be made at the end of the concretization process, serving as a definitive reason for the decision ruling the case. Let us take into account, for example, Article 37.X of the Brazilian Federal Constitution, which ensures an 'annual

[148] Alexy, 1986, 121 (Engl. trans. 2002, 83). See p. 54 above.

general review' of the remuneration of civil servants. To this provision a rule was assigned whose content has been understood as a requirement to recover inflation-related loss of value. One can then confront this rule with constitutional rules that require the allocation of a minimum percentage of the tax revenue for the maintenance and development of education by all unities of the federation (Article 212 BFC). It is clear that the factual possibilities are relevant in this case, but not exclusive. In such a normative context, a situation can arise in which the remuneration review, considering the revenues assigned by the constitutional rule, may lead to the removal of this rule. It depends on weighing or balancing considerations. The denial of the remuneration review at the percentage level of inflation by virtue of giving precedence to the rule that determines the percentage of revenue assigned to education involves a weighing: the consideration that, in a given situation, the public interest served by this rule would be seriously affected under a highly precarious public system of education, while the restriction on remuneration revenue will not bring significant harm to civil servants in view of the high standard of remuneration already existing. But in another situation, an orientation in the opposite direction would be imaginable. Considering the excellent conditions of the public education system, the respective rule that assigns a percentage of revenue to education could cede to the full application of the remuneration review of civil servants in poor material living conditions under inflation. In both cases, the rule that eventually cede to the other does not lose its validity.

An equivalent situation occurs in the relationship between the rule attributed to Article 19 of the Brazilian Fiscal Responsibility Law—based on article 169 of the Federal Constitution—according to which 'the total personnel expenditures in each period of assessment and each member of the Federation (Union, States, Federal District, and Municipalities) may not exceed the percentage of net current revenue' of 50 per cent at the federal level and 60 per cent in the States and municipalities, and the rule derived from the case-law of the High Court of Justice (STJ), a rule attributed to the constitutional text by a broad interpretation of the provisions of Article 37.III–IV of the Brazilian Federal Constitution, in accordance with which, within the number of vacancies established in the relevant civil service announcement, those who pass an entrance examination have a right to be appointed.[149] It is clear that the first rule

[149] 'The precedents of the High Court of Justice are that the applicant approved within the number of vacancies provided in the civil service announcement has not a mere "expectation of a right", but a real subjective right to be appointed to the position for which she applied and was selected' (STJ, RMS 31,611/SP, 2nd T, judgment 04/05/2010, DJe 17/05/2010; the precedents are as follows: RMS 27,311/AM, 5th T, judgment 04/08/2009, DJe 08/09/2009; RMS 27,508/DF, 5th T, judgment 16/04/2009, DJe

can be seen as an exception to the second. But nothing prevents that under certain specific conditions the rule of fiscal responsibility cedes to the rule of mandatory appointment. This follows from the fact that the relationship between rule–rule and rule–exception can always include a dimension of weight, even to determining which one is the exception. In the case under appreciation, the weight given to the rule of mandatory appointment may increase because, in the concrete situation, the positions may relate to an essential and immediately needed service (e.g. in health) requiring qualified professionals to perform it. To give preference to this rule over that determining the limit of total personnel expenses does not mean that the latter has lost its validity, but it has ceded momentarily in solving the case. Of course, to remedy the situation the body in charge of interpreting and applying these rules to the case may, for instance, also order that the public institution required to appoint the new personnel to the positions take measures to reducing personnel occupying 'commission offices declared by law as being of free appointment and discharge' (Article 37.II BFC). However, this does not exclude the fact that a balancing posture has been fundamental to the precedence of a rule over another, which, at first, could be presented as an exception. This means that, except in the mere everyday observance or routine application of law, the complete statement of the rule to be applied, as a definitive reason for the decision, can only be achieved at the end of the concretization process, presupposing a conflictive plurality of argumentative controversies upon the case settlement, in which the dimension of weight plays a role. It seems to me that Alexy somehow, by accepting incomplete rules, dependent on weighing, implicitly admits that, in this particular case, the difference between rules and principles is rather gradual, although this is not his intention.

Yet it is not only in relation to legal possibilities (their weight in the face of competing rules or principles) but also in view of the factual possibilities that constitutional rules can be evaluated for their application in the process of constitutional concretization. In this respect, the requirements of suitability and necessity are also relevant to them. Having stablished a reservation clause as an exception to a constitutional right rule, it is essential to consider whether the application of the measure seeking to satisfy the exception clause is suitable and necessary for the purpose for which it is intended. In this regard, it is worth considering the case of an explicit and qualified reservation clause contained in Article 13(7) of the German Constitution ('Basic Law'), authorizing,

18/05/2009; RMS 30,459/ PA, 5th T, judgment 03/12/2009, DJe 08/02/2010; AgRg RMS 30,308/MS, 5th T, 23/02/2010, DJe 16/03/2010).

among other restrictions on the inviolability of the home, measures that on a statutory basis infringes or limits this inviolability to 'combat the danger of an epidemic'.[150] In such cases, the legal measure based on the constitutional rule-exception must establish the suitable and also necessary (for lack of a less burdensome) means to reach the end.[151] Otherwise, the restrictive statutory rule should be deemed unconstitutional by virtue of illegitimately violating the constitutional rule that guarantees the right to the inviolability of the home, in terms of the first and the second criterion of proportionality, that of suitability and that of necessity.

If, on the one hand, comparing, balancing or weighing constitutional rules in the face of the legal and factual possibilities present in the concrete situation may always arise in the constitutional concretizing process, on the other hand, it does not seem appropriate to define principles as optimization requirements or requirements to be optimized. I will return to this issue in the next chapter but it seems appropriate to advance a brief comment here. The fact that prima facie norms may be subject to weighing or balancing in the concretization process does not mean that one can speak of optimization as a result of the practice of weighing principles. It is true that the concept of Alexy is not empirical but counterfactual. It points to an 'ideal ought'. In this sense, it resembles the idea of a single right decision or the best judgment, as advocated by Dworkin.[152] But even from a counterfactual perspective, the optimization model is weak, as it neglects the fact that we live in a complex society with many vantage points

150 In regard to other exceptions to the 'inviolability of the home', see Alexy, 1986, 114 ff., 263 ff. (Engl. trans. 2002, 77 ff., 189 ff.).

151 According to Habermas, the 'pragmatic discourse' directed to seek suitable means for achieving certain goals would be pertinent in this context (1992, 197–8 (Engl. trans. 1996, 159–60)).

152 Based on Alexy (1986, 149 (Engl. trans. 104 ff.)), Virgílio Afonso da Silva (V.A. Silva, 2007, 221–2) insists on the opposite direction with the following argument: 'The mere existence of an extensive catalog of constitutional rights to be optimized does not allow a single right answer for collisions between constitutional rights. Because of the many variables and levels of insecurity in many empirical and normative premises it is not only possible but also likely that the same problem can be given several solutions.' He invokes then the 'parity theory' to affirm 'that there can often be multiple solutions to the same problem in a parity zone within which an answer is to be considered optimal'. See also V.A. Silva, 2002, 103, 149, 204–6. It seems to me, however, that he does not distinguish between the levels. First, the question of a single right answer or the best decision (the two formulations are similar) is not at the level of 'requirements to be optimized' (the principles as 'objects of balancing'), but on the level of the 'optimization requirement' in the strict sense, implicit in the notion of 'optimizing weighing' (see p. 60 above). Therein, one seeks, if not the single right decision, the best ought-judgment. Based on the model of Pareto (1965 [1906], 102–4, 110–11, 116, 147–9, 158 ff., 337 ff.), Sieckmann himself (2006, 131) notes that 'an optimizing weighing applies when on both sides of the collision there are mandatory goals to be met by the one who weighs *in the best way possible*' (emphasis added). Second, the notion of a single right answer or the best decision is not, contrary to what the formulation of Silva suggests, an empirical concept, but a regulative ideal (see Habermas, 1992, 277 (Engl. trans. 1996, 226)). Therefore, it can be said that in the context of a theory that deals with principles as an 'ideal ought', the optimizing weighing is driven to find the best solution within the context of the respective case. On 'parity', see my critical objections in Chapter 3 section 4, pp. 116–17.

depending on the social spheres from which one observes social problems (economy, science, technology, politics, law, health, religion, art, sport, family, etc.), and the fact that we deal with a legal system that translates this plurality of perspectives internally, according to its own criteria. What is optimizing in one perspective may not be so in another. The optimization model assumes a (counterfactual) subject able to achieve the optimum point between competing principles, similar to the way the theory of rational choice assumes an idealized individual able to maximize value through calculation of costs and benefits.[153] Yet the collision between principles is based on the competition between different social spheres which, in turn, results in competition between different individual rights and collective interests protected by constitutional norms. Although the proceeding of articulating constitutional principles and rules includes the practice of weighing or balancing, this occurs in the context of a complex social and legal process that seeks paradoxically to ensure both legal consistency and social adequacy of the law, but such a process does not serve to ensure, even from a counterfactual perspective, the optimal result to be obtained from a model based on a rational choice of the subject (ideal) of weighing.

After raising those restrictions on Alexy's theory of principles, it is now worth pointing out an aspect of his theory that can be incorporated into the model that will be developed in the next chapter, provided that it be duly reviewed: the principles, as principles, are prima facie 'reasons' or criteria, while the rules are definitive reasons or criteria for a normative answer to legal issues. But here one should depart from Alexy's ambivalence,[154] maintaining that the principles cannot be direct or immediate reasons for concrete decisions since, even in the case of weighing, one has to define a 'derivative' constitutional right rule in order to settle the case. Therefore, the principles are indirect reasons for legal issues decisions because between the former and the latter there will be always a rule, whether directly attributed to the text produced by the legislative procedure (including constituent and amendment procedures), whether indirectly attributed to a normative text by the body in charge of legal adjudication or application, especially by judicial constructing. Principles as principles mark out existing rules and serve for the construction or unfolding of rules indirectly attributed to the constitution. The rules, even when they are meta-rules, can become reasons or definitive criteria for the decision of a specific legal case, being irrelevant whether that decision relates to the solution of

[153] See below pp. 113–14.
[154] See pp. 57–8 above.

a concrete conflict between certain individuals or legal entities, whether it is interlocutory or resolves a controversy in the framework of an abstract judicial review. In short, while principles as prima facie reasons or criteria serve as mediate reasons for legal dispute decisions, rules, beyond their prima facie character at the starting point of the concretization process, only play their full role when, at the end of this process, they transmute into definitive reasons. Thereupon, the difference has functional-structural significance in passing from determinable (stucturable, organizable) complexity to determinate (structured, organized) complexity within the legal system.

Regarding the aforementioned critics, with whom Alexy engaged when his theory was at the height of its development and dissemination, some critical notes also seem fruitful. Klaus Günther starts from a strict difference between justification discourses and application discourses,[155] a distinction that makes sense under the assumptions of a universal moral founded in absolute and unconditional principles but which proves to be inadequate for the analysis of a particular positive legal order. According to the model, moral principles—as unconditional requirements related to the categorical imperative in the sense of the Kantian tradition—would serve the justification discourse and would be ultimately fixed, but their appropriateness for the context of the subjects involved would require an application discourse.[156] In the field of law, this would mean that the legal—especially constitutional—principles would have absolute validity and therefore be prima facie ready, whereas the case in the application discourse would be to seek their appropriate subsumption according to the corresponding context. In a way, there would not be indeed any difference between a prima facie norm and a definitively and completely stated norm at the end of the concretization process. Günther seems to be unaware that the concretizing process also implies a hermeneutic construction of norms. The institutional norm-making by constitution-makers and ordinary law-makers relates reciprocally to the hermeneutic construction of the norm by the bodies responsible for the legal concretization. Strictly speaking, the application—which occurs at the end of the concretizing process and enables the subsumption of the case, by a concrete ought-decision, under one or more legal rules (and at times indirectly under one or more legal principles)—presupposes a norm-constructing activity during this process. Despite being supported in

[155] Günther, 1988 (Engl. trans. 1993). Concerning this distinction, see, relativizing it critically, J.P. Müller, 1993, 89 ff.; Alexy, 1995, 52 ff., 170–2, who holds: 'The fact that any application discourse necessarily involves a justification discourse, from which its outcome depends, prevents opposing application discourse and justification discourse as two autonomous discursive forms' (70; see also 172).

[156] See, for instance, Günther, 1988, 16–18 (Engl. trans. 1993, 5–7).

moral philosophy, the view that the distinction between rules and principles is related to how norms are treated in application discourses, and concerns the 'conditions of action', assumes a touch of classical positivist hermeneutics when transplanted into positive law: the norm is already fixed in advance, with the relevant authority being responsible only for interpreting or discovering it in order to appropriately apply it to the case. So it is not considered the circular process between institutional production and hermeneutic construction of the norm.

Sieckmann's model, making use of the infinite reiteration of validity requirements to clarify the role of principles as normative arguments, seems to me not only overly complicated but also somewhat artificial.[157] After all, it comes down to an attempt of uncovering something like a rule of recognition of the principles as validity requirements. This rule would then be the endless reiteration of their validity. Yet of course, the constitutional principles construct and reconstruct themselves in a permanent circular process of constitutional self-foundation of law, not appearing to have practical relevance or be theoretically fruitful to seek or determine a rule of recognition to constitutional principles and rules.

In turn, the distinction of Atienza and Manero between 'principles in strict sense' and 'principles' as 'policies or programme norms' seems rather simplistic. According to it, the former could only be fulfilled or not fulfilled, while the latter could be complied with to varying degrees. But the general reservation clause that Atienza and Manero introduce in the statement of the principle of equality expressed in Article 14 of the Spanish Constitution ('and there is no countervailing principle of higher weight in the case at hand'),[158] in order to reach the binary conception of this principle regarding the indispensability of full compliance or noncompliance, would have the same effect as if it were introduced in the statement of any principle relating to collective purposes ('policies or norm programmes'). Nonetheless, a rule indirectly attributed to the constitution would have to be built along the concretizing process in which the conflicting principles were collated.

Regarding the objections of Habermas, it is appropriate to restate the rebuttal made of Klaus Günther's view. The criticism of the balancing of principles also presupposes in Habermas a moral philosophy with a universalist claim, in which principles are presented as absolute and unconditional requirements of 'duties' valid for any person, in a tradition dating back to the

[157] See p. 60 above.

[158] Atienza and Manero, 1998, 9. See p. 61 above.

Kantian categorical imperative.[159] It is true that, in relation to the principles so understood, the values as individual or collective preferences would be the object of weighing and would be transformed from case to case.[160] But the understanding of Habermas that the notion of collision between legal principles makes them in a misrepresented way subject to a simple weighing of values does not consider the specificity of a legal theory of principles. While the legal principles serve the justification of norms and, indirectly, of action within the legal system, the values need to be incorporated into the law by principles or rules in order to have the binding force of a systemic program or criterion for justification. Therefore, the systemically structurable collision between legal principles is not the same as the collision between *unstructured* values that can guide or influence the law. Moreover, the notion of the binary nature of the norms, as opposed to the gradual nature of values, has a strictly moral meaning, implying a deontology with a universal validity claim. In the legal system, although the binary character at the level of the code 'lawful/unlawful' is fundamental, there is a plurality of criteria and programmes that admit tensions and conflicts among themselves.[161] Albeit the law is oriented towards determining ultimately if something is lawful or unlawful, before an answer to this question is reached, a complex chain or network of arguments develops in each case (except in mere everyday observance and pure routine application), which are articulated on the basis of various criteria put forward to resolve the legal dispute. In this argumentative process, the comparison of criteria that present themselves as appropriate for decision-making is recurrent, involving even the weighing between occasionally competing norms. Therefore, the binary character of law is associated with a selective attitude towards different normative criteria invoked to settle a case, comprising the balancing of principles, which, however, is neither intended nor appropriate to lead to their optimization.

[159] See e.g. Habermas, 1992, 200 (Engl. trans. 1996, 161–2). About categorical imperative, see Kant, 1965 [1785/1786], 34, 36–7, 40 ff. [414, 416, 419 ff.] (Engl. trans. 2012, 28, 30, 32 ff.).

[160] Habermas, 1992, 315 (Engl. trans. 1996, 529); Habermas, 1996, 1531.

[161] About the combination of codes ('coding') and criteria or programmes ('programming'), see Luhmann, 1986a, 82–3, 89 ff.; as regard specifically the legal system, 1986b, 194 ff.; 1993 165 ff. (Engl. trans. 2004, 173 ff.).

3

To the Search of Another Model of Difference Between Constitutional Principles and Rules

1. Locating the Problem and Conceptual Contours

The distinction between constitutional principles and rules cannot be naively defined based on the formulations of the norms in the constitutional provisions, be these contained in a codified constitutional law, in various non-codified constitutional laws,[1] or in sparse statements that express norms resulting from an established practice, whether these statements are found in precedents or in official documents, including legislative compilations.[2] By interpreting the constitutional provisions, as advanced in Chapter 1, we assign to them one or more norms, whether rules or principles. Strictly speaking, the hermeneutic discussion lies in establishing which normative expectations are expressed as valid constitutional norms in those provisions. Often a norm, in its minimal structure, can only be stated by way of interpretation through the coordination of several constitutional provisions. For example, while Article 198.1 of the Brazilian Federal Constitution states that 'the unified health system shall be financed as set forth in Art. 195', it cannot, in itself, be assigned any norms before we take into account one or more of the provisions contained in Article 195 of the Brazilian Federal Constitution, which addresses the funding of social

[1] They are written constitutions, but they consist of several basic laws such as the Belgian Constitution of 1830 and the French Constitution of 1875 (see Hauriou, 1929, 332 ff.; Pinto Ferreira, 1971, 80).

[2] That is the case of the legally flexible (but sociologically stable) English Constitution, which, although usually called 'customary' in textbooks, is formed not only by the common law as a background, but also by written laws voted on by Parliament (statutory law), as emphasized by Hauriou (1927, 301). See Dicey, 1982 [1915], cxliii, warning, however, that some rules of common law became the content of statutory law, such as the one that regulates the descent of the Crown (cxliii–cxliv). But there are laws that radically changed the British constitutional system, breaking with tradition, such as the Parliament Act, 18 August 1911, which *basically* transferred the legislative authority (not the 'sovereignty') from the King (or Queen) and the two houses of Parliament to the King (or Queen) and the House of Commons, essentially reducing the legislative power of the House of Lords (see with another view Dicey, 1982 [1915], xxxvii ff.).

Constitutionalism and the Paradox of Principles and Rules. Marcelo Neves, Oxford University Press. © Marcelo Neves 2021.
DOI: 10.1093/oso/9780192898746.003.0004

welfare. In turn, there are constitutional provisions to which more than one norm can be assigned, such as the two rules derived directly from Article 8.VII of the Brazilian Constitution, which provides that 'retired members shall be entitled to vote and be voted on in unions', and the heading of Article 1, even if we only consider the portion that establishes that the Federal Republic 'is a democratic rule-of-law state', since both the rule-of-law principle and the democratic principle, which are in a paradoxical relationship of complementarity and tension, can be immediately assigned to this part of the provision.

These examples are less problematic because they relate to norms immediately attributed to constitutional provisions. The question becomes more relevant when it comes to norms assigned indirectly to constitutional texts, especially constitutional principles. In this case, it is not only about norms assigned to specific constitutional provisions but also norms attributed to the constitutional text as a whole (or to the set of statements considered constitutional when there is no codified constitution). Several subprinciples and rules can be indirectly derived from the provisions related to the rule of law. Not only the principle of equality can be assigned to the head provision of Article 5 (equal treatment clause), but also, indirectly, *sub*principles, according to the social sphere, such as the equal tax treatment, regardless of whether it is expressly enshrined in the constitution. Rules may also be developed from the equality clause, such as those that determine whether affirmative action policies are constitutionally allowed (or forbidden!). However, when it comes to rules and especially principles indirectly attributed to the constitutional text as a whole, being impossible to specify a particular provision or a precisely defined combination of provisions, as with the principle of reasonability and the standard of proportionality,[3] the loose relationship between constitutional provisions and norms becomes more apparent and constitutes a particularly difficult constitutional problem. In this regard, one has to consider the old maxim that law should be interpreted as a whole of meaning ('system'), or that the constitution

[3] The three partial criteria of proportionality (suitability, necessity, and proportionality in the strict sense) are not to be confused with the principle of reasonability, which prohibits unreasonable or extremely absurd measures (see V.A. Silva, 2002b, esp. 29–30; Guerra Filho, 2001, 283), although one also speaks of 'extreme disproportionality' to refer to reasonability in this sense (see Holländer, 2007, 194, referring to the US Supreme Court's case-law). Reasonableness as a 'duty of congruence' is also distinguished from proportionality (Ávila, 2003, 102 (Engl. trans. 2007, 110–11)). However, care should be taken so as not to restrict this discussion to a mere terminological debate. In Germany, the term '*Verhältnismäßigkeit*' ('proportionality') was initially used only to refer to the requirement of suitability of means and ends (Lerche, 1961, 19). In the United States, 'proportionality' is also used to refer specifically to the suitable relationship between means and ends (see Hamilton and Schoenbrod, 1999, 473). See also Thomas, 2007; in comparative perspective, Jackson, 2004; Jackson and Tushnet (eds), 2018; Sweet Stone and Mathews, 2019; Kremnitzer, Steiner, and Lang (eds), 2020.

must be considered in its unity.[4] The question that becomes delicate in this case concerns the limits of this indirect assignment of norms to the constitutional text (or, as a functional equivalent, to the set of constitutional provisions or statements in constitutional systems without a constitution codified by a constituent decision).

As previously mentioned, the distinction between norms directly attributed and norms indirectly attributed to the constitutional text, which is similar to the difference between the implicit and the explicit meaning of normative provisions and texts, is relative. However, care should be taken in this case, lest we fall into sterile nominalism. At one extreme, it can be observed that the direct attribution means that the reconstruction of provisions through interpretive statements is just a matter of restructuring their grammatical form. Thus, for example, Article 5.XLVII.a of the Brazilian Constitution, by determining that '*there shall be no*' death penalty ('save in cases of declared war'), engenders the interpretive statement 'the death penalty *is prohibited*'.[5] At the other extreme, assigning a principle to the constitutional text as a whole must not be done arbitrarily, according to the taste of each interpreter/applicator of law. In this case, the bodies officially in charge of the binding interpretation and application of the constitutional text, or rather, normative concretization of the constitution, build statements that play the role of constitutional provisions, but they must be at least compatible with the set of constitutional provisions. The test

[4] And here the issue of the 'principle of unity' of the Constitution (Hesse, 1969, 28; Canotilho, 1998, 1096–7; Barroso, 1996, 181–98) reappears, which rather concerns a condition of possibility for the consistent functioning of a Constitution. In this regard, V.A. Silva (2005, 121–7) argues critically that the 'principle' of unity of the constitution is a mere requirement of systematic interpretation (the former adds nothing to the latter), and criticizes the understanding that such 'principle' is an expression of the lack of hierarchy between constitutional norms (there is formal hierarchy between norms protected by the entrenchment clause and those concerning the constitutional amendment procedure, as well as material hierarchy because of the possibility of weighing between constitutional norms). Although one can agree with the terms in which Silva poses the question, the 'principle of unity', at least in this last sense ('hierarchical unity'), is already part of the Brazilian constitutional precedents (see STF, ADI 4,097–AgR/DF, judgment 8 October 2008, TP, DJE 7 November 2008).

[5] The prima facie intensity of the normative force of this provision arose, leading to an embryo of preventive judicial review, in the Writ of Mandamus No. 21,231/DF, filed by Congressman José Genoíno and other parliamentarians 'against an act of the Board of House of Representatives, which made possible the examination of the "Proposed Amendment to Federal Constitution No. 1 of 1988", presented by late Congressman Amaral Netto, "instituting death penalty for cases of theft, kidnapping and rape followed by death, which shall be submitted to the electorate, through a referendum, within 18 (eighteen) months of approval of the Amendment"'. The then General Attorney of the Republic 'opined in favour of the issue of the requested writ of mandamus, in order for the filed legislative body to definitively interrupt the voting procedure for the amendment in question'. In a monocratic decision, Justice Neri da Silveira, for considering that the Committee on Constitution and Justice of the House of Representatives had quashed the proposal on its unconstitutionality, judged the writ of mandamus as no longer being relevant due to the loss of the object, determining its filing (MS 21,231/DF, judgment 13 May 1999, DJ 25 May 1999).

of coherence is obviously difficult,[6] implying an argumentative overburden. Common to any complex constitutional issue, this difficulty does not affect the requirement that any principle to be introduced by indirect assignment to the whole constitutional text not be an odd body that destroys the consistency of the legal system. In this sense, the principle of racial segregation in a democratic constitutional state and the parliamentary principle of political responsibility of the head of government before the parliament in a strictly presidential state cannot be indirectly attributed to the constitution, and therefore must be rejected for not belonging to the corresponding legal system or for being declared invalid because they entered it irregularly. Otherwise, the 'impotence' of 'constitutional legislators' (constitution-makers or constitutional amendment-makers) comes to light owing to a sort of 'judicial constitutional positivism' that makes them invisible and marginalizes them.[7] Thus, the double contingency between the instance that institutionally produces the norm, giving its provision a prima facie meaning (the constitution-maker or the amendment-maker as alter), and the instance that hermeneutically constructs the norm to be applied with binding force (the judge or constitutional court as ego) is broken. The question of a direct or indirect attribution of rules and principles to the constitutional text implies exactly how to maintain the constitutional identity under the paradoxical alterity between the constitutional legislator and the bodies in charge of concretizing the constitution. On the one hand, focusing merely on the identity between the two would lead to a naive constitutional-legalistic positivism, which despises the social adequacy of law, holding onto a pure model of rules as a direct expression of constitutional provisions. On the other hand, completely denying that identity, focusing exclusively on the bodies responsible for the constitutional concretization, especially those that have the 'last word', the constitutional courts, would lead to a realistic constitutional positivism or judicial decisionism, which disregards legal consistency.[8] At both ends, the functioning of a constitutional order developed through the

6 The test of coherence relates to the legal certainty and is the matter of *the* specifically legal discourse according to Habermas (1992, 207 (Engl. trans. 1996, 167–8)), but there are other dimensions of the legal argumentation.

7 Jestaedt, 2002, 188 ff.

8 With other well-known procedural implications (judicial review as a means to 'policing the process of representation', 'clearing the channels for political change' and 'facilitating the representation of minorities'), Ely (1980) criticized these two positions based on the distinction between 'interpretivism' and 'noninterpretivism', drawing attention to constitutional provisions that seem 'insistently to call for a reference to sources beyond the document itself and a "framers" dictionary'—concerning 'interpretivism' (13); and 'the fallacy of transformed realism', i.e. to draw from the 'earth-shattering insight' that 'judges were human and therefore were likely in a variety of legal contexts consciously or unconsciously to slip their personal values in their legal reasonings' 'an easy inference that that is what judges *ought* to be doing'—concerning 'noninterpretivism' (44).

dynamics of the paradoxical relationship between rules and principles within an overly complex society would be impossible.

Another aspect to be considered concerns the plane of legal action and communication on which the distinction between principles and rules as categories of norms becomes relevant. As mentioned above, when it comes to mere everyday compliance and pure bureaucratic application, the difference between principles and rules has no practical significance.[9] It may be added that, when it comes to the routine exercise of private autonomy within the framework of 'legal-statutory offers of regulation',[10] this distinction remains unimportant as well. In these situations, the people involved either fulfil or violate rules without questioning the way they are binding. If it is not relevant to distinguishing whether it is a principle or a rule that is being fulfilled, norms as behavioural patterns are followed out of habit because they have been internalized, by virtue of the agent's identification with their values, or in view of a rational calculation of costs and benefits driven by the weight of the sanction in case of noncompliance.[11] In turn, if there is no reason to follow them, norms tend to be unfulfilled also without differentiating between the violated principles and rules. The difference between rules and principles become relevant in practical and theoretical terms only when there is a controversy about the norm to be applied to the case in the context of a concrete interpersonal conflict or in the scope of abstract judicial review. Therefore, this distinction can only be problematized when the plane of the legal argumentation is reached.

The issue of establishing the plane on which the distinction between principles and rules is placed can be understood based on the distinction between action and discourse, as per Habermas's theory of communicative action. According to this view, at the level of action, which is part of our everyday practice, validity claims[12] are naively accepted, not being problematized.[13] The action in this sense is developed in everyday practice with the 'lifeworld' as

[9] See p. 64 above.

[10] Here I distinguish analytically the use of 'legal-statutory offers of regulation' (suppletive law) in private law both from factual compliance or observance (autonomous fulfilment) and enforcement (heteronomous imposition) of law and from the application of law in the narrow sense (concrete decision-making for ruling a case or situation) (see Neves, 1998, 43–6; 1992, 83–5; Blankenburg, 1977, 36–7).

[11] Rehbinder (2000, 141–3) defines orientation to sanctions, identification, and internalization as the reasons for the fulfilment of norms.

[12] On the distinction between the three validity claims, truth (concerning the objective world), rightness (related to the social or intersubjective world), and truthfulness (concerning the subjective world), see Habermas, 1982a, vol. 1, 427 ff. (Engl. trans. 1984, 319 ff.); 1983, 147 ff. (Engl. trans., 1990, 136 ff.); 1986, 137 ff., 426–7, 462 ff., and 588–9.

[13] Habermas, 1971, 25 (Engl. trans. 1974, 18); 1986, 131. See also Alexy, 1983, 138–9 (Engl. trans. 1989, 105).

background, which is defined 'as the horizon within which communicative actors are "always already" moving',[14] mutually and tacitly sharing the validity claims involved in their expressions and statements without questioning them. From this perspective, the claims that the Earth is round and that bodies are subject to the law of terrestrial gravity are part of unquestionable truths in our everyday practice. Likewise, the assertion that we must fight paedophilia corresponds to a rule whose legitimacy is unquestioned in the context of our contemporary lifeworld. However, when the validity claims implicitly held in actions or speech acts are problematized in a concrete interaction, and justification from the actor or speaker is required, we enter the level of discourse, at which, unlike the level of action, no new information is exchanged but there is an exchange of arguments.[15] So, the very validity claims that had been problematized become the subject or topic of discussion and need to be substantiated. What was naively assumed to be true or right on the action plane is now susceptible to questioning and criticism. From this perspective, it can be observed that actions and speech acts that implicitly assume the rightness of conduct of parents who vigorously beat their children, part of our everyday life a few decades ago, have been questioned by a new pedagogical discourse gradually developed during the second half of the twentieth century. Therefore, the discourse breaks with the naïve consensus existing in everyday practice and founded on the lifeworld as background, introducing dissent. However, in the terms of the theory of communicative action, the discourse is oriented towards the search for a new consensus on the questioned validity claims.[16]

Since the discourse requires foundations or justifications, involving reasoning, of course, from Habermas's viewpoint, the distinction between rules and principles can only be thematized at the discursive level. Strictly speaking, principles can be articulated only at the discourse level. Nevertheless, Habermas's model, which requires action and discourse oriented towards consensus, seems inappropriate for a complex society in which the structural dissent with regard to normative expectations is striking.[17] Moreover, Habermas

[14] Habermas, 1982a, vol. 2, 182 (Engl. trans. 1987, 119, the term '*Handelnden*' (namely 'actors') has been translated as 'actions'); cf. 1986, 593. In this regard, see Neves, 2000, 61–8.

[15] Habermas, 1971, 25 (Engl. trans. 1974, 18); 1986, 130–1. See also Alexy, 1983, 139–40 (Engl. trans. 1989, 105–6).

[16] In this sense, the treatment of the dissent that the discourse allows to 'emerge', 'in the interests of fundamental formation of consensus' (Apel, 1987, 71), is reduced to a means of consensus-building (see J.P. Müller, 1993, esp. 27, 35, 65, 79–80, 84; 1999, 25–6, 41).

[17] See Neves, 2000, 100 ff.; 2011. Despite his emphasis on dissent, Sunstein (2003, 91) qualifies it as a 'reasonable dissent': 'What we want to encourage is not dissent as such but reasonable dissent, or dissent of the right kind.' But the question becomes more challenging in today's society when we take into consideration the paradox of what 'reasonable dissent' means in concrete conflicts or controversies. For a

bases his position on communicative actors in intersubjective relations, not properly taking into account the involvement of the argument in a systemic connection of communications. Constitutional principles are normative artefacts that serve precisely to absorb dissent and, paradoxically, to enable and promote its emergence under the conditions of a complex legal system.

Hence, it seems to me that the systemic notion of first-order and second-order observation[18] is more appropriate to understand where the distinction between principles and rules lies in terms of legal argumentation.[19] In the mere everyday observance of law, in the pure routine application of legal rules by the state bureaucracy, or the use of 'legal-statutory offers of regulation' (suppletive law) in the ordinary exercise of private autonomy, those involved act and communicate at the level of a first-order observation of the standards to be applied. They do not question the meaning or validity of the norms to be followed, applied, or used in the corresponding context.[20] Alter and ego assume their habitual meaning, but this does not necessarily imply consensus. For example, ego (any person) does not smoke in a premise because there is a ban, sometimes even posted on a sign, or alter (a policeman or another administrative authority) orders and enforces the order to stop someone from smoking. Ego (an official responsible for authorizing expenditures) applies the routine norm that determines the payment of salaries shall be made on a certain day of the month, or alter (a civil servant in the corresponding government department) comes with an administrative complaint. Ego (a lessor) prepare the lease contract to adjust the rent within the limits of the corresponding tenancy law, or alter (a lessee) does not sign the contract. These alternatives are relatively simple. The legal-systemic difference between principles and rules unfolds only when controversies arise with regard to the norms to be applied and the argumentation level is reached. This implies a second-order observation.

In the second-order observation, those involved in the legal communication move on to another plane on which they discuss the norms to be applied, their validity, meaning, conditions of compliance, etc. With regard to contemporary society and law in a constitutional state, reaching an ultimate, 'ontological', underlying reality is not the point. A second-order observation with this assumption existed in the 'old world', especially in the Aristotelian-Thomist

less restrictive view on the dissent while considering its role 'in a system of living constitutionalism', see Balkin, 2009, 609–11.

18 Luhmann, 1997, vol. 2, 766 ff. (Engl. trans. 2013, 102 ff.).

19 Luhmann, 1993, 339 ff., 403 ff. (Engl. trans. 2004, 306 ff., 353 ff.).

20 At this level, 'One lets oneself be guided by the understanding that one is applying the law correctly in the form of given text-based norms' (Luhmann, 1993, 340 (Engl. trans. 2004, 306)).

tradition.[21] In the legal realm, it may have significance in a classic natural law model. Resorting to a plane of ultimate truths and principles, whether meta-legal or 'legal' meta-positive, allows for a second-order observation of behaviour patterns. However, in this case, the observation is externalized; strictly speaking, it is not a second-order observation as self-observation within the legal system. This is only made possible, as explained below,[22] with the functional differentiation of law.

In a functionally differentiated legal system, the second-order observation makes it possible to permanently rediscuss the rules to be applied and the conditions for their fulfilment. Thus, one might question the smoking ban in the light of constitutional freedoms, including economic freedom, contest the salary of highly paid civil servants in the light of 'morality', 'impersonality', and 'lawfulness' as 'principles' guiding the public administration (head provision of Article 37 of the Brazilian Federal Constitution)[23] and review the rent adjustment by turning down legal rules in the light of the financial balance requirement. Thus, the system is constrained to increase its irritability and permanently construct and reconstruct its own reality, its own world.[24] Principles and rules are norms reconstructed at the level of second-order observation in the legal argumentation processes.[25] This does not mean that principles and rules are not categories of norms, as Klaus Günther would suggest.[26] No norm is from the start a finished work and ready to be applied either as a rule or as a principle. The opposite understanding presupposes an externalization of the normative justification to a moral order with a universal pragmatic validity claim. Yet, in the first-order observation, the difference between rules and principles is still irrelevant. When, in the second-order observation, an argumentative controversy arises around the meaning, validity, and conditions for the application of norms, the difference between principles and rules gains vital significance for the consistent and proper development of law. Legal

[21] See Luhmann, 1997, vol. 2, 766–7 (Engl. trans. 2013, 102).

[22] See section 2 of this chapter.

[23] In this regard, an interesting example is the preliminary decision of the Councilor José Adonis de Araújo, ratified by the Brazilian National Council of Justice, determining, based on the principles of lawfulness, impersonality, and morality of the public administration, that the payment of additional remuneration provided by the State of Bahia Court of Justice according to a state law that attributed broad powers to the board of the Court for granting such benefits should be suspended (PCA No. 0005230-38.2009.200.0000). Against this decision, a preliminary injunction was granted by Justice Carlos Britto in Writ of Mandamus No. 28,924, on 7 July 2010.

[24] Luhmann, 1997, vol. 2, 766–7 (Engl. trans. 2013, 102).

[25] 'We have said that argumentation always sees itself in the context of a second-order observation. What matters is always the elaboration of an argument—for other observers' (Luhmann, 1993, 403 (Engl. trans. 2004, 353)).

[26] See pp. 59 and 69–70 above.

argumentation occurs at the intersection between the justification and the application of norms. With it, as opposed to what Günther proposes, one leaves the plane of mere application or observance (which also occurs in various ways and conditions according to the situation) and attempts to shed new light on the application by discussing the systemic-internal justification of the norms to be applied. And this is especially relevant in the case of constitutional law, that is in determining which constitutional principles and rules are applicable to the solution of controversial legal issues.

The third aspect to be taken into account concerns the character of the classification between principle and rule as categories of norms: is that a weak (quantitative) or strong (qualitative) demarcation? It seems to me that this question has been posed in inappropriate terms. If this is about the possibility of extracting the 'principles–rules' dichotomy from the legal materials (repertoires of legislation, case law, administrative acts, and established legal practices), any demarcation, whether strong or weak, qualitative or quantitative, would have no meaning. What is called a principle or a rule in legal texts does not correspond to the difference between principles and rules in an argumentative chain.

The distinction between principles and rules could be presented as a difference in the strict sense of systems theory, that is a 'two-sided form', such as system/environment, equal/unequal, validity/invalidity, lawful/unlawful (or legal/illegal).[27] Thus, a norm would formally be either a principle or a rule. But the difference between principle and rule is constructed and operates in the framework of two concepts of content, not exactly being a two-sided *form*.[28] More appropriate is to admit that those are *approximatively* ideal-typical constructs in the terms of Weber's tradition.[29] 'In its conceptual purity', the ideal type—defined by Weber as an epistemological 'utopia'—'cannot be found empirically anywhere in reality', rather serving as 'a purely ideal limiting concept' for the interpretation of 'reality' with 'the one-sided accentuation' of certain elements that are most relevant for the knowledge to be obtained.[30] In Weber's conception of the ideal type, the elements considered 'accidental' or 'non-essential' for the formation of the hypothesis are excluded.[31] However, Weber's concept of the ideal type is based on 'the fundamental ideas of modern

[27] See Luhmann, 1997, vol. 1, 60 ff. (Engl. trans. 2012, 28 ff.); 1993, 104, 111 ff., 174–5 (Engl. trans. 2004, 127, 132 ff., 180–1). Luhmann uses the concept of form defined by Spencer Brown, 1971, esp. 1 ff. In this regard, see Foerster, 1993.

[28] See Luhmann, 1997, vol. 1, 62 (Engl. trans. 2012, 30).

[29] Weber, 1973 [1904], 190 ff. (Engl. trans. 1949, 89 ff.); 1968a, 67–9, 157–9, 163–5.

[30] Weber, 1973 [1904], 190–1, 194 (Engl. trans. 1949, 90–1, 3).

[31] Weber, 1973 [1904], 201–2 (Engl. trans. 1949, 100–1); 1968a, 163–4.

epistemology which ultimately derives from Kant; namely, that concepts are primarily analytical instruments for the intellectual mastery of empirical data and can be only that';[32] it goes back to the notion of the transcendental subject. From another perspective, I conceive the 'ideal type' as a cognitive selection structure of the social sciences in relation to reality-environment, which, compared to them, appears more complex and unstructured.[33] This means that every area of knowledge constructs conceptual schemes to the reality, at first chaotic, which it claims to control as its knowledge material. This selective ordering involves the construction of its own object of knowledge, its reality. Kant's distinction between the (sensory, random) data and the (intelligible) objects of the transcendental subject[34] is here transformed into the difference between the disordered data of the environment of science and the objects selectively and neatly constructed by science. In his distinction between legal-rational, traditional, and charismatic domination, Weber clarifies this point by stating that these ideal types are not to be found in 'pure' form in historical reality.[35] The concept of capitalism, so dear to the Marxist tradition, as opposed to socialism, is also a scheme that serves the interpretation of a plurality of economic experiences as found, for example, in the United States, Scandinavian countries, Africa, etc.

In the normative framework, however, the 'ideal types' do not primarily serve to guide cognitive expectations but to stabilize normative expectations, and therefore to arrange selectively normative provisions and statements. Legal scholars and interpreters/applicators of law alike—given the repertoires of legislation, case-law, administrative acts and established practices (legal customs), especially in the event of disputes regarding the pattern to be followed—have to structure the normative material.[36] Principles and rules play this role in terms of legal argumentation. A norm presents itself schematically as either a principle or a rule. Principles are norms on the reflexive plane, enabling the marking out and construction or reconstruction of rules. While being immediate reasons for concrete ought-decisions, rules are conditions for the application of principles to case solutions.[37] In the argumentative process, a norm typically appears as a principle or as a rule. It is impossible to define beforehand whether a norm is a principle or a rule. That depends on the manner in which

[32] Weber, 1973 [1904], 208 (Engl. trans. 1949, 106).
[33] See Neves, 1992, 110–11.
[34] See, for instance, Kant, 1990 [1781^{A}/1787^{B}], vol. 1, 139–141, 168 [B 137–139, A 107] (Engl. trans. 1998, 249–50, 232–3).
[35] Weber, 1985 [1922], 124 (Engl. trans. 1968, vol. 1, 216).
[36] In this sense, Bydlinski (1996, 5–9) speaks of 'the "legal stuff" to be structured'.
[37] I will return to this issue in section 3 of this chapter.

the norm will be incorporated into the argumentative process according to the functional-structural point of view. Obviously, a standard can be established as either a principle or a rule in the system (the dignity of the human person, the prohibition of torture, respectively),[38] and this stabilization often relates to its constitutional wording. But the emergence of new principles or rules in the argumentative process is at first inexhaustible. It should also be noted that because both are normative concepts analogous to the ideal types as cognitive categories, they cannot, strictly speaking, be immunized from any mutual contamination in legal practice. This is why one can speak of hybrids, norms found in an intermediate situation between principles and rules.

Hybrids are accepted even by authors who have established a strong demarcation between principles and rules. In this sense, Dworkin argues: 'Sometimes a rule or a principle can play much the same role, and the difference between them is almost a matter of form alone.'[39] In this regard, he refers to the interpretation that the Supreme Court of the United States gave to the first section of the Sherman Act, which determines that every contract containing a restraint of trade shall be avoided. The Supreme Court interpreted the provision as expressing a rule, but by introducing the term 'unreasonable' in the statement of the rule ('"unreasonable" restraints of trade'),[40] the Court gave it a dimension of principle:

> This allowed the provision to function logically as a rule (whenever a court finds that the restraint is 'unreasonable' it is bound to hold the contract invalid) and substantially as a principle (a court must take into account a variety of other principles and policies in determining whether a particular restraint in particular economic circumstances is 'unreasonable').
>
> Words like 'reasonable', 'negligent', 'unjust', and 'significant' often perform just this function. Each of these terms makes the application of the rule which contains it depend to some extent upon principles or policies

[38] In relation to human dignity, Alexy distinguishes a rule and a principle (1986, 95 ff. (Engl. trans. 2002, 62 ff.); in the same sense, see Barcellos, 2005, 193–4). But when it comes to 'balancing the principle of human dignity against other principles in order to establish the content of the rule of human dignity' (Alexy, 1986, 96 (Engl. trans. 2002, 64)), nothing gets modified in the distinction between principles and rules, with regard to any principle: after the concretizing process, one can extract a corresponding rule from any principle. In this regard, V.A. Silva (2009, 201–2) raises objection to Alexy's formulation, rather drawing attention to directly constitutional rules, such as the prohibition of torture and degrading treatment (Article 5.III BFC), which set absolute limits to the intervention in the scope of the dignity of the human person.

[39] Dworkin, 1978, 27.

[40] Dworkin (1978, 28) cites the following decisions: *Standard Oil v United States*, 221 US 1, 60 (1911); *United States v. American Tobacco Co.*, 221 US 106, 180 (1911).

lying beyond the rule, and in this way makes that rule itself more like a principle.[41]

These assumptions correspond to what Aarnio called 'principle-like rules', pointing out examples such as 'those flexible legal rules that have a scope of application that is cognitively or evaluatively open in the same way as is the scope of value principles'. And he adds another category of hybrid, the so-called rule-like principles, exemplifying it with the principle of freedom of speech, which, when applied alone—without colliding with another principle, such as the principle of protection of one's private life—may be applied directly to the solution of a case, as in the assertion of the right 'to publish an article without being stopped by censorship'.[42] Similarly, Larenz refers to 'principles in the form of legal propositions' (as opposed to 'open principles'), 'which are condensed into an immediately applicable rule'.[43] Alexy himself resorts to this concept in the initial formulation of his theory of principles.[44]

It can be said that the norms Dworkin refers to as being 'logically' rules and 'substantially' principles, and which Aarnio calls 'principles-like rules' are incomplete rules in the narrow sense of Alexy because, as far as these norms explicitly or implicitly establish exceptions or application conditions, they are susceptible to balancing with principles in order to be applied immediately to the solution of a case. This clearly implies the possibility of a collision between a rule and a principle.[45] But anyway, dimensions of principles are present in that type of rule. In practice, therefore, to say that the ideal type 'rule' is a complete fit to such situations makes no sense to me. Of course, at the end of the concretizing process, after a possible balancing of the exception clause or condition clause with the competing principles, we have a complete rule, under

[41] Dworkin, 1978, 28. Alexy (1979, 70–1) refers to such situations, mentioning the same passage, in order to criticize the 'all-or-nothing' thesis.

[42] Aarnio, 1990, 184, 186; see also, Aarnio, 1997, 179–80; 2011, 122–3.

[43] Larenz, 1983, 461; 1969, 465–6. He uses as an example the constitutional maxim '*nulla poena sine lege*' (ibid.), which Alexy later defines simply as a rule (Alexy, 1986, 92–3 (Engl. trans. 2002, 61)). See p. 25 above.

[44] Alexy, 1979, 67, note 62.

[45] Alexy, 1986, 121 (Engl. trans. 2002, 83). For a different view, see V.A. Silva, 2009, 51–6, especially for understanding that, 'once the exception is created, the reasoning of definitive *right or duty*, typical of rules, also applies to it' (56). It seems to me, however, that nothing precludes that the definition of an exception prescribed in the rule depends on the balancing with a competing principle in the concrete case, so that the rule prima facie presents itself as incomplete in the strict sense. So, its definitive character can only be set at the end of the concretizing process, with the full statement of the rule to be applied. However, it should be noted that in controversial cases, depending on the legal argument regarding the definition of the norms to be applied, the (complete) rule that determines the definitive right or duty only appears at the end of the concretizing process, in order for the case to be subsumed thereunder.

which the case is subsumed by a concrete ought-decision. Nevertheless, prima facie, it is a hybrid, because a dimension of the rule competes with principles.

Similarly, it can be stated that the 'rule-like principles' in Aarnio's terms and the 'principles in the form of legal propositions' in Larenz's view are ultimately rules. But in this case, the situation is reversed. Although prima facie the norm can be seen as an immediately applicable rule (which determines the right to publish uncensored article in the case of freedom of speech), it can transmute into a principle during the concretizing process, provided that there are competing principles, requiring a collision solution rule to decide the case. In this sense, also in the so-called rule-like principles, we are confronted with normative hybrids within the ideal-typical difference between constitutional principles and rules.

This reference to hybrids may suggest a search for other categories. For instance, Humberto Ávila introduces the category of 'normative applicative postulates', defined as 'metanorms' or 'second-degree norms' that structure the application of principles and rules, establishing a bond between elements and imposing a certain relation among them.[46] In these terms, he distinguishes between non-specific postulates, which 'can be applied regardless of the elements subject to interrelationship' (weighing, practical accordance, prohibition of excess), and specific postulates, whose application 'depends on the existence of some elements and is defined by certain criteria' (equality, reasonableness, proportionality).[47]

In his own formulation, Ávila does not refer with this category to each and every metanorm, as he does not include, for example, the 'superprinciples' (better: meta-principles) in the category of postulates.[48] Other principles can be deduced from or justified based on them. This is what happens, for instance, in relation to 'the principle of a functioning criminal justice system as a subprinciple of the rule-of-law principle'.[49] There are also meta-rules, which refer to other rules and comprise several types: rules immediately related to the *solution* of inter-normative conflicts concerning time (*lex posterior derogat legi priori*), hierarchy (*lex superior derogat legi inferiori*), space (renvoi in private international law), and degree of generality (*lex specialis derogat legi generali*); renvoi rules in general and reservation rules in particular;[50] constitutional reservation rules referring to rules that can limit constitutional rights;[51] rules of

[46] Ávila, 2003, 79 ff. (Engl. trans. 2007, 83, 91 ff., 96 ff.).
[47] Ávila, 2003, 85 ff. (Engl. trans. 2007, 98 ff.).
[48] Ávila, 2003, 80–1 (Engl. trans. 2007, 83).
[49] Alexy, 2000, 33–4 (Engl. trans. 2000, 296).
[50] See Guastini, 1995a, 67 ff.
[51] See Alexy, 1986, 112 ff., 263 ff. (Engl. trans. 2002, 76 ff., 189 ff.).

procedural law in relation to the corresponding substantive law; and even rules of a higher degree in relation to the norms made based upon them (constitutional rules in relation to statutory law,[52] the latter in relation to ordinances, etc.). All those rules serve as immediate criteria for resolving inter-normative conflicts or solving concrete interpersonal conflicts. They are not to be confused, therefore, with principles, because they can be definitive reasons for decisions settling legal disputes, whether in the form of concrete interpersonal disputes, preliminary questions concerning the norm to be applied or conflicts in the abstract judicial review.

Moreover, the category of the so-called normative applicative postulates implies a variety of norms that can be characterized as principles, rules, or hybrids. The introduction of this category stems from the scanty definition of principles as 'immediate[ly] finalistic norms', referring to 'ideal states of affairs', as formulated by Ávila borrowing from Von Wright, Aarnio, and Hage.[53] The conceptual framework proposed in this work does not include a third 'ideal type' of norm (although I do not reject the existence of other standards in the legal system beyond binding norms, such as legal consultative opinions, legal advice or recommendations, and expert opinions). Norms are either at the reflexive level of the legal system, serving to both mark out and hermeneutically construct other norms, not being definitive reasons for deciding legal issues, and being therefore classified primarily as principles; or they work as definitive reasons for settling legal disputes, not functioning as a reflexive mechanism and being therefore classified primarily as rules. If we cannot fit them primarily in any of the categories, we are confronted with hybrids.

Let us take the criterion of proportionality as an example. In relation to this criterion, the terminological contention about the correct translation of the German term '*Grundsatz*',[54] which can be translated either as principle or as maxim or postulate, is not of importance here.[55] Alexy himself in the past referred to proportionality as a principle in literal terms (Verhältnismässigkeits*prinzip*, and not Verhältnismässigkeits*grundsatz*).[56] Later on, he maintained that proportionality is a rule: it is a norm that is either fulfilled or not fulfilled.[57] It seems to me that, strictly speaking, proportionality

[52] See e.g. Guastini, 1995b, 254 ff.

[53] See pp. 27–9 and 32 above

[54] See V.A. Silva, 2009, 168–9.

[55] Jakab (2006, 57, note 36) warns that, in most European languages, the distinction between the terms '*Grundsatz*' and '*Prinzip*' would be untranslatable. It is worth adding that, in German, sometimes these terms are synonymous, other times they involve very different concepts. See note 101 of Chapter 2 above.

[56] Alexy, 1979, 80.

[57] Alexy, 1986, 100, note 84 (Engl. trans. 2002, 66–7, note 84), citing, in this regard, Haverkate, 1983, 11.

can be considered a *condition of possibility* for the effective and consistent functioning of an order of rules and principles, as well as of an order of constitutional rights in particular. Ultimately, it appears as a condition of possibility for the functioning of the constitution of a rule-of-law and democratic State. Nevertheless, this understanding should not be over-interpreted in the sense of defining 'proportionality as a universal constitutional principle'.[58] As a condition of possibility it is a *form* of the purposive or instrumental rationality serving the efficient functioning of any cognitive or normative order. The three sub-requirements of proportionality (suitability, necessity, and balancing) are originally seated on the means–end rationality.[59] As a form (like the form of equality),[60] proportionality is compatible with any social, legal, or political order. In order to function rationally well and be efficient in the pursuit of their purposes, both National Socialism and Stalinism had to consider the technique of proportionality. To be rationally efficient according to a costs-and-benefits model, an economic organization has to take into account the three requirements of proportionality. Thus, as a *form*, proportionality is void, being able to contain very contradictory contents and comporting with very different institutional arrangements.

To say that proportionality is a *norm* seems inappropriate at first sight. A condition of possibility for something cannot constitute that something. However, if within the legal system the use of the proportionality test comes to be viewed as a duty to be performed by those in charge of normative interpretation/application, the imposition of this duty becomes a norm of the system. Obedience to proportionality is determined by 're-entry': what is a condition of possibility for the order becomes a norm within the order. As a norm, the meaning and relevance of proportionality can vary immensely among different orders: at one extreme, proportionality can be widely removed from the competence of the courts and other bodies in charge of the concrete interpretation

[58] Klatt and Meister, 2012b; 2012a, 1–2. They claim not only the universalism of the 'principle' of proportionality, but also of the schema of proportionality in the terms of Alexy's principle theory, as they—following Zucca, 2008, 28——also pontificate about Alexy being the 'prophet of structured balancing' (Klatt and Meister, 2012a, 4). For a critique of their view, see Reimer, 2013, who asserts that 'proportionality is a category of positive law (or at least of its doctrine)' (ibid., 30–1). In the words of Beatty (2004, 162), 'proportionality is 'a universal criterion of constitutionality'. In turn, according to Sweet Stone and Mathews (2008/2009, 160), 'proportionality is today a foundational element of global constitutionalism'.

[59] It is worth pointing out that in the process of reducing complexity the purposive/instrumental models are only 'employed when the problems have already gained more specific structures, when thus the complexity has already been broadly absorbed' (Luhmann, 1973, 156; see also 1983b, 223). This is related to the limits of proportionality as a form.

[60] On the distinction between equality as a form and as a norm, see Luhmann, 1991; 1993, 111–12 (Engl. trans. 2004, 132–3).

and application of law, remaining mainly as a political issue of law-making bodies; at the other extreme, the legal order can attribute enormous power to the courts and other law-applying officials to deal with proportionality. Between these two extremes, there is a wide range of solutions. This issue is dependent not only on a definition by the constitution-making power or decision in a system with a written constitution (there are constitutional orders that were not grounded by a constitution-making power and do not have a written constitution), but also on the self-understanding of the legal order by legislators, the executive branch, courts, and the public.[61]

Yet, is the proportionality *norm* a principle or a rule? A distinction needs to be made here. Norms that impose the use of the suitability and necessity criteria, norms that require pragmatic rationality of means and goals[62] for the application of constitutional rights, can be clearly seen as rules. They serve directly to resolve a dispute, presenting themselves as definitive reasons for deciding whether a measure that limits constitutional rights (or constitutionally protected collective interests) is suitable and necessary for reaching the goal it claims to attain. With regard to proportionality in the narrow sense, which includes in its content the balancing requirement (although the latter must not be confused with the former),[63] the situation does not seem so simple. Of course, if the measure has been proven to be disproportionate in the strict sense, declaring its unconstitutionality is required. This implies a typical characteristic of rules. Nevertheless, proportionality in the narrow sense involves the incidence of the balancing requirement. In Alexy's formulation, there is a reciprocal relationship between this requirement—which, he said, involves the optimization requirement in the strict sense—and the principles, which he calls, in more precise terms, 'requirements to be optimized'.[64] Once the optimization claim is removed, as exposed below,[65] it can be observed that between the weighing or balancing requirement—an integral part of the proportionality

[61] Anyway, it seems inappropriate to suggest that 'the development over time of a larger experiential base in other regimes might be predicted to produce methods more similar to the American ones', that is to expect a convergent development from 'the more flexible and open-ended balancing approach that generally rides under the banner of "proportionality"' to 'the American approach characterized by an emphasis on rule-based categorization' (Schauer, 2005, 31–2, dealing with freedom of expression controversies). Experiential bases and contexts vary considerably, so that a uniform methodology is unlikely to develop world-wide, much less in terms of the 'American exceptionalism'.

[62] It is worth recalling Habermas's concept of pragmatic questions, which 'pose themselves from the perspective of an actor seeking suitable means for realizing goals and preferences that are already given' (Habermas, 1992, 197 (Engl. trans. 1996, 159)). In our context, one may add '*more* suitable means', which are therefore less burdensome for the interested parties (necessity of a certain rights' restrictive measure).

[63] See V.A. Silva, 2009, 178–9.

[64] Alexy, 2000, 38–9 (Engl. trans. 2000, 300–1: 'commands to be optimized'). See p. 60 above.

[65] See section 4 of this chapter.

test in the narrow sense—and principles, there is a circularity that implies a certain contamination of the levels: determination by the balancing requirement of which principle has the precedence or highest weight assumes the precedence or highest weight of the selected principle for the case, and vice versa. This supports the understanding that proportionality in the strict sense, which includes the weighing requirement itself, is a hybrid: from the structural point of view, it is a rule, that is a criterion or a definitive reason for the solution of the case (only in so far as it solves a conflict between norms); under the functional aspect, it is a principle because it acts on the reflexive level of the legal system, in articulation with the principles it attempt to weigh or balance.

Finally, it should be noted that not all *conditions of possibility* for the functioning of a normative order or for the application of a norm become norms by re-entry. Just as the concepts of matter and energy as conditions of possibility for physics do not constitute themselves law of physics, the logical principle of non-contradiction as a condition of possibility for the consistent application of norms (because it is impossible to do and not do something at the same time) is not, in itself, a rule, working rather as a criterion for the laying down of rules aimed at solving normative conflicts. Similarly, some criteria are in place for the application of the principle of equality (for example, to define what is equal and unequal, as well as the relationship between equal and unequal) that are not themselves norms but conditions of possibility for the application of this principle. The same goes for any principle (or rule): criteria that are intrinsic conditions of possibility for their application can always appear, but that does not mean they will necessarily result in legal norms. Otherwise, from the static aspect of law, they will be either typically rules or principles, or atypically hybrid norms. The practical and theoretical relevance of this difference is greater on the constitutional plane.

2. Constitutional Principles as a Result of the Positivization of Law: Principles and Rules as an Internal Difference of the Legal System

Constitutional principles cannot be conceived without the phenomenon of positivization of law in modern society. This means they only arise and have practical significance when there is a functional differentiation of law as a social system.

In archaic forms of society, neither the difference between action and norm nor correspondingly the difference between cognitive and normative was present. Strictly speaking, law was not instrumentally *applied* or *enforced* by procedures but expressively *maintained* by retribution or reciprocity, whether directly by those involved or by tribal rituals.[66] This implied the notion of a self-evident law, mixed not only with moral but also with the unquestionable claims about the objective world. Truth and normative validity were indistinguishable.

Ancient cultures and civilizations already distinguished between norm and action, but law remained tied to a religious morality that is inseparably associated with representations of the truth.[67] This led to a situation in which conventional rules of the community were unquestionable[68] because they were directly linked to *unchangeable* and *true* values.[69] In this regard, the immutability of traditional law prevents a clear distinction between rules and principles. Application procedures are restricted to dogmatically shared norms, directly anchored in the moral and religious values of their community.[70]

With the introduction of the concept of natural law in the evolution from the ancient society through the Middle Ages to the threshold of modern society, it became possible to distinguish between rules and principles. In a way, this distinction is the same as the difference between natural law and positive law. In this new context, one already admitted the existence of a mutable law, which involved a change in the social structure. But the mutable, positive law, was subject to the immutable, natural law.[71]

Only when the law started to be made basically by decisions, that is with its positivization in modern society, it became permanently alterable.[72] The decidability and mutability of law are associated with the problem of its functional differentiation and autonomy in modern society.[73] As law differentiates from morality, institutionally overcoming its support in natural law representations, the question arises of its foundation as an operatively autonomous

66 See Weber, 1985 [1922], 445–6 (Engl. trans. 1968, vol. 2, 760–1); Schluchter, 1979, 146; Habermas, 1982a, vol. 1, 349, 351; vol. 2, 261–2 (Engl. trans. 1984/1987, vol. 1, 257–8; vol. 2, 175–6); 1982b, 135; Luhmann, 1993, 257 (Engl. trans. 2004, 243–4); 1987b, 150, 154–7 (Engl. trans. 2014, 117–18, 120–3); Neves, 1992, 25; 2000, 26–7, 49–50.

67 Luhmann, 1987b, 185 (Engl. trans. 2014, 143–4).

68 See Habermas, 1982a, vol. 2, 290 (Engl. trans. 1987, 194–5).

69 Luhmann, 1987b, 183 (Engl. trans. 2014, 142–3).

70 Even in Roman law, which intensely develops complex procedures of legal case solutions, 'The law remains embedded in general social arrangements, remains dependent on structures that also serve other functions (for instance, the family or a religiously founded morality)' (Luhmann, 1993, 58 (Engl. trans. 2004, 92)).

71 See Luhmann, 1987b, 186 (Engl. trans. 2014, 144); 1981, 119–20; Teubner, 1989, 73 (Engl. trans. 1993, 57–8).

72 Luhmann, 1987b, 203 (Engl. trans. 2014, 156); 1983b, 141; 1981, 125; Neves, 1992, 27–30; to similar effect, see Weber, 1968b [1922], 215–16; 1985, 125 (Engl. trans. 1968, vol. 1, 217); Schluchter, 1979, 146.

73 Luhmann, 1993, 38–123 (Engl. trans. 2004, 76–141); 1988; 1983a; Neves, 1992, 34 ff.; 2000, 69–73.

social system. In summary, three types of responses have been addressed regarding the problem of the foundation of the law after its positivization.

Habermas admits that positivization implies the difference between law and morality, as well as the direct justification of legal norms by legal principles.[74] Nevertheless, he relates the principle of enactment to the principle of justification.[75] From his perspective, law needs to be justified in the framework of a post-conventional or universal morality. In the context of the tension between 'facticity' and 'validity', the political instrumentality of law has its moral 'indisponibility' as a counterpoint.[76] 'Emancipated' from its 'sacred foundation',[77] law has to be legitimized by rational morally justifiable procedures. This model can be designed as a justification or foundation model.[78] From the standpoint of legal principles, this means that their validity is closely related to their compatibility with moral principles.

The opposite model can be called a de-foundation or de-justification model. Authors such as Derrida and Lyotard can be classified as belonging to this stream. From Derrida's deconstructive perspective, an act of force characterizes the starting point of any constitutional order. Every attempt at formulating a moral foundation of constitution, law and politics engenders a myth to be deconstructed.[79] From Lyotard's postmodern viewpoint, the different 'language games' are hermetically closed and develop an 'agonistics' among them, leaning towards 'damaging' and 'victimizing' one another.[80] Politics would not be a language game (a 'genre'), let alone a 'supreme status', but rather 'the multiplicity of genres', and therefore 'the threat of the differend'.[81] Thus, from this perspective, it is not appropriate to present foundations or to provide a justification for the constitutional order based on moral, ethical, or political principles.

Luhmann's systems theory can also be framed in the de-foundation model.[82] Positivization leads to the autopoiesis, and therefore to the operative closure of law, leaving no room for questions regarding the foundations of law. However, another reading of the systemic model is possible. According to this interpretation, it can be observed that the closure of the legal system derives from the

[74] See Habermas, 1982a, vol. 1, 351–4 (Engl. trans. 1984, 259–61); 1992, 565; 1988, 244.
[75] Habermas, 1982a, vol. 1, 354 ff., vol. 2, 266 (Engl. trans. 1984/1987, vol. 1, 261 ff.; vol. 2, 178); 1992, 97 (Engl. trans. 1996, 72).
[76] Habermas, 1992, esp. 582 ff.; 1988, 261 ff.
[77] Habermas, 1992, 582–3; 1988, 261–2.
[78] Cf. Habermas, 1982a, vol. 1, 354; vol. 2, 536 (Engl. trans. 1984/1987, vol. 1, 261; vol. 2, 365; 1992, 599); 1988, 279. In this regard, see Neves, 2000, 88 ff.
[79] Derrida, 1990, 941 ff.
[80] Lyotard, 1983, esp. 29, 52 (nos 21, 42) (Engl. trans. 1988, 12–3, 30); 1979, 20 ff. See Teubner, 1996b, 903–4, 1996a, 210; Welsch, 1996, 303 ff.
[81] Lyotard, 1983, 200 (no. 190) (Engl. trans. 1988, 138).
[82] So it is classified by Kasprzik, 1985, 368 ff.

constitution in the modern sense, which serves to 'replace external support, such as those postulated by natural law'.[83] Therefore, constitutionalism implies the claim to the constitutional self-foundation of law. Although the constitution can be seen as the structural coupling[84] between law and politics, or as a mechanism of transversal rationality between these systems,[85] it acts –from the internal viewpoint of law as the most comprehensive reflexive mechanism ('the norming of norm-making')[86] of the legal system.[87] Of course, this notion of constitution is incompatible with pre-modern social formations, in which law was directly subordinate to the amalgam composed of the political domination structure and the moral-religious semantics, and it is also incompatible with contemporary autocratic regimes, in which law is immediately subject to the ideology of the actual holder of power at any given time. And the constitution, as here understood, does not work satisfactorily in cases of symbolic constitutionalization,[88] in which constitutional norms show a very low degree of social efficacy, combined with the strong invocation of their texts within the legal and political rhetoric. Under these circumstances, the consistent reproduction of law is blocked by diffuse intrusions of political, economic, and relational factors in the process of concretizing and realizing law. So, the constitutional self-foundation of law presupposes a satisfactory functioning of both the rule of law in the legal field and democracy in the political sphere.

The issue of self-foundation presents itself initially in terms of the dynamic aspect of law in the sense of Kelsen's construction.[89] In addition to the distinction between 'legislation' (statute-making) and 'jurisdiction' (adjudication) or enforcement, it is important to distinguish between constitutional and statutory law. Thus, the code 'lawful/unlawful' (or 'legal/illegal') is duplicated with the introduction of the internal difference 'constitutional/unconstitutional'. The constitutional self-foundation of the system should not, however, lead to a linear hierarchical understanding of the legal system because although constitutional norms serve as reason for the validity of the other legal norms, the normative meanings of the constitution depend on both the legislation and the

[83] Luhmann, 1990a, 187.

[84] Luhmann, 1990a, 193 ff.; 1993, 470 ff. (Engl. trans. 2004, 404 ff.).

[85] Neves, 2009, 62 ff. (Engl. trans. 2013, 42 ff.).

[86] Luhmann, 1987b, 214 (Engl. trans. 2014, 164).

[87] In previous works, I referred rather to *constitutionality* as a reflexive mechanism or as the broadest reflexivity of the legal system (see, respectively, Neves, 1998, 125–7; 1992, 193–5).

[88] Neves, 1998.

[89] Hans Kelsen's concept of 'the dynamic aspect of law' matters here with regard to the *processes* of creation and application of norms (as opposed to 'the static aspect of law', concerning the normative *content*) (Kelsen, 1960; 72–3, 114, ff., 196 ff. (Engl. trans. 1967, 70–1, 108 ff., 193 ff.)), but not with respect to the hierarchical structure (*Stufenbau*) of the legal order (ibid., 228 ff. (Engl. trans. 221 ff.)).

acts of concrete interpretation/application of the constitution. Therefore, from the very constitutional self-foundation of the legal system a 'tangled hierarchy' is developed in the dynamic process of normative concretization.

Whereas from the dynamic aspect of law the primary difference arising from positivization and the corresponding constitutional self-foundation of law lies in the distinction between constitutional and statutory law, from the static aspect of law, although less evident, the basic difference that results from the same historical process is the distinction between constitutional principles and constitutional rules. Since the models of natural law lose their institutional significance in an increasingly complex society, which is marked by great dissent between various moral and evaluative perspectives, meta-legal principles practically fail to act as a normative guidance criterion. The answer to this problem is provided by the gradual construction of constitutional principles. Thus, constitutional principles, while presented as norms of norms from the static aspect of law, become a key filter in the face of the plurality of normative expectations that exist in the legal system environment and sometimes claim moral comprehensiveness. Rules—including constitutional ones—designed to act ultimately as definitive reasons to settle legal disputes, are incapable of fully performing this selective task immediately. In a sense, they are under-complex to providing selective criteria before a disorderly and conflicting plurality of normative expectations in the framework of morality, values, and the various functional systems of society. A constitution formed only by rules would be inadequate in a hyper-complex social context. Constitutional principles, by implying a certain distance from the case to be decided and a more flexible relationship between antecedent (norm conditions) and consequent (norm conclusion), are better suited to address the diversity of normative expectations circulating in society. In turn, principles are under-complex in relation to the case to be decided. Rules, in its structure, are more appropriate to offer an immediate reason for the case decision.

We can consider the issue from the static aspect of law resuming the distinction between unstructured (indeterminate, disorganized), structurable (determinable, organizable), and structured (determinate, organized) complexity.[90] This distinction refers to the relationship among the elements: it can be highly flexible, allowing for many different combinations and possibilities (the limit case is chaos), or slightly flexible, establishing and specifying the acceptable combinations between the elements. In this respect, the

[90] See pp. 3 and 69 above.

'smoke and crystal' metaphor, formulated by Henri Atlan, is opportune.[91] Systems generally reproduce between variety (smoke) and redundancy (crystal). With regard to constitutional principles and rules within the legal system of a democratic constitutional state, the *unstructured* complexity of the environment, which implies a plurality of conflicting values, interests, and normative expectations, passes through a selective sieve formed by legal or constitutional principles, and turns into *structurable* complexity. However, complexity becomes *structured* only with the determination of the rule to be applied to the case, making it possible to subsume the case under the rule through a concrete ought-decision.

It is worth opening a parenthesis at this point. From another perspective, it can be said that constitutional principles and rules are legal-doctrinal categories. But this does not mean they only exist at the descriptive proposition level of legal doctrine or jurisprudence. Strictly speaking, the radical distinction between descriptive meta-language ('science of law') and object-language (law) is unsustainable.[92] The legal doctrine is a form of reflection of the legal system within the system itself, intending to reflect its identity.[93] Principles and rules work as legal norms in argumentative practice, but conceptually they are defined more precisely by the legal and constitutional doctrine, understood as an instance of the legal system itself. Thus, a rigidly hierarchical distinction between meta-language and object-language becomes diluted, since there is a reciprocal reference between the language used by the authorities responsible for legal interpretation-application and the legal-doctrinal language with respect to constitutional principles and rules: doctrine relates to the legal practice (especially of courts and judges with constitutional functions) of applying constitutional principles and rules in order to conceptualize these normative categories; the authorities responsible for constitutional concretization resort to the legal-doctrinal concepts of constitutional principles and rules in order to apply the corresponding norms.

Having closed this parenthesis, it can be said that just as the difference between constitutional and statutory law from the dynamic aspect of law does not imply a linear hierarchy but rather a circular relation, the difference between constitutional principles and rules from the static aspect of law entails a relationship of reciprocal presupposition, as shall be seen below.

[91] Atlan, 1979.
[92] In the sense of Hofstadter's critique of Russell's theory of types (see note 7 of Chapter 1). In this regard, see Neves, 2009, 295–7 (Engl. trans. 2013, 183–4); 1998, 64; 2000, 146.
[93] Luhmann, 1974. See Neves, 1992, 204 ff.

3. The Circular Relationship Between Constitutional Principles and Rules

Based on the assumption that the distinction between constitutional principles and rules is an internal difference of the legal system, consisting of two legal-doctrinal categories, it can be observed that rules are first-degree 'general norms', that is placed at the first-order observation level in relation to the ought-decision of a case (or the ruling of a case as an 'individual norm'). This is not related to a first- or second-order observation concerning the elements (communications), which I addressed when considering the legal argumentation as a second-order observation in relation to the everyday observance and routine bureaucratic application of law. The question concerns first- and second-order observations at the level of structures (expectations). Rules condense normative expectations immediately directed at settling a case.

Let us consider the rule immediately attributed to Article 5.XLVII.b of the Brazilian Federal Constitution, which prohibits, without exception, the punishment of life imprisonment. From the observation of the case to be decided according to this rule, the ought-judgment can be extracted without intermediation, even when it comes to the analysis of other legal systems, as has occurred in innumerable decisions about extraditions to countries where a life sentence is expected for the offender: extradition ought to be granted only under the condition that the state requesting it undertakes to commute a life sentence to imprisonment for not more than thirty years within the limits of Brazilian criminal law.[94] And it seems to me that this constitutional prohibition cannot be mitigated in cases subject to the Rome Statute of the International Criminal Court,[95] whose Article 77 (1, b) establishes a 'term of life imprisonment when justified by the extreme gravity of the crime and the individual circumstances of the convicted person' for the 'the crime of genocide', 'crimes against humanity', 'war crimes', and 'the crime of aggression' (Article 5, 1, a–d). Indeed, in this context, the situation becomes rather complicated, since two

[94] The case-law experience has confirmed the precedents. See the following cases of extradition, all of which were decided unanimously by the Brazilian Supreme Court: Ext. 1548/DF, judgment 19 March 2019, DJe 1 April 2019; Ext. 1533/DF, judgment 12 March 2019, DJe 22 March 2019; Ext. 1104/UK—United Kingdom of Great Britain and Northern Ireland, judgment 14 April 2008, DJe 23 May 2008; Ext. 1103/US–United States of America, judgment 13 March 2008, DJe 07 December 2008; Ext. 1060/PU—Peru, judgment 15 October 2007, DJe 31 October 2007; Ext. 1069/US—United States of America, judgment 09 August 2007, DJe 14 September 2007. These precedents are now expressly supported by Law No. 13,445, 24 May 2017, Article 96.III.

[95] The Statute was adopted on 17 July 1998 and entered into force in the international order on 1 July 2002, having been approved in Brazil by Legislative Decree No. 112, 6 June 2002, and promulgated by Decree No. 4,388, 25 September 2002. It entered into force in Brazil on 1 September 2002.

other constitutional rules come into play: Article 5.4 of the Brazilian Federal Constitution, introduced by Amendment No. 45 of 2004, states that 'Brazil accepts the jurisdiction of an International Criminal Court to whose creation it has expressed its adhesion'; Article 60.4.IV of the Brazilian Constitution prohibits any proposal of constitutional amendment aimed at abolishing individual rights and guarantees. However, if we consider that a life-term imprisonment ban is included among the entrenchment clauses, or rather that it is part of the constitutional identity core provided by Article 60.4.IV, then Article 77 (1, b) of the Rome Statute does not prevail over it, even if we go beyond the position settled by the Brazilian Supreme Court in the conjoint judgment of HC 87,585/TO and Extraordinary Appeals (RE) 466,343/SP and 349,703/RS.[96] In this trial the Supreme Court defined the 'supra-legality' (the supra-statutory rank), but, at same time, the 'under-constitutionality' of human rights treaties ratified by Brazil that do not meet the procedure laid down in Article 5.3 of the Brazilian Federal Constitution, a procedure equivalent to that of a constitutional amendment. An interpretation in favour of the constitutional status of the human rights treaties or the choice for the procedure laid down in Article 5.3 would not remove the character of entrenched clause from Article 5.XLVII.b of the Brazilian Constitution. It would only be possible to overrule this rule as partly invalid (under the Rome Statute) if we adopted the thesis of the supra-constitutionality of human rights treaties or conventions, which would imply the absorption of domestic law by international law, an untenable situation in a world society with many different perspectives of human rights.

Anyway, although the argumentation concerning the life-term imprisonment ban by a constitutional rule may involve conflicts with rules of public international law, making the issue even more complex, arguments only in the light of rules make a first-order observation of the case to be decided feasible. Determining the applicability of a rule excludes other rules to be applied (since the case is not within their spheres of validity), immediately making it possible to shape a definitive reason for the ought-decision of the case, in other words, the construction of a complete statement of the rule to be applied.

The situation becomes much more complex or, stated rather better, the degree of structuring the complexity of the case is reduced when one falls back on the level of principles. Invoking principles leads to a second-order observation of the case to be decided and of its ought-judgment. It is not about denying that the constitutional principles, including the so-called open principles, have

[96] RE 466,343/SP, RE 349,703/RS, HC 87,585/TO, judgment 3 December 2008, TP, DJ 12 December 2008.

structure or 'propositional character',[97] that is to say they can be expressed in a statement that contains an antecedent (norm conditions) and a consequent (norm conclusion).[98] If they could not be expressed in normative statements, they would not have the character of legal norm. It turns out that the relationship between antecedent and consequent is flexible, involving an incomplete 'legal causality'. Based only on a principle as a principle, one cannot directly observe and determine the relationship between a legal fact and its concrete legal consequence. In this sense, we can say that principles prima facie solely hold a wide norm scope.[99] The norm scope is only delimited in the development of the concretizing process in the light of a rule, enabling the transformation of the fact situation into a legal fact that brings about the corresponding concrete legal consequences. But the issue of a flexible 'propositional' structure regarding the bond between normative antecedent and consequent, and therefore of a normative structure that is incomplete for the purposes of subsuming the fact under the norm, does not equal a lack of 'propositional' dimension in principles. As norms, they need to be expressed in normative statements with a 'propositional' structure.

This issue must be related to the distinction between principles and meta-rules, as addressed above. Meta-rules are norms that refer to norms and thus are also norms of norms, such as: *lex posterior derogat legi priori*, *lex superior derogat legi inferiori*, *lex specialis derogat legi generali*, renvoi rules in general and reservation rules in particular, constitutional rules of reservations of constitutional rights, rules of procedural law in relation to the corresponding substantive law, and rules of a higher degree with regard to the norms made

[97] Larenz (1983, 461; 1969, 465–6) maintained the opposite view. See also Sieckmann, 2006, esp. 85.

[98] Canaris, 1983, 51. See pp. 37-8 above.

[99] Here one could point to an approach to the notion of wide 'scope' as opposed to narrow 'scope' of constitutional rights, which is closely linked to the distinction between 'external theory' and 'internal theory' of the limits of constitutional rights, since these 'theories' are respectively associated with compatibility or incompatibility with balancing (Alexy, 1986, 290 ff. (Engl. trans. 2002, 210 ff.); Borowoski, 2007, 315 ff.; V.A. Silva, 2009, 79 ff.; 2006, 31 ff.). I am not convinced that there is an intrinsic relationship between the so-called internal and external theories and balancing. Those who start from a narrow 'scope' can also admit balancing. In this orientation, the inherent limits (concerning the field of what is limitable) would be balanced with the relative 'core'. For example, there is no impediment for an advocate of the 'internal theory' to weigh the 'social function of property' (Article 170.III BFC), as an immanent limit of the property right, against a relative 'core' of that right in order to determine its dimension that is non-limitable by the requirement of social function. The question would involve establishing, in specific cases, the measure or weight of the social function as an immanent limit. It would be just another terminological and conceptual clothing, distinct from that used by a supporter of 'external theory', who admits the weighing in the same terms. In this respect, the distinction in itself would have no practical significance for the problem of weighing or balancing. Unlike this model that stems from Alexy's work, I use the distinction between wide and narrow norm scope only to distinguish between the norm scope at the beginning of the concretizing process (prima facie) and the norm scope at the end of this process, the latter featuring the construction of a definitive and complete rule, attributed directly or indirectly to the constitutional text.

according to them in terms of the dynamic aspect of law (constitutional rules concerning ordinary laws, ordinary laws in relation to ordinances, etc.),[100] as well as the rules related to the first and second proportionality criteria (suitability and necessity). But rules of this type, although one can speak of 'second-degree norms',[101] are not related to, in the strict sense of systems theory, second-order observation of the cases to be decided or of the concrete legal ought-judgments. Meta-rules (or, in a more comprehensive formulation, rules that refer to general norms) serve as a definitive reason for the settlement of legal disputes. The settlement in this case can take various forms, such as a preliminary or abstract solution to an inter-normative conflict, a solution to a controversy about what norm has to be applied to a certain case, an answer to a question concerning the sphere of validity of other norms, a procedural solution to a normative conflict of substantive law or even procedural law, etc. Based on meta-rules, it is always possible to shape an ought-decision of the case immediately, which might even configure an abstract conflict of rules. Thus, in the light of them, one can always make a first-order observation of the case to be decided and of its ought-judgment. Principles, by contrast, always remain structurally at the second-order observation level, not providing definitive criteria for the solution to a case.

It must not be inferred from the characterization of the principles as norms of norms at the second-order observation level that principles are normative arguments, unlike normative statements, which is said to express definitely valid norms.[102] It is worth distinguishing between arguments as system elements, that is on the plane of communications, and principles, which, as norms, are located on the plane of system structure. Of course, as stated above, argumentation implies a second-order observation in the dimension of system elements, that is in terms of legal communication. The principles imply a second-order observation at the level of structures, namely, of the normative expectations stabilized as legal norms. In fact, the distinction between principles and rules only becomes relevant at the level of argumentation. Albeit arguments serve the system redundancy by reducing the 'surprise value' of other arguments and eventually of decisions, they distinguish themselves from the redundancy itself, since they lead to asymmetrization in the system by referring to grounds or reasons.[103] In this view, arguments are communications that relate to both principles and rules, which are programs as reasons for deciding.

100 See pp. 84-5 above.
101 Ávila, 2003, 80 (Engl. trans. 2007, 83).
102 Sieckmann, 2006, esp. 85. Later, he formulates otherwise, stating that principles are 'fundamental premises of a legal argument' (2009, 24), in a conceptually confusing style.
103 Luhmann, 1986c, 35 and 37.

One way would be simply to hold that constitutional principles are not legal norms, as these arise only at the end of the concretizing process.[104] From this perspective, legal norms would only be complete rules as definitive reasons for the ought-decision of the case. Although this thesis—as mentioned above with respect to norms in general[105]—has a seductive force, it seems to me that it disregards an important question: if legal norms arise only at the end of the concretizing process, judges and other officials in charge of interpreting and applying the law would not be subject to any legal norm in their activity of law concretization; the double contingency between the institutional instance of *production* of norms (legislature in the broad sense) and the instance of binding hermeneutic *construction* of norms (judge in the broad sense) implies cross-references in meaning-giving (alter: 'I say that you shall say this'; ego: 'I say that you said this'). The authority responsible for interpreting and applying normative texts cannot break with this double contingency, ignoring the body responsible for the institutional production of law (at least in a democratic constitutional state). Legal interpretation and argumentation are text-dependent.[106] And those who produce normative texts always give them meaning. The legislator and the constitution-making body produce more than just signifiers (much like the judge creates more than just a meaningless text of a judicial decision, for the meaningful ruling of a case does not only arise with its interpretation by the parties or by the officials in charge of its enforcement). It is assumed that they give meaning to the text, which will then be discussed in the concretizing process as being constructive of legal norms. In this context, the authorities responsible for normative interpretation-application assign principles to the constitution, defining them as legal norms to which they are bound while determining the legal rule that will be the definitive reason for the case decision: 'In the light of the valid principles of the constitutional order, I ought to determine this rule as a definitive reason for the settlement of the present case.'

The constitutional principles as norms concerning the second-order observation of the cases to be decided and of the concrete legal ought-judgments present, in the chain of argumentation, a greater capability of developing external references. In a way, they always point to something that already existed outside of the legal system (values, moral principles, general interests, etc.). Yet, this formulation can be misleading in the sense of denying the autonomy of

104 F. Müller, 1994, 202.
105 See pp. 14–15 above.
106 Luhmann, 1993, 342 (Engl. trans. 2004, 308). See also Möllers, 2015, 281 ff.

the legal system as a characteristic of the constitutional state.[107] In this regard, the paradoxical formulation that principles are external, becoming legal only when stamped by the relevant legal authority, is very common. Accordingly, Esser, on the one hand, says: 'the precedent is not only the means by which a hitherto unknown principle becomes visible—no, this would not exist without that'.[108] On the other hand, he maintains, in relation to the 'Continental system' specifically, that the precedent is not 'binding by virtue of the formal authority of "stare decisis", but by virtue of the imposition of a principle confirmed by it'.[109] This circular model,[110] however, suggests a certain immediate relation in the absorption of external elements by the law.[111] The judge would have the power to recognize the pre-existing principles, giving them legal force. Seen in this way, the question implies a stance that ignores the functional requirement of autonomy of the legal system in a complex society. Legal principles, especially those of constitutional kind, have the fundamental task of selecting, from the internal point of view of law, normative expectations with a claim to moral validity, group preference values or identity values, interests in establishing regulatory standards, as well as the most diverse atypical normative expectations that are articulated in conflicting ways in the environment or context of the legal system. What is a moral principle to a group is not the same for others; the values of a group are opposite to those of others; not only are the interests of a group opposed to those of others, but also the public or general interests for certain sectors of society clash with general interests from the perspective of others. With regard both to rules in general (in terms of the static aspect of law) and to under-constitutional principles (in terms of the dynamic aspect of law), constitutional principles display greater mobility to play a selective role before this inconsistent diversity that shapes a public sphere characterized by structural dissent. And they are not only hermeneutically *constructed* by precedents. They can arise immediately from the constitutional text or be directly assigned to a normative provision of the constitution. But the mobility and the scope of constitutional principles do not preclude external conflicts from being reproduced internally, so that the same principle can be often taken as a reason for antagonistic decisions.[112] This is related to the danger of abusing principles, which arises from the likelihood that, in certain contexts, they

107 See Luhmann, 1993, 347 (Engl. trans. 2004, 312).
108 Esser, 1956, 284.
109 Esser, 1956, 275.
110 Pascua (1996, 21) speaks of 'circular reasoning' [Zirkelrschluß].
111 'Principle and case-law reasoning form a functional unit' (Esser, 1956, 275).
112 Luhmann, 1993, 347 (Engl. trans. 2004, 312).

serve rhetorically to cover up manipulations that block the constitutional self-consistency of the legal order in question.[113]

From the static aspect of law, constitutional principles, as general legal norms under which a second-order observation develops with respect to constitutional cases to be decided and their ought-judgments, function as reflexive mechanisms or, more precisely, are the more comprehensive structures of reflexivity in the legal system.[114] Reflexivity concerns the reference of a process to systemic processes of the same kind. Thus, one can point to decisions on decision-making in organizations, 'the norming of norm-making' in law, the teaching of teaching (or the education of the educator) and the learning of learning in education, power over power in politics, the exchange related to exchange (monetization or, at a further level, the financing of the use of money) in economy, love communication about love itself.[115] Reflexivity relates immediately to the self-reference of processes, but it has a meaning in terms of structures. For example, the exchange (process), by involving currency (structure), relates to reflexivity at the structural level, that is a second-order 'having property' (money) referring to a first-order 'having property' (goods). Arguments concerning principles are reflexive processes in the light of principles as reflexivity structures, namely, as norms that are reflexive in relation to norms.

The reflexive mechanisms or processes and their reflexivity structures enhance the dynamics of the corresponding system in a hyper-complex environment. In less complex societies, the development of reflexive mechanisms is very limited.[116] The exchange of goods was sufficient for the dynamics of the economy. The lack of formal education in school made it irrelevant to educate the educator. The religion-based domination was not likely to be subordinate to controls by other instances of political power. The foundation of law on immutable truths rendered 'the norming of norm-making' dispensable. 'Decisions' were taken outside of organizational structures, depending either on standards set by tradition or on concrete and diffuse criteria chosen by the occasional holder of power. Love did not reflect on itself, because, paradoxically, on the one hand, it had the character of spontaneity and, on the other, it was immediately subject to religious, familial, and political determinations.[117]

113 This problem will be tackled again in Chapter 4.

114 From the dynamic aspect of law, the constitution is presented as the most comprehensive reflexive instance of the legal system (see p. 91 above).

115 Luhmann, 1984, 93–9; 1987a, esp. 612–3 (Engl. trans. 1995, 451–2).

116 Luhmann, 1984, 92.

117 The William Shakespeare's tragedy 'Romeo and Juliet' can also be read as an artistic expression concerning the crisis of the transition to the institutionalized form of 'modern love', characterized by a claim to autonomy in relation to religion, politics and family (although it serves to found a family), which implies the development of reflexive mechanisms in the love relationship itself, and the

As social complexity increases, thus implying the requirement of functional differentiation and specification, the autonomy of the social systems grows dependent on the development of reflexive structures and processes. Given the social hyper-complexity, first-order observation mechanisms and structures become insufficient to enable a socially adequate reproduction of the corresponding systems. If we consider the monetary mechanism, this situation will be very clear. What would happen with the abolition of the monetary mechanism in today's economy? Undoubtedly, a reversion to barter in a world of intense transactions in financial terms would mean a global catastrophe. But currency and financial transactions, like any reflexive structure and process, have a diabolical side. If the monetary or financial mechanism decouples too much from 'having' goods that are capable of directly satisfying human needs, that leads to a serious social crisis: not only the economy loses its consistency but it also becomes socially inadequate. Excessive orientation to goods designed to satisfy direct needs tends to undermine the monetary consistency of the economic system; excessive orientation to monetary and financial mechanisms can lead to the inadequacy of the economy before its social (and—dare we say—natural) environment. In these contexts, there is inflation, deflation, stagnation of the productive sector, 'bubbles', etc.

Similarly, this occurs with constitutional principles as reflexive structures of the legal system. The implications here are obviously different because, unlike the economy, which is primarily a cognitive system, law is primarily normative. Principles are reflexive mechanisms in relation to rules. They can serve to mark out, construct or develop, strengthen or weaken, restrict or extend the content of rules. With regard to the rules directly attributed to a constitutional or legal text, their function of marking out, strengthening or weakening, extending or restricting the content of rules stands out. With regard to the rules assigned indirectly to a constitutional or legal text ('derivative' constitutional or legal norms), their function as criteria for the hermeneutical construction or development of rules stands out. Thus, constitutional principles fortify the legal system's capacity to reproduce itself in a socially adequate way. Rules—especially those of constitutional kind, due to their claim to be comprehensive—without the reflexivity of constitutional principles, are under-complex as isolated criteria for the treatment and solution of highly complex constitutional cases. They are better at serving the consistency or self-reference of the legal system but are limited in terms of social adequacy of law. On the

romanticization of love ('one loves love for the sake of love', Luhmann, 1997, vol. 1, 372 (Engl. trans. 2012, 223)).

contrary, although constitutional principles cannot overlook the consistency of the legal system, they play their role especially in relation to the social adequacy of law, particularly in more complex controversial cases. It can be said that an argumentation oriented primarily by constitutional rules is a formal reasoning, with which the legal system practices self-reference, with 'the necessity at all levels to come to a decision and to avoid submersion in the full complexity of the factual world' being fundamental.[118] In turn, an argumentation oriented primarily by constitutional principles can be seen as a substantive reasoning, with which the system practices external reference, even towards 'a given society's morals', thus preventing 'from isolating itself in formal argumentation'.[119] Therefore, the importance of constitutional principles relates to their ability to allow for a adequately complex reproduction of the legal system in relation to society as a whole, or rather to the social (and natural, at least as the content of communications) environment of law.

Yet, as money is to economy, constitutional principles (and other reflexive structures of social systems) are also 'diabolical'. It is true that a modern legal system that overestimates rules at the expense of constitutional principles tends to an excessively rigid consistency, isolating itself from its environment: such rigidity makes it socially inadequate before a highly dynamic and complex society. However, the fascination with constitutional principles to the detriment of rules tends to block legal consistency, dissolving law amorphously in its environment and subordinating it immediately to particularistic intrusions of power, money, intolerant moralism, excluding, non-negotiable values, etc. The amorphous character of the 'smoke' derived from the excessive use of principles makes law inconsistent and simultaneously inadequate to the social factors of its environment as well as immediately subordinate to them. This results in the inflation of principles, which can ultimately lead to the destabilization of normative expectations, legal insecurity, and distrust in the functioning of the constitutional order itself. In this context, principles are presented as argumentative *topoi* of a rhetoric that covers the inconsistencies of law. This situation is related to the fact that principles can be understood as 'formulae for redundancy' (they reduce the degree of surprise of decisions), 'which appear to be compatible with any degree of variety in the system'.[120] This feature should not, however, lead to a disregard for principles in defence of a formalistic return to

[118] Luhmann, 1993, 393–4 (Engl. trans. 2004, 346).

[119] Luhmann, 2013, 281; 1993, 394 (Engl. trans. 2004, 346). With respect to these two modes of argumentation, see Summers, 1992, who characterizes their relationship as 'a complex and intriguing mystery' (153).

[120] Luhmann, 1993, 348 (Engl. trans. 2004, 312).

the model of rules,[121] since this would result in legal over-consistency and the social inadequacy of law. The principle-overestimating model of constitutional law in terms of the static aspect of law (normative content), understood as a model that disregards constitutional rules (beside 'constitutionalization of law' in terms of the dynamic aspect of law—law-making process—understood as a model that underestimates statutory law),[122] can be contrasted with a model of articulation between constitutional principles and rules (besides a constructive articulation between constitutional law and statutory law).

From this perspective, the issue of circularity between principles and rules comes to light in the constitutional concretization process. There is no linear implication between reflexive structures or processes and 'reflected' structures and processes. Reflexivity in general implies a circular relationship. Let us take money again as an example: does money have any value in the absence of goods or if its purchasing value is eroded? And what is the economic value of goods with no monetary value in a complex society? This mutual implication is similar in the relationship between constitutional principles and rules in terms the static aspect of law (as well as between constitution and statutory law or between constitution and constitutional adjudication in terms of the dynamic aspect of law). Constitutional principles serve to mark out, construct, develop, weaken, and strengthen rules, and occasionally to restrict and extend their content. In short, we can say with due care that they act as reason for or ground for rules, including constitutional rules, in complex legal disputes. In turn, rules are conditions for applying principles in the settlement of constitutional cases (see Figure 3.1). That is, if there is neither a rule directly assigned to constitutional or legal texts nor a judicially constructed rule under which the case can be subsumed by a concrete ought-judgment (i.e. a ruling), principles lose their practical significance or only serve the rhetorical manipulation to remove the application of complete rules, thus concealing the inconsistency of the legal system. The inflation of principle-overestimating arguments entails the loss of importance of constitutional principles as criteria to solve cases. The circular reflexive relationship between principles and rules implies a mutual fortification of the corresponding structures (norms) and processes (arguments).

[121] In a way, it can be said that the defence of legal formalism reappears as a reaction to the excess of substantive reasoning invoking principles and correspondingly using balancing. In this sense, one may understand the contribution of Schauer, 1998b. In turn, regarding international law, Koskenniemi (2002, 494 ff.) advocates a 'culture of formalism' as opposed to realism in international relations.

[122] In a way, one can see a certain affinity and co-originality between the overestimation of constitutional principles to the detriment of constitutional rules and the 'constitutionalization of law' to the detriment of legal statutes.

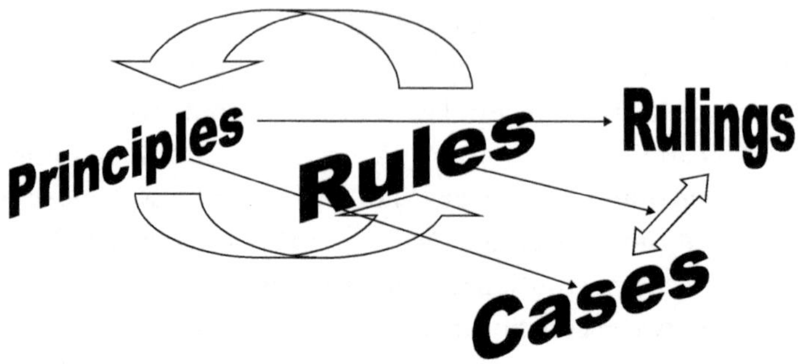

Figure 3.1 The Circular Relationship Between Constitutional Principles and Rules.

However, when constitutional rules need to be articulated in the light of constitutional principles during the course of the concretizing process, they become incomplete in the narrow sense, since some of their dimensions become liable to be collated and weighed with the principles in question. This situation brings up once again the question of the norm that appears as an immediate criterion for the settlement of the case and the construction of the pertinent ruling.[123] In more complex constitutional cases, in which various constitutional principles and rules are engaged in a chain of argumentation, some norms are invoked and some norms are applied directly and indirectly as a definitive reason or criterion to settle the dispute. As per figure 3.2, a contradictory diversity of values, moral claims, interests, and atypical normative expectations is present in the social environment of the constitutional concretization process. In the network or chain of constitutional argumentation, constitutional principles and rules are invoked. By invoking principles, an initial selective step is taken towards structuring the complexity of the case in the face of values, moral claims, and interests circulating in the social environment of the concretizing process: a way is sought to go from an unstructured to a structurable complexity. By invoking rules, a further step is taken: one seeks to make the complexity of the case structured. Nonetheless, the invoked rules and principles, particularly on a legal board in which opinions are formally drawn up individually (*in seriatim*), are not susceptible to offer case solution criteria. During the course of the concretizing process, a new selection appears, determining what principles and rules should be applied. The former are applied medially, that is by means of complete rules as definitive criteria

[123] See section 3 of Chapter 2 above, esp. pp. 68–9.

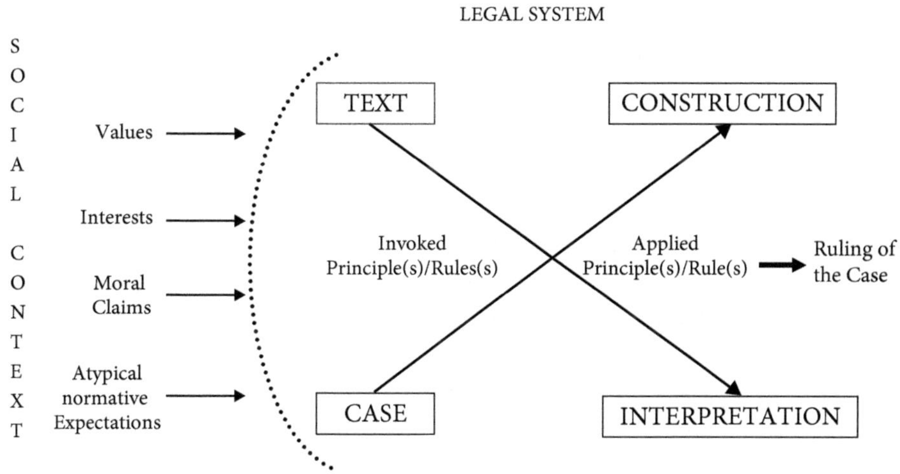

Figure 3.2 Constitutional Concretization through Principles and Rules.

for solving the case and constructing the relevant ought-decision. The theoretical strategy that only complete and definitive rules are legal norms—whereas principles and incomplete rules are only normative meanings of arguments and statements—seems problematic, as mentioned above because it may lead to the misconception that the constitutional concretization process and the judges involved therein are not subject to any legal norm, which results in the invisibility of the constitutional legislator, and therefore a denial of the double contingency between the institutional instance of norm production and the instance of its hermeneutic construction with binding force.

Let us consider the *Ellwanger* case, in which the Brazilian Supreme Federal Court decided that publishing a book with anti-Semitic content constitutes 'practice of racism', and therefore 'a non-bailable crime not subject to the statute of limitations', according to Article 5.XLII of the Brazilian Constitution.[124] This case dealt with the controversy around the application of the criminal rule assigned to Article 20 of Law No. 7,716, 5 January 1989, in the wording amended by Law No. 8,081, 21 September 1990, which stated as follows: 'To practice, induce or incite, through the media or publication of any kind, discrimination or prejudice based on race, religion, ethnicity or national origin. Penalty: confinement from two to five years.'[125] Moreover, it was about subsuming the case under the rule expressed in Article 5.XLII of the Brazilian Constitution, which

[124] HC 82,424/RS, judgment 17 November 2003, TP, DJ 19 March 2004.
[125] This provision was amended again by Law 9,459, 15 May 1997.

provides that the 'practice of racism' is a crime 'not subject to the statute of limitations'. First, the question was posed of whether the fact pattern involving the publication of a book denying the Holocaust was consistent with the criminal rule; second, assuming that fact pattern was subsumed under the rule, whether this rule set forth the elements of the crime of racism, that is an offence 'not subject to the statute of limitations' under Article 5.XLII BFC. The question, at first glance, could be converted into an 'easy' case of subsumption under constitutional and legal rules. But the matter was referred to the plane of principles. The convicted defendant invoked the principle of freedom of expression. In litigation in the Supreme Court, competing principles were cited, such as human dignity and non-discrimination.[126] Through the invocation of those principles, the pertinent constitutional and statute-law rules became incomplete. The issue could be considered under three aspects:

(1) the constitutionality or unconstitutionality of the statute-law rule on the basis of principles, in order to determine whether this rule, by considering the publication of books with discriminatory content against ethnic or religious groups as a crime of racism, has exceeded the scope of Article 5.XLII of the Brazilian Constitution, interpreted in the light of either the principles of human dignity and non-discrimination or the principle of freedom of expression;
(2) the exclusion or inclusion of the fact pattern from or in the scope of the criminal legal rule, also definable in the light of constitutional principles;
(3) assuming that the fact pattern fits the statutory elements of the crime, the inclusion or exclusion of the statutory crime definition (assumed its constitutionality) in or from the scope of the constitutional rule regarding the no-limitation of the crime of racism (would it be a crime of discrimination but not a crime of racism?), also definable in the light of constitutional principles.

In the first and third possibilities of treatment of the case, the principles are in a mediate relation to the concrete ought-judgment because one had to define the constitutionality of the criminal legal rule directly in the face of Article 5.XLII BFC, interpreted in the light of constitutional principles, or to subsume the statutory elements of the crime under the rule assigned to this constitutional provision, also interpreted on the basis of the principles to be applied. Yet, even in

[126] See pp. 157–9 below.

the second alternative, regardless of the constitutional provision on the crime of racism, it is possible to speak of a mediate relation between principle and concrete ought-judgment since the case solution cannot be derived directly from principles, but rather from the criminal rule, concretized in the light of constitutional principles. Furthermore, it can be maintained that the solution to the controversy on the constitutionality of the criminal rule, the subsumption of the fact situation under this rule, or the allocation of statutory elements of the crime in the constitutional framework requires the construction of a rule assigned indirectly to the constitutional text, as follows: 'The criminal qualification [as a crime of racism in alternatives 1 and 3] of the publication of books that deny the Holocaust is allowed from the point of view of the constitutional principle of human dignity [or non-discrimination].' In a way, a rule with this content was constructed by most Justices of the Brazilian Supreme Court in the *Ellwanger* case and was attributed indirectly to the constitutional text. As a general norm defined by precedents, it reduces the 'surprise value' of the decision for future cases in which the fact situation has the same core as of the fact situation in Ellwanger's crime: a publication denying the Holocaust. However, this does not exclude the possibility that, in future cases, legal facts with identical characteristics and the corresponding legal and constitutional rules will be understood in reverse, in the light, for example, of the freedom of expression or of scientific freedom. This relates especially to the fact that the decisions made based on principles that oppose one another express a rationality that is strongly marked by fallibility,[127] so they can be overruled with the introduction of new arguments tied to principles: the Hydra generates new heads.

In short, to conclude this section: constitutional principles as norms at the level of second-order observation of cases and of their corresponding ought-decisions are reflexive structures in relation to rules; the relationship between principles and rules involves a circular reflexive implication in the dimension of the static aspect of law; constitutional concretization requires a complete rule as an immediate criterion for the solution to the case through an ought-decision; there is a practical impossibility of immediate application of principles without the use of rules, whether the latter are attributed directly to legal

[127] The term 'fallibility' should not be understood here in the sense of 'defeasibility', widely used in the debate on rules, principles and legal arguments, with a strong normative charge and an appeal to logic (in this regard, see among many Hart, 1949; Baker, 1977; Alchourrón, 1996; Schauer, 1998a; Weinberger, 1999, 246–8; Hage and Peczenik, 2000; Tur, 2001; Atria, 2001, 37–44, 122–40, 172–84; Prakken and Sartor, 2004; MacCormick, 2005, esp. 239–53; Sartor, 2008, 1994, 185 ff.; Vale, 2009, 116–20). I use 'fallibility' here in association with the systemic concept of contingency, referring broadly to the social structure: 'By *contingency* we would like to understand that the indicated possibilities of further experience can turn out differently from what was expected', meaning 'danger of disappointment and the necessity to take risks' (Luhmann, 1987b, 31 (Engl. trans. 2014, 25)).

or constitutional provisions or indirectly to the constitutional text by case-law constructions;[128] an argumentation focused excessively on constitutional principles is greatly fallible, leaving ample space for the very constitutional rules developed from it to be overcome.

4. From Optimization to Competition: Limits of 'Balancing'

There is no doubt that the requirement of weighting or balancing in a collision between constitutional principles (and, in general, between norms) is, *tout court*, irremovable. But balancing is just one of the techniques that enable the consistent application of constitutional principles. In addition, the bond between balancing and optimization, that is the idealistic notion of optimizing balancing requirement, underestimates the complexity of constitutional cases in which one argues primarily in the light of principles.

Alexy starts from a counterfactual model of optimizing balancing. In this sense, as already stated above, his model approaches Dworkin's notion of a single right answer or a best decision.[129] Optimizing means finding the best decision within the legal and factual conditions concerning the case. This requirement could only have a practical significance if we were based on a monological judge (Hercules in Dworkin), the sovereign subject of the case decision, or from an intersubjectivity consensually oriented to the search for a case solution through rational arguments, with reference to an 'ideal speech situation'.[130] These two perspectives seem both descriptively and prescriptively very simple for understanding and intervening in social (in general) and legal (in particular) action and communication arrangements in a hyper-complex society. The social and legal variables that lead to determining a solution to the so-called hard cases are very different. The double contingency manifested in the communications of the parties involved in legal disputes in which the discussion and the arguments around competing constitutional principles are prevalent always entails different and opposing perspectives of the case, being impossible to be confident that all current and potential addressees ('universal

[128] In the same vein, but based on different assumptions, see Larenz, 1983, 405, 461; 1969, 465–6, in relation to 'open principles' (as opposed to 'principles in the form of legal propositions').

[129] See above pp. 67–8, esp. note 152.

[130] In this sense, cf. Alexy, 1983, 155 ff. (Engl. trans. 1989, 119 ff.), based on Habermas, 1986, 127–83 (article '*Wahrheitstheorien*' ('theories of truth'), originally published in 1972).

audience') of the constitution will be convinced, or that those effectively implicated in the case solution (particular audience) will be persuaded.[131]

This issue of double contingency may be related to different perspectives of observation of a legal order by individuals and groups. In this respect, the question of values, interests and moral expectations that are contradictory and conflicting among themselves leads to a structural dissent, allowing for several readings of the principles. To a certain extent, a sort of agonistics develops around competing principles. This is not a matter concerning only the relationship between the parties involved in a constitutional procedure, necessarily partial from the legal point of view; nor is it restricted to the public sphere as an arena of dissent. It often involves the members of the judiciary in general, and the members of a court in charge of ultimately concretizing the constitution in particular. The challenge that arises in such circumstances refers to the selective ability to absorb dissent and reorientate normative expectations in the face of decisions, leaving, however, open space for criticism and the possibility of future perspective transformations of decision-makers. This clearly implies, in the double contingency, an opening to the position of the other, with a willingness to learn (alterity); but this should not lead to the illusion of an optimizing consensus, for the unity of alterity and identity (alter/ego) around the understanding of principles presupposes a *difference* in the perspectives of alter and ego regarding the constitution. What is needed—instead of optimization—in the collation or balancing of competing constitutional principles, taking into account the double contingency regarding individuals and groups, is the overwhelming task of preventing the expansion of alter's perspective towards the elimination or permanent subjection of ego's perspective, and vice versa. Therefore, balancing is, in these terms, one of the constitutional techniques of absorbing dissent while simultaneously developing and promoting it.

Besides being related to the plurality of perspectives of groups and individuals, constitutional principles as reflexive structures of law under both the static aspect of law (for being principles) and the dynamic aspect of law (for being constitutional) correspond to diverse observation perspectives of a legal order. In this regard, there is a certain affinity between principles and constitutional rights. These relate to the 'danger of dedifferentiation' or, positively expressed, to the maintenance of 'a differentiated communication order'[132] and, one

[131] On the distinction between 'universal audience' and 'particular audience', see Perelman and Olbrechts-Tyteca, 1988, 34 ff.; Perelman, 1979, 107–8, 122 ff. As observed by Alexy (1983, 206 (Engl. trans. 1989, 163)), Perelman's 'universal audience' corresponds to Habermas's 'ideal speech situation'. Alexy adds (ibid.): 'Perelman's agreement of the universal audience is Habermas's consensus arrived at under ideal conditions.'

[132] Luhmann, 1965, 23–5.

might add, to the promotion of this order. In other words, constitutional rights can be seen as responses of the legal system to the functional differentiation of society: economic freedoms and the right to work, political rights, religious freedom, scientific freedom, right to education, right to health, etc. And also as a response to the differentiation between society and human beings: right to personality, general right to liberty, and human dignity. The explicit denial of constitutional rights is directly related to the experiences of dedifferentiation, in particular to the ideological politicization of law (authoritarianism) and all spheres of society (totalitarianism).[133] Moreover, the inefficacy of the concretizing process is related to the blocking of the self-consistency of constitutional law by dedifferentiating intrusions of very different social variables, such as political (government/opposition, power/not power), economic (having/not having), relational (friend/enemy), and familial (kin/not kin) factors.

Constitutional principles—which, in part, fall short (since there are rules that lay down constitutional rights) and, in part, go beyond (because there are principles concerning the organization and structure of the state and principles referring to political and institutional goals) the basic constitutional rights—are also associated with the functional differentiation of society into operatively autonomous systems, as well as the differentiation between human beings and society. They are established and understood based on the requirements of all social systems, which are in a conflicting relationship with one another in a hyper-complex society. In addition, they involve the opposition between the demands of the person and those of society or, to be more specific, the individual and the collective. They involve basic questions associated with constitutional rights, such as those related to the collision between economic freedom ('free enterprise', Article 1.IV BFC) and the right to health and to an 'ecologically balanced environment' (Articles 6 and 225 BFC),[134] or between freedom of the press or of speech and human dignity.[135] In these cases, the collision of principles is linked with conflicts among communication spheres or, ultimately, with the 'human beings–society' conflict. There are scenarios where the public debate around this issue involves a plurality of simultaneously present social perspectives. Let us take as an example the judgment of Direct

[133] Loewenstein (1957, 55 ff.) distinguished two basic types of autocracy: the authoritarianism, which 'refers rather to the structure of government than to the structure of society' and 'confines itself to the political control of the state without aspiring to the complete domination of the socioeconomic life of the community' (56); totalitarianism, which 'refers to the socioeconomic dynamism, the way of life, of a state society' and whose 'ambition is "total"' in relation to society and the individual (58). From the perspective of systems theory, cf. Neves, 1992, 70.

[134] ADPF 101/DF, judgment 24 June 2009, TP, DJe 4 June 2012.

[135] HC 82,424/RS, judgment 17 November 2003, TP, DJ 19 March 2004; ADPF 130/DF, judgment 30 April 2009, TP, DJe 6 November 2009.

Action of Unconstitutionality (ADI) No. 3,510/DF on 29 May 2008, in which the decision was in favour of the use of embryonic stem cells for research and therapy, rejecting the claim to declaration of unconstitutionality of Article 5 of Law No. 11,505, 24 May 2005 (Biosafety Law).[136] In this case, different perspectives from religion, healthcare, family, and science were directly involved. The right to life understood from a religious perspective was countered by both the right to health in terms of medicine and the right to family planning and scientific freedom. One could say in simple terms that, in the constitutional settlement of the case, science, health, and family prevailed over religion. Nevertheless, this result was not reached only by taking into account the requirements of the pertinent social systems. The question was of a legal and constitutional nature, which therefore led to a new reading from the viewpoint of the constitution. On the one hand, the Brazilian Supreme Court maintained the right to 'family planning' as based on the principles of 'human dignity' (Article 1.III BFC) and 'responsible parenthood' (Article 226.7, BFC), also associating it with the 'freedom of choice' and the 'right to maternity'; it defined the 'right to health as a corollary of the fundamental right to a dignified life'; it resorted to 'the constitutional right to freedom of scientific expression and the Biosafety Law as a densification of this freedom', defining this law 'as a means to combine the right to health with science itself'. On the other hand, it rejected the religious view of human life as starting from the moment of conception, adopting instead the theory that it starts with the birth, and concluding that the human life is the life of the human person with the following peremptory assertion: 'the embryo is the embryo, the foetus is the foetus and the human person is the human person'.[137] It is evident that in this trial not only were aspects of subjective rights to be occasionally reached by the decision taken into account but also the impact of the judgment on the various social spheres involved in the dispute.

The question that arises in such a case is whether it is meaningful to speak of optimization through the balancing of the invoked principles. It seems to me that the issue should rather be seen with a view to limiting the expansion of social spheres. In this case, the expansive tendency of religion could lead to the suffocation of science, healthcare, and family. Besides noticing that a political balancing by the democratic legislature had already taken place, it should be noted that the danger of religious dedifferentiation of society would have been stimulated by a contrary decision, in a sense of returning to pre-modern forms

[136] ADI 3,510/DF, judgment 29/ May 2008, TP, DJ 5 June 2008.
[137] The quoted passages are part of the judgment's summary.

of social structure and semantics to the detriment of constitutional rights. We are facing here with a turning point in terms of matching social adequacy and legal consistency in complex constitutional cases like this.

The example of religious expansion points to the requirement of limiting the tendency towards 'regressive' dedifferentiation. But the expansion of economic rationality to the detriment of other social rationalities implies a trend towards 'progressive' dedifferentiation, which often reverberates in the constitutional concretization in the light of principles. The case of Claim of Non-Compliance with a Fundamental Precept (ADPF) No. 101/DF, regarding the importing of used tyres, whose judgment was decided expressly based on the balancing between the requirements of health and environmental protection and the requirement of free exercise of economic activity (free enterprise and free competition), determining the precedence of the former over the latter, points to a reaction of the state legal system to the expansion of the global economic system. Of course, there was mitigation, considering the variables of regional Mercosur norms that led an exception to be allowed. But with regard to this exception, the quantitative element and the negligible impact of the retreaded tyres were taken into consideration. We are not talking about an optimization of principles here either, but rather a reaction to the danger and trend of economic dedifferentiation of society at the expense of a constitutional rights order. Again, in this case, the question was not limited to the individual interests of any of the involved parties (economic right versus right to health) but extended its impact on the relationship between social spheres: the health system, inseparable from a healthy environment, in the face of the economy. In this regard, Ladeur is right when, in criticizing the dominant balancing model, he stresses the importance of guaranteeing the fundamental rights through a constitutional practice so as to ensure the 'self-organization of society in various functional fields' (and not functional areas—I add—as organizations not bound to a specific functional sphere, protest movements, etc.), in such a way that the respective autonomies are maintained by means of 'relation networks' among them.[138] From this perspective, he argues that the paradigm of the optimizing balancing is strongly linked with positions assumed by groups and, therefore, 'focuses, both cognitively and normatively, above all on the short-term effects, neglecting the long-term ones'.[139] And he critically points to the 'devaluation of fundamental rights through a balancing without limits'.[140]

[138] Ladeur, 2004, 79.

[139] Ladeur, 2007b, 367.

[140] Ladeur, 2007b, 343. He seems to be wrong, though, when he intrinsically links the model of 'balancing without limits' with the welfare state and confines himself to the libertarian paradigm of society (cf. 2007b, esp. 371; in the opposite direction, Christodoulidis (2013, 180 ff.) links 'the "solution" of

Of course, all balancing strategies concerning constitutional principles, even without the optimizing claim, are fallible. In a way, this problem relates to the *incommensurability* of perspectives concerning the legal reasoning process.[141] Treated originally in science, incommensurability is related, first of all, to the fact that 'the proponents of competing paradigms will often disagree about the list of problems that any candidate for paradigm must resolve', framing standards or definitions that 'are not the same'. In addition, it is associated with the incorporation of the vocabulary and apparatus of the new paradigm, thus causing misunderstanding. Finally, and this is the most fundamental aspect for Kuhn, incommensurability concerns the fact that scientists carry out their activities and practices in different worlds, seeing 'different things when they look from the same point in the same direction'.[142] Setting aside the assumptions from which Kuhn starts and the consequences that he gives to this issue in science,[143] it is worth adding that the incommensurability does not occur only at the level of scientific paradigms but also in the relationship among value orders, rationality systems, reasoning models, and, finally, among social systems.[144] It is not just a question related to the diversity of individual perspectives as it also involves mainly complex communication constellations. And there is no supreme instance to resolve or mediate conflicts and misunderstandings between the partial spheres of a multicentre society.[145] What can happen is the development of transversal rationalities between them, with the construction of 'transition bridges',[146] which always involve reciprocal filtering.

proportionality' by the European Court of Justice with '"total market" thinking'). Jestaedt (1999, 49 ff.) uses a similar formulation ('unlimited balancing') to criticize the impotence of the legislator and the constituent in the face of judicial positivism (see also Jestaedt, 2002). In turn, Luhmann (1993, 268 (Engl. trans. 2004, 252)) questioned the use of 'the "balancing of interests" as the Trojan horse of all juridical reasoning', which makes balancing one of the forms of argumentation that comes 'dangerously close to *ad hoc* and *ad hominem* arguments'. For critiques of the balancing model, see also, among many, from various assumptions and with different consequences, Schlink, 1976, 127 ff.; 2001, 458 ff.; 2012, 724–5; Alleinikoff, 1987; Kahn, 1987; F. Müller, 1994, 208 ff.; 1995, 62–3; 67–8; Leisner, 1997 (concerning the optimizing balancing); Böckenförde, 2003, esp. 190; Poscher, 2003, 94–96; Ladeur and Augsberg, 2005, 158 ff.; Christensen and Fischer-Lescano, 2007, 148 ff.; Webber, 2010 ('The result is perhaps nothing short of a loss of rights' (202); Bernstoff, 2014 (against ad hoc balancing).

[141] Christensen and Fischer-Lescano, 2007, 199 ff., based on Kuhn, 1996, esp. 148 ff., 198 ff. See also Sunstein, 1994, associating (without conflating) incommensurability with diversities of valuation in law.

[142] Kuhn, 1996, 148–50.

[143] Kuhn, for instance, associates the change of scientific paradigms exclusively with real persuasion techniques at the 'subjective' level, completely disregarding the 'objective' question of concerning proof (see Kuhn, 1996, 152).

[144] In this regard, cf. Christensen and Fischer-Lescano, 2007, 200–1.

[145] See Teubner, 1996a, 2008.

[146] Welsch, 1996, esp. 754 ff., under the concept of 'transversal reason'. See Neves, 2009, 39 ff. (Engl. trans. 2013, 28 ff.).

An optimizing balancing model of competing constitutional principles does not take into account the problem of incommensurability, for it starts from a subjective or intersubjective superordinate instance, which is able to determine what definitely fits each sphere of life. Alexy reacts to this criticism, arguing that there would be commensurability and comparability of constitutional rights from a 'unitary point of view: the point of view of the Constitution'.[147] But the problem of incommensurability arises exactly because of the diverse perspectives from which the constitution can be observed in a society differentiated in a variety of social spheres, each with its own claim to autonomy. In this regard, it should be added that, according to Alexy's own model,[148] the constitution (its principles) is the object of balancing.[149] And the problem of incommensurability emerges precisely by virtue of this paradox: the constitution is at the same time a criterion and an object of balancing. It is true that with a 'weight formula', in which the variables are formalized ('triadic scale'), one can make them measurable.[150] However, if we return to the dimension of the content, the problem of incommensurability, then repressed, reappears in an uncontrollable fashion.[151]

The optimizing balancing model—I insist—overlooks the fact that constitutional principles arise and are developed from normative expectations circulating in various social spheres, in which there are understandings of the meaning and value of each principle that are incommensurable among themselves, whether from an abstract point of view or under the concrete conditions of a case to be decided. Incommensurability leads to principles always being able to do 'injustice' to other principles in the constitutional concretization process, thus enabling a 'language game' to destructively override another at the expense of 'heterogeneity of language games'.[152] The legal argumentation is, in this particular instance, always fallible. It can only either establish limits to the expansion of the 'logic' of a language game and the 'rationality' of a social system, removing the danger of dedifferentiation, or offer means and parameters of 're-entry' between the language games that underlie the competing

147 Alexy, 2003b, 781.

148 Alexy, 2000, 38 (Engl. trans. 2000, 300).

149 See p. 60 above.

150 Cf. Alexy, 2003b, esp. 782; see also 2002, 405 ff.; 2003a, 443 ff.

151 For a critical analysis of the 'weight formula' proposed by Alexy, see Schuartz, 2005, 218 ff. On the limits of the mathematical models of optimization and maximization rationally oriented to the search for the best decision or the only right decision, see Simon, 1956a, 136 ff.; 1956b; 1955, 110 ff. With an odd view of this issue, V.A. Silva (2011, 282 ff.; 2016, 110–11) maintains that balancing and optimization are only possible in the case of incommensurability (see my criticism to Silva: Neves, 2019, 288–9).

152 Teubner, 1996b, 903–4, borrowing from Lyotard, 1983, esp. 29, 52 (nos 21, 42) (Engl. trans. 1988, 12–13, 30); 1979, esp. 20 ff. See also Welsch, 1996, 312 ff.; Teubner, 1996a, 210.

principles. But there is no guarantee of success, and a model of optimizing balancing is under-complex to address the delicate issue of competing principles. This should not lead to the simplistic thesis of regression to a model of rules, which is incompatible with a complex society,[153] but rather point to the fact that falling back on the level of principles should not lead to illusions, requiring caution and restraint: principles are remedies that are presented as a panacea, but their immoderate use can lead to poisoning. They are, I repeat, somewhat diabolical.

Obviously, incommensurability is not to be confused with incomparability.[154] However, it does not follow that what is comparable is always optimizable. Optimization presupposes not only comparability but also commensurability. Thus, the concept of weighing or balancing should not necessarily be linked with optimization.[155] It is possible to speak of a comparative balancing as opposed to a balancing with an optimization claim.[156] But in this case, considering the differentiation of society, the corresponding comparisons are constructed from each perspective of observation,[157] being impossible to attain a rational (monological or dialogic) super-instance ultimately to set the comparison criteria (ideals or norms), nor even as 'measures of approximation'.[158] What may happen is the development of entanglements that enable the emergence of transversal rationalities, under which there is the possibility of constructing mechanisms of 're-entry' among the various comparisons. In this

[153] See pp. 102-3.

[154] In this sense, see Kuhn, 1982, 670–1; Sunstein, 1994, esp. 793, 798, 800, 805 ff.; V.A. Silva, 2011, 282 ff.; 2002a, 173 ff., based especially on Chang, 1997, 2, 18. See also Chang, 2001; 2002a; 2002b. It seems, however, that according to Ruth Chang comparison in itself does not imply optimization, that is 'it goes beyond optimizing', particularly because, 'unlike optimizing, it denies that all justifying reasons are comparisons of the alternatives; a justifying reason needs not be the fact that the alternative is optimal with respect to the choice value' (Chang, 2002b, 60). Moreover, Chang argues from a theoretical perspective of the 'rational choice' (Chang, 2016) of an autonomous subject who is able to define a 'covering value' (2002b, 3 ff.) to justify their choices rationally in a 'choice situation' (2002b, 44–5), not from a systemic-theoretical perspective considering transsubjective social processes of decision-making under the conditions of high complexity. Finally, albeit Chang points out that 'being "good enough" is, on the face of things, a noncomparative fact' and that 'satisficing isn't a plausible theory about the structure of rationality' (2016, 228, 230), she admits that 'although, in at least one interpretation, it presents an alternative for optimization, satisficing does not undermine the comparativist thesis', since 'it poses a genuine challenge for comparativism' (2002b, 51). From another perspective, I do think that 'satisficing' ('good enough') is not entirely incompatible with comparison, at least in very impersonal processes of decision-making involving a complex institutional apparatus and a range of unstructured expectations of the public. This is the reason why, under these circumstances, counting on 'all things considered' (Chang, 2004) is inappropriate. The comparison is thus precarious. See Neves, 2019, esp. 299–300. Cf. note 162 of this chapter.

[155] In the opposite direction, Alexy (2002, 401) states that 'optimization relative to competing principles consists of nothing other than balancing'.

[156] Based on different assumptions, Sieckmann (2006, 131–2) refers to a 'comparative balancing', but gives it a secondary standing in relation to optimizing balancing.

[157] Cf. Luhmann, 1987a, 16–17 (Engl. trans. 1995, 2–3).

[158] Luhmann, 1997, vol. 1, 42–3 (Engl. trans. 2012, 17–18).

context, when observing (also from a partial point of view) several different perspectives of comparison conflicting with each other, a path can be provided to 'make dissensions compatible'[159] and promote heterogeneity. But this comparison is not optimizing; it is ready to face a plurality of comparative possibilities and cannot stop the emergence of new unpredictable possibilities in the contingent context of the law of modern (or postmodern?!) society. In these terms, admitting the problem of incommensurability of the various readings of the constitution and constitutional rights, one may admit a comparative balancing in order to find ways beyond self-reference, thus enabling a reciprocal observation from different perspectives. The argumentation within this framework reduces the 'surprise value' of the decision (thus excluding decisionism) but always involves a contingent solution, which can not only cause disappointment but also trigger an avalanche of criticism based on other readings of the constitution.

These observations do not imply that it is necessary to adopt a model of the 'constitution as a framework' as opposed to the conception of the constitution in terms of optimization requirements.[160] Choosing one of these two extremes seems simplistic. The incommensurability of the models of constitutional argumentation and interpretation relates, especially in the light of constitutional principles, to permanent 'change of the framework'.[161] This variation of the constitutional 'framework', meaning that constitutional structures (norms) and operations (communications, acts) or processes (procedures) condition one another circularly, is not related to any optimizing orientation of subjects or intersubjective discourses, but to conditions for the reproduction of a complex and contingent interconnection of communications. Under these conditions, a permanent competition between (transsubjective) spheres of society develops around constitutional principles, just like the perspectives of individuals and groups faced with the 'double contingency' in the reading of the principles vary. The constitutional structure reconstructs itself, to some extent, in each constitutional operation or process. In this context, the use of 'parity' between the legislative and the judicial solution as a 'regulative idea'[162] (a notion

159 Ladeur, 1986, 273.

160 As regards the understanding of the 'constitution as a framework', see Wahl, 1981, esp. 507; Grimm, 1991, 17–18; Starck, 1992, 193–4; Isensee, 1992, 128; Jestaedt, 1999, 72 ff.; Böckenförde, 2003, 186–7.

161 See Christensen and Fischer-Lescano, 2007, 212–17.

162 V.A. Silva, 2007, 221 ff. (230); see 2002a, 194 ff. Silva relies on Chang's concept of parity (Chang, 2002a), which relates rather to the proposal of—beyond 'epistemicists', 'incomparatibilists', and 'semantic indeterminists' in the field of ethics of comparison in assigning values—a 'fourth relation of comparability beyond "better than", "worse than" and "equally good"' (ibid., 688), but does not refer specifically to the relationship among institutional instances (see also Chang, 2002b, 121 ff.). Cf. later Silva, 2011, 293 ff. See my criticism to Silva: Neves, 2019, esp. 296–300. Cf. note 154 of this chapter above.

concerning ideal moral orders as a transcendental or universal model) seems rather simplistic. The double contingency between legislator and judge always entails a plus in communication, or 'triangulation' in Davidson's sense,[163] not being susceptible to be reduced to one perspective or to a convergence of perspectives. The 'intertextuality' of the interpretation means that this is to be understood 'as the creation of new texts with the help of older texts, as the expansion of the basic text'.[164] In the relationship between alter (the legislator) and ego (the constitutional court), each side starts from the language and the criteria of each of the systems with which it is primarily linked, namely, politics and law. The 'parity' could be understood as the horizontality of democracy and the rule of law, implying that the constitution is a structural coupling between politics and law.[165] Yet, this does not favour an optimizing (idealistic) conception of the constitution but it instead points to relations of tension and complementarity between both systems and therefore between legislators and judges or courts, involving the constant transformation of the constitutional structure.

The model of optimizing balancing of constitutional principles becomes even more problematic when it goes beyond the constitutional state and the relationship between legislature and the judiciary in its specific context, and when one considers the variation of understandings of principles in the courts of several legal orders simultaneously involved in the solution of the same constitutional problem in the transconstitutional context.[166] The issue of transconstitutionalism is broad and involves transversal entanglements among legal orders of the same kind and among orders of different types, namely, state, international, supranational, transnational, and local extra-estate orders, as well as various tangled levels in the relationship between principles and rules: principle–principle, rule–rule, principle–rule (if more than two orders are involved, the possibility of entanglement increases).[167] This is not the place to return to this issue in a comprehensive manner. Nevertheless, it is worth drawing attention to the fact that the pursuit of an optimizing balancing in the

[163] Although Davidson starts from other assumptions, his idea of 'triangulation', which implies a level other than that of the communicators, i.e. the social or communicational level (Davidson, 1982, 327; 1991, 159–60), is in a way similar to the communication concept of Luhmann (1987a, 193 ff. (Engl. trans. 1995, 139 ff.)), understood as a 'three-part selection process' of information, message, and understanding that emerges 'from above' (1987a, 43–4 (Engl. trans. 1995, 22–3)), under the double contingency between alter and ego (cf. above pp. 15–16).

[164] Luhmann, 1993, 340 (Engl. trans. 2004, 306).

[165] Luhmann, 1990a, 193 ff.; 1993, esp. 470 ff. (Engl. trans. 2004, 4004). See Neves, 2000, 80 ff. To go even further, one can define the constitution of the democratic constitutional state as a mechanism of transversal rationality between politics and law (Neves, 2009, 62 ff. (Engl. trans. 2013, 42 ff.)).

[166] Neves, 2009 (Engl. trans. 2013).

[167] Neves, 2009, 275 (Engl. trans. 172–3).

relationship between radically different 'constitutional identities' can lead not only to illusions, but also to reciprocal narcissistic paralyses. The key in this case is to construct mechanisms that serve to rearticulate identities via the observation of the solution offered by the other order for a given problem. The permanent reconstruction of the 'constitutional identity' becomes indispensable by virtue of a permanent consideration of alterity.[168] This does not mean a denial of the identity according to a naive model of pure convergence,[169] rather the readiness not only for a cognitive but also for a normative opening to other intertwined orders in specific cases. An uncertainty regarding the outcomes obviously remains, but only with that readiness can the original dissent be absorbed. The opposite path leads to mutual blocking when solving relevant constitutional problems in terms of both human or fundamental rights and the organization (control and limitation) of power. Rather than affirming the optimization, it is appropriate to speak of containment as the first step of the transconstitutional method.[170] But this containment is not an end in itself. It relates to the double contingency, the ability to be surprised by others, the acknowledgement of the possibility of an open future, which cannot be predetermined by any of the orders entangled in the case. A willingness to seek out the normative 'findings' of others is crucial[171] in order to fortify one's own capacity to offer solutions to common problems.

Within the plurality of cases that I have treated in my work on the subject, there is an emblematic one that deals strictly with the application of the technique of the optimizing balancing. In the judgment of *Caroline of Monaco II*, on 15 December 1999, while analysing the disclosure of Caroline of Monaco's photographic images by the media, the German Federal Constitutional Court gave greater weight to freedom of the press at the expense of privacy of prominent people.[172] This ruling was flatly rejected by the European Court of Human Rights (ECtHR) in *Caroline von Hannover v Germany*, which found that the

[168] From an entirely different perspective grounded on psychoanalytic assumptions, Rosenfeld (1998, 144 ff.) associated the 'identity of the constitutional subject' with the viewpoint of 'the other'.

[169] On the distinction between convergence, resistance, and engagement models in the relationship between legal orders and their corresponding courts, see Jackson, 2005. In this regard, cf. Neves, 2009, 258–60 (Engl. trans. 2013, 162–3).

[170] It is relevant to note here the tendency of the various social spheres or discourses to maximize their own rationality to the detriment of others', as emphasized by Fischer-Lescano and Teubner (2006, 25 ff.). See also Teubner, 2008, 32–3 (Engl. trans. 2009, 23; 2012, 15 (Engl. trans. 2012, 4).

[171] Based on other assumptions ('modern *ius gentium*'), but in the same sense, Waldron (2005, 133 ff.) points to the challenge with which lawyers of various orders are confronted today: to share experiences and knowledge, as scientists from all over the world are sharing their empirical findings. In this regard, see Neves, 2009, 260–1 (Engl. trans. 2013, 163–4).

[172] BVerfGE 101, 361 (1999). As regards this decision, see the critique by Ladeur (2007a), supporting the debatable thesis that 'the right to prominence should be considered primarily as a property right' (146).

right to privacy overweighed the public's right to information in this case.[173] Subsequently, the German Federal Constitutional Court consolidated its position in *Görgülü* (14 October 2004)[174] in regard to establishing limits to the domestic application of ECtHR decisions, considering the hypothesis that they may be contrary to fundamental rights and the principle of the rule of law established in the German Constitution: the German Federal Constitutional Court must take ECtHR decisions into account but is not bound by them.[175] According to this understanding, the European Convention on Human Rights and the ECtHR jurisprudence are considered auxiliary means of interpretation to determine the content and scope of fundamental rights and rule-of-law principles, providing they do not lead to a reduction or limitation of the protection for fundamental rights laid down in the German Constitution.

Yet, concerning the relationship between *Caroline of Monaco II* (domestic) and *Caroline von Hannover v Germany* (international), the two understandings of what is the limitation to fundamental rights clash openly with each other. It is undeniable that there is no way to censor the position of the German Court for not showing willingness to submit without restrictions to the ECtHR guidelines in every single case brought before it, as this would mean the denial of its own 'constitutional identity', and not its reconstruction in the light of alterity. It does not seem appropriate, however, to solve these cases of constitutional entanglement by insisting merely on the model of 'association between collision of fundamental rights, balancing, rationality, and burden of argumentation'[176] under the optimizing posture of the German constitutional case-law. This model would only make sense if we assumed the existence of an intersubjective deliberating forum oriented consensually towards an ideal relationship between the two courts. Rather, it is worth considering in this context the fact that the 'narcissistic' denial of the ECtHR decisions by state courts, based on the optimizing balancing of the respective constitutional principles, does not seem bearable considering the degree of European integration. This is why the development of a transversal rationality in the face of the legal order of the European Convention on Human Rights is essential also for the domestic courts involved in addressing issues concerning human and fundamental rights. Any

[173] *Caroline von Hannover v Germany* (*Application* No. 59320/00). In this regard, see Rudolf, 2006; Hedigan, 2007.

[174] BverfGE 111, 307 (2004). The case relates to the application by a German court of an ECtHR ruling against Germany based on Article 8 of the European Convention on Human Rights: *Görgülü v Germany* (Application No. 74969/01), 26 February 2004. See Hartwig, 2005, 870–3.

[175] See V.A. Silva, 2010, 106 ff.; Hoffmeister, 2006; Hartwig, 2005, 874 ff.; Hofmann, 2004, 30 ff.; Wahl, 2007, 880–3.

[176] V.A. Silva, 2010, 110, analysing the collisions between the German Federal Constitutional Court and the ECtHR in light of Alexy's theory of principles.

unilateral path can have destructive or irrational effects on European integration in the field of human and fundamental rights. For this reason, the German constitutional case-law seeks to invoke Article 53 of the European Convention on Human Rights: 'Nothing in this Convention shall be construed as limiting or derogating from any of the human rights and fundamental freedoms which may be ensured under the laws of any High Contracting Party or under any other agreement to which it is a Party.' But this provision must be understood in the light of the ECtHR's own competence to ultimately interpret the European Convention on Human Rights. The problem is not simply to establish whether a provision of the Convention has been interpreted so as to limit the fundamental rights constitutionally laid down by a state, but to determine which court has jurisdiction to decide this limitation by interpretation. This requires openness to the other's perspective, willingness to be surprised, to learn from each other, reconstructing the very constitutional identity in the light of alter's perspective. Balancing principles with optimizing claims, against this background of immense incommensurability, may have catastrophic effects on European integration. What is required in such circumstances, instead of using regulative ideas, is a transconstitutional communication that seeks transversal rationality, always precarious, fallible, and limited.

In short, the constitution of the democratic constitutional state involves a complex and dynamic articulation between principles and rules. The balancing of competing principles is one of the techniques of constitutional argumentation and interpretation, allowing for the comparison of different perspectives on constitution and fundamental rights. However, we must pay attention to the competition and the incommensurability of argumentation models around principles, related to both the double contingency concerning the groups or persons involved in the process of constitutional concretization and the heterogeneity of perspectives on principles developed by different functional systems. This situation becomes more complex when the perspectives of other legal orders involved simultaneously in solving common constitutional problems are considered. Competition and incommensurability make the optimizing balancing model rather unsuitable to theoretically understand and doctrinally orientate the settlement of constitutional cases that entail a collision of principles. The most controversial constitutional issues involving principles and rules shall be treated more appropriately in a constitutional practice that is able to react to the dangers of dedifferentiation (in terms of social systems and legal systems intertwined around constitutional problems) and to avoid the denial of double contingency (in terms of persons and groups). This requires that this practice, by absorbing dissents about principles with the exclusion of perspectives that underlie them, be able to reorient and stabilize the corresponding normative expectations. But, paradoxically, the reorientation of normative expectations in these terms is only legitimized if it serves to maintain and even promote structural dissents about constitutional principles, not only in the public sphere related to the democratic constitutional state, but also in the society that encompasses the 'multilevel' or multicentric world legal system.[177]

5. Intra-Principle Collision, Double Contingency, and Functional Differentiation of Society: Towards a Complex Theory of Principles

The dominant theory of constitutional principles presupposes a less complex social reality. In addition to the competition between colliding principles, it should be noted that, even when one starts from the same principle (human dignity, general liberty, equality, etc.), the readings thereof may be the most diverse, and the argumentative models may be incommensurable with each other, resulting in the possibility of intra-principle collisions.

This question can be examined initially from the basic alterity of the social world in general and of the legal field in particular, which is inseparable from the double contingency between those involved in any communication. The principle of general liberty conceived of by alter can collide head-on with the same principle coming from the vantage point of ego. This question can lead to complex constitutional disputes.[178] For a more specific principle, for example, the constitutional principle of free competition (as admitted in Brazilian constitutional law, Article 170.IV BFC), even if it invokes detailed expertise of financial mathematics, there can be extremely different views on its content, both by virtue of abstract models in terms of economic knowledge and the very application of a model chosen for a specific case. The economic analysis of law has not demonstrated in this regard any Herculean ability to safely maximize or optimize this principle in legally complex situations involving different perspectives of economic organizations.

[177] See Neves, 2009, 235 ff. (Engl. trans. 2013, 148 ff.); 2000, 99 ff.

[178] In this regard, Sunstein (1998, 267) warns: 'Thus people who disagree on pornography and hate speech can accept a general free speech principle, and those who argue about homosexuality and disability can accept an abstract anti-discrimination principle.' When associating this question with the valuation of goods and incommensurability, he points out that '[t]his problem does not entail paralysis, indeterminacy, or arbitrariness', concluding that eliminating it 'would be a sort of tragedy, not least because it would make the very fact of tragedy puzzling or even incomprehensible' (1994, 860).

The issue of intra-principle collision treated in terms of basic social alterity requires care and caution when one affirms the prima facie unlimited character of the 'scope' of constitutional rights anchored in principles, particularly the general right to liberty. In other words, this means that this right in particular would only be limited after its balancing with competing principles.[179] Although Alexy has clarified this formulation[180] and, in a sense, provided a caveat to it,[181] it is worth pointing out that the general right to liberty also implies a limitation resulting from the general right to liberty of the other. It does not seem appropriate to maintain that there is a prima facie unlimited right, but rather legal criteria or programs that depend on operationalization by persons and roles: principles are reflexive legal criteria. There is no right (founded on a principle) of ego without the right (based on the same principle) of alter, and vice versa. The basic alterity of law precludes the idea of prima facie unlimited right based on a principle to be limited only through its balancing with other principles. There may also be intra-principle collisions arising from the invocation of the same principle as simultaneous reason of the parties involved in the process of constitutional concretization. Hereupon, it is apposite to speak of intra-principle balancing, given the different perspectives on the same principle by those involved in a constitutional strife. Strictly speaking, however, the key is that, prima facie (i.e. before any balancing with competing principles), every right founded on a principle, when affirmed by a party, will always be intrinsically limited by the same right claimed by another, being irrelevant whether or not it is a 'negative' right: the one's general right to liberty affirmed with respect to the same right pleaded by the other; human dignity alleged

[179] Alexy, 1986, 342–3 (Engl. trans. 2002, 248–9).

[180] Alexy, 1986, 343 ff. (Engl. trans. 2002, 249 ff.). It seems problematic to me, however, to associate the general right to liberty with the freedom of the state of nature. In fact, Alexy (1986, 346 (Engl. trans. 2002, 251)) also assigns to it a role in securing the status quo, stating that 'the general right to liberty brings into the overall state of liberty both something of the freedom of the state of nature as well as a securing of the status quo'. But the issue of the overall state of liberty and the status concerns, according to Alexy himself, 'the formal structure of the complete legal position of the citizen' (1986, 247 (Engl. trans. 2002, 176)), involving other rights and duties of citizens and therefore, strictly speaking, not a general right to liberty prima facie, whose 'scope' is defined by him as unlimited. Thus, the general right to liberty prima facie would have rather something in common with liberty or right in general in the state of nature in Hobbes's terms, implying 'the absence of externall Impediments'—also in relation to the liberty of others—and unlimited right: 'Right, consisteth in liberty to do, or to forbeare . . . Naturally every man has a Right to every thing; even to one anothers body' (Hobbes, 1991 [1651], 91 [64], Chapter XIV). Otherwise, based on Locke, according to whom the liberty of the state of nature, unlike 'a state of licence', means that 'no one ought to harm another in his life, health, liberty, or possessions' (Locke, 1980 [1690], 9, Chapter II, section 6), the general right to liberty would be limited prima facie, including by other rights.

[181] 'No right to liberty is unlimited. It finds its limits, at least, at the point that goes against the liberty of others' (Alexy, 1998, 253).

by one in relation to that claimed by the other;[182] the right to life claimed by someone in view of the same right invoked by the other;[183] the general right to equality adduced by one in the face of that held by the other. These observations are, in a way, trivial, but serve to avoid misunderstandings when addressing this subject.

The intra-principle collision becomes relevant when considering the differentiation of society in various spheres of communication. Principles should not be defined according to a simple model of understanding modern society and the democratic constitutional state: principles vary according to the sphere of communication in which they are applied. In this sense, the multicentric character of society engenders a competition between different and incommensurable readings of the same principle. This could be addressed in terms of spheres of justice, as defined by Walzer, who considers the issue of 'complex equality' in particular as follows: 'What the equality norm demands is a society in which those men who have more money, power or technical knowledge—and such men will always exist—are prevented from taking possession of any other social good just because they have more money, power or knowledge.'[184] But Walzer addresses this subject in terms of spheres of goods.[185] We should instead consider communication systems that reproduce themselves autonomously (or at least claim to autonomy) based on own codes and criteria. Moreover, Walzer's formulation concerning complex equality can lead to the understanding that it would involve many subprinciples of equality: economic, political, those related to the access to knowledge and education, etc. The aim here is to draw attention to something more radical: the general right to liberty, the general right to equality, human dignity, as well as economic equality and liberty, the principles of free enterprise and competition, religious freedom, and the right to education may be subject to the most diverse readings from the social sphere in which the constitutional problem may arise. Of course, the understanding of the general right to liberty from the viewpoint of the economic system may conflict with the interpretation of this right in religious or familial circles. The same way, familial, educational, or religious views of the principle of equality can oppose the economic or political conception of

[182] Kai Möller (2007, 466–7) refers to this possibility, but his argument is based on a very controversial position of Brugger (2000), who not only considers the collision that results from the invocation of the human dignity *principle* by disputing parties, but also restricts the ('nearly') absolute and prima facie ('nearly') complete *rule* that forbids torture, making it relative and prima facie incomplete.

[183] See Kumm, 2007, 155–6. Klatt and Meister (2012a, 38 ff.) also admit these possibilities, in an attempt to subsume them under Alexy's balancing model, which was rather constructed to tackle inter-principle collisions.

[184] Walzer, 1998, 12. See Walzer, 1983, 3 ff. Similar to Walzer, Sunstein (1994, 825 ff.) relates 'social differentiation' ('appropriate spaces for different kinds of valuation') to the 'incommensurability'.

[185] Walzer, 1983, 6–10.

the same principle. Also the economic self-understanding of the principle of free enterprise can clash with the perception of this principle in the political, educational, scientific, or religious system. Finally, the understanding of the principle of human dignity varies according to the vantage point of each social system.[186] Regarding the latter, I would like to present two fictitious examples.

Let us imagine, in terms of the binding effects of constitutional rights on private actors,[187] an angry reprimand of a mother or a father challenged by behaviours of their young child at home, in a strongly objectionable moral and cultural context (e.g. engagement in sexual acts, use of illicit drugs, excessive consumption of alcohol, all carried out in the parents' bedroom). This rebuke would hardly be characterized as an offense to human dignity. The legislator, in principle, could not intervene and establish penalties to parents based on the principle of human dignity. It would be an illegitimate intervention in family relationships (in this regard, an objection could be made that it is a collision with other constitutional principles regarding the family, but this contingent issue is not relevant here). The same situation practiced by a domestic worker (housekeeper) within the workplace (physically identical), with the same verbal reprimand delivered by the employer, could give rise to compensation for moral damages according to statutory or case-law based on the principle of human dignity. In contrast, requiring domestic service of a child as a condition for the payment of the weekly allowance (excluding here the specific child labour issue) may ultimately appear as a strong disregard for the principle of human dignity, whereas asking a housekeeper to perform unpleasant services (e.g. cleaning a toilet), provided the due reward for the service has to be paid, is not understood as an offense to human dignity.

These fictitious examples illustrate that it is worth speaking not only of 'complex equality' but also of 'complex liberty or freedom', 'complex human dignity', 'complex solidarity', etc., with each principle varying according to the social sphere in which the constitutional controversy comes to light. If in a concrete constitutional dispute the perspective of one of the social spheres confronts

[186] Similarly, in relation to the applicability of the balancing formula, see Schlink, 1976, 195–6. In my view, this matter cannot be appropriately approached using the conception of 'a constitution of many minds' (Sunstein, 2009), especially in the sense of the 'Condorcet Jury Theorem', which—supposing 'that many people are answering the same question with two possible answers, one false and one true', and assuming 'that the probability that each person will answer correctly exceeds 50 percent, and that these probabilities are independent'—'says that the probability of a correct answer, by a majority of the group, increase toward 100 percent as the group gets bigger' (ibid., 8–9). The question goes far beyond the sum of individual 'minds', involving complex social and legal structures and processes underlying and shaping the constitution. Moreover, a model like the 'Condorcet Jury Theorem' would perhaps demand commensurability of the involved variables, which goes against Sunstein, 1994.

[187] In the vast literature on the so-called horizontal effect of constitutional rights, see Sajó and Uitz (eds), 2005; Sarmento, 2004; V.A. Silva, 2008; Steinmetz, 2004; 2005; Sarlet, 2000.

the other in the face of the same principle, then the intra-principle collision arises. Incommensurability reappears with the reciprocal misunderstandings about the principle. Speaking of optimization in this case is already conceptually problematic because there are no competing principles. One could then refer to maximization.[188] But by claiming to maximize the principle based on the model of an ideal subject-judge or in the counterfactual terms of a rational intersubjective discourse, there is a tendency towards the primacy of a certain understanding of the principle to the detriment of others. The question that arises here is how to avoid the danger of hypertrophy of a particular reading of the relevant principle at the expense of others.

This issue comes to the fore with regard to transconstitutionalism as well. The fundamental right to life, as established in a constitutional principle in competition with other principles, gives rise to conflicts between different understandings of protection of life and its value in the corresponding order. One of the most sensitive cases appeared in the relationship between the Brazilian state law and the normative order of the Suruwaha people who live in Tapauá, a municipality located in the state of Amazonas, and remained voluntarily isolated until the end of the 1970s.[189] Under Suruwaha customary law, children born unhealthy or disabled must be killed. Another case involved the Yawanawa living in Acre, a state on the border between Brazil and Peru, among whom a customary normative order required the killing of one newborn twin. At first sight, the question can be seen as a collision between the right to life and cultural autonomy. But it can also be analysed as intra-principle collision in relation to the right to life. The public impact of the Suruwaha custom led to Bill No. 1,057 of 2007, intended specifically to criminalize (or 'ultra-criminalize')[190] this practice. Albeit the National Congress has not taken further steps to pass this Bill, the context in which it was drafted and the discussion that followed constitute a unique instance of transconstitutional 'dialogue' between the state legal order and the normative orders of indigenous communities. The bill's drafters and advocates took as their basic starting point the idea of absolute primacy of the individual's fundamental right to life in accordance with Western Christian morality. Rita Laura Segato is one of the anthropologists who participated intensely in the debate, including the public hearing held on 5 September

[188] Cf. Alexy, 1986, 80–1, 37 (Engl. trans. 2002, 51, note 37).

[189] For an analysis of the case from the legal and constitutional point of view, see Neves, 2009, 222 ff. (Engl. trans. 2013, 139 ff.); from an anthropological perspective, Segato, 2011.

[190] Segato, 2011, 361, 368–9. Later, an alternative draft significantly changed the Bill, reducing it to general statements and promises of support for the respective communities. The Bill 1,057/2007 was approved by the Chamber of Deputies and is now being considered by the Federal Senate as Bill 119/2015 (https://www25.senado.leg.br/web/atividade/materias/-/materia/122998?o=t).

2007 in the Chamber of Deputies.[191] Her remarks were a great help in clarifying the implication of this collision and pointed to the need for a transversal communication between normative orders in terms that can be considered appropriate to a constructive model of transconstitutionalism. In her view, the meaning of life and death for the Suruwaha deserves as much respect as the meaning attributed by Christianity: 'We also found a complex, sophisticated vision of great philosophical dignity that owes nothing to Christianity.'[192] The argument is fortified by reference to Yanomami practice giving women absolute autonomy to decide whether their children should live. The mother withdraws into the forest to give birth, so that delivery occurs outside the context of social life, leaving the choice to the mother:

> If she does not touch the new-born or welcome it into her arms, but leaves it on the ground where it fell, that means it has not been accepted into the world of culture and social relations. It is therefore not human. Thus, it cannot be said that a homicide has occurred from the viewpoint of this indigenous group, since one who remains on the ground is not a human life.[193]

This very different idea of human life (not related to conception, birth, or 'personality', but rather to a social or cultural meaning) genuinely entails a delicate problem, which I also consider incompatible with the mere imposition of external views of life and death by means of what in another context I have paradoxically called 'human rights imperialism'.[194] This is valid not only from an anthropological-cultural or anthropological-legal viewpoint but also from the specific constitutional law perspective that is sensitive to transconstitutionalism.

This delicate problem is not confined to the dilemma between ethical relativism (oriented to particular cultures) and moral universalism (oriented to human rights). It also points to the possibility of coexistence between legal orders based on distinct historical experiences,[195] requiring moderation, especially on the part of the constitutional state, with regard to its claim to concretize its specific norms when they collide with the norms of indigenous communities with essentially different cultural foundations. Discretion and

[191] Cf. Segato, 2011, 369 ff.
[192] Segato, 2011, 364.
[193] Segato, 2011, 365.
[194] Neves, 2007, 432, 436.
[195] Segato, 2011, 375–7; see also 2006 for a broader treatment. On the intrinsic relationship between universalism and difference, see Neves, 2002.

self-restraint seem in this case to be the right way to go about engaging in constructive 'conversations' capable of stimulating internal self-transformations by indigenous communities so that they have a less conflictual relationship with the state order. An attempt to pursue internal models of optimization in accordance with the theory of principles could be disastrous under these circumstances. Instead, when dealing with the 'other', with the different order of indigenous people, it is advisable to adopt a transconstitutional instance of self-containment with regard to the fundamental rights whose optimization could lead to disintegration of life forms, with destructive consequences for the minds and body of the members of the communities involved.[196]

The intra-principle collision in terms of double contingency related to persons (including legally personified entities) and groups, at the level of autonomous functional systems as well as at the level of the relationship between various legal systems involved in common constitutional problems, is not susceptible to be adequately resolved from a monological (rational subject-judge) or dialogical (discourse oriented towards consensus) super-instance. In general, the model of optimizing balancing by the judicial state authority is under-complex to face issues of this magnitude in an over-complex society. Nevertheless, a legislative repoliticization of these issues according to the model of constitution as a framework[197] is not appropriate. The constitution of the democratic constitutional state always implies structural interpenetration and operative interference between law and politics. Moreover, constitutional problems go beyond the domain of state and therefore its specific democratic process of political legitimization. Nor does it appear appropriate simply to remove the balancing with the argument that this would stimulate antithetical legal positions and undermine the legal limitation of power.[198] The comparative balancing between the different perspectives on the same constitutional principle is fundamental to the social adequacy of law. In the same vein, simply returning to a model primarily oriented by rules in the name of security is unsustainable. On the one hand, it is unsustainable because such a model, by overestimating legal consistency, would tend to suppress fundamental controversies surrounding the constitution, and thus to exclude peremptorily and definitely certain constitutional understandings that are relevant in the public sphere. On the other hand, because it starts from an illusory belief in that rules have the ability to ensure legal certainty and thus security, while in fact they also

196 Neves, 2009, 228–9 (Engl. trans. 2013, 143–4).

197 Böckenförde, 2003, esp. 186–7. See pp. 116–17 above.

198 Ladeur, 2004, 79, assuming a critical stance on Böckenförde, 2003.

involve uncertainties and, ultimately, can produce insecurities ('good public and private behaviour' for the purposes of criminal rehabilitation?).[199] The crucial question facing the constitutional interpretation-application body in cases of intra-principle collisions, in the same manner as in the inter-principle collision, is how to reorient the normative expectations of those directly and indirectly involved in the corresponding dispute. This also implies a re-articulation of principles in the light of rules (both from statutes and from case-law). But make no mistake: all these tasks imply a selective and excluding absorption in the face of the structural dissent around the meaning of the constitution, its principles and rules. In these circumstances, the decision is all the more justified the greater its ability to prevent the hypertrophy of a social sphere (economic, political, media, scientific, religious, etc.), as well as the vantage point of a group, organization, person, or legal order in the understanding of constitutional principles, without repressing the structural dissent, but rather allowing and even stimulating its emergence in future cases.

In short, within their limits, judges and constitutional courts (in the broad sense) also play a role in reacting to the dangers of dedifferentiation (politicization, economization, religious fundamentalism, scientification, corporatism, moralism, media domination, etc.) and to the denial of the double contingency (the elimination of alter by ego or vice versa) in the constitutional concretization process. To do this, they have to permanently face the paradox of the relationship between legal consistency—associated primarily with the formal argumentation based on rules—and the social adequacy of law, linked primarily with the substantive argumentation based on principles.

[199] See pp. 19–20 above.

4

The Use and Abuse of Principles

From Doctrine to Practice in Brazilian Constitutional Law

1. From Doctrinal Fascination . . .

In the late twentieth century and early twenty-first century, Brazilian constitutional doctrine was enthralled by the theory of constitutional principles and, in this context, the balancing of principles, an approach that, although with outstanding exceptions, has been contributing to an oversimplification of complex issues concerning the relationship between principles and rules. This fascination could simply be associated with the democratization and constitutionalization processes that occurred in Latin America in general, and in Brazil in particular, in the last quarter of the twentieth century, after a period of authoritarian regimes with disastrous effects on civil and political liberties. Just as there was a broad debate on democratic transition and consolidation in political science and theory,[1] a debate around the 'constitutionalization of law'[2] and 'neo-constitutionalism'[3] emerged in the legal field.

However, this connection between legal-political changes and emerging constitutional doctrines cannot be so closely and directly understood as a 'stimulus/response' reaction. Firstly, because corresponding concepts were originally developed in other contexts, in which democratic experiences were already stabilized, not having arisen in periods of transition from authoritarianism to democracy.[4] Even in Mexico, where the debate on

[1] See, among others, O'Donnell, Schmitter, and Whitehead, 1986; Mainwaring, O'Donnell, and Valenzuela, 1992; Alcántara and Crespo, 1995. Despite being one of the main advocates of the model, O'Donnell later warned of 'illusions about consolidation' (1996).

[2] For the debate in Brazil, see Souza Neto and Sarmento (eds), 2007. Cf. also Barroso, 2010, 352 ff.; V.A. Silva, 2008, focusing, however, on the effects of fundamental rights on private relationships (18). With a contrary conclusion regarding antitrust law, Schuartz (2009) points to its 'de-constitutionalization'.

[3] For the debate in Brazil, see Quaresma, Oliveira, and Riccio de Oliveira (eds), 2009. Cf. also Maia, 2007; 2009; Barroso, 2006; 2007a, linking neo-constitutionalism with the constitutionalization of law; Schier, 2007; Moreira, 2008; Sarmento, 2009; Streck, 2009; Dimoulis, 2009; Ávila, 2009; Vale, 2009, 21 ff.

[4] See e.g. Favoreu, 1996; Mathieu and Verpeaux (eds), 1998; Schuppert, 1998; Schuppert and Bumke, 2000; Jarass, 2008; Guastini, 1998b; Pozzolo, 1998, 2001. In France, the topic of constitutionalization

Constitutionalism and the Paradox of Principles and Rules. Marcelo Neves, Oxford University Press. © Marcelo Neves 2021.
DOI: 10.1093/oso/9780192898746.003.0005

'neo-constitutionalism' in Latin America was initially promoted,[5] the context was not of transition from authoritarianism to democracy, despite the limits and shortcomings of the democratic constitutionalism developed in Mexico since the 1910s. In any case, it should be noted that between political-constitutional experience and legal-constitutional doctrine there is always a certain asymmetry, particularly because in democratic states, several different constitutional theories clash with one another, some being more 'formalist', others more 'substantive'.

Secondly, because a more pronounced choice between principles or rules–for a primarily substantive or formal argumentation–has no relation whatsoever with the dichotomy 'democracy/autocracy' or 'constitutionalism/authoritarianism', especially when principles are associated with axiological, teleological, or moral models. Historical experience is resounding in this regard. At the time of National Socialism, the jurists who proclaimed the importance of principles guided by values and teleology, especially within the Hegelian tradition, were precisely those who pontificated in academic circles.[6] Authors deemed 'formalists', which Hauke Brunkhorst suggestively related to 'democratic legal positivism',[7] among whom Hans Kelsen stands out, were banished from the chairs they held or had no access to the academic sphere.[8] Obviously, for the '*Führer*', a model with emphasis on constitutional and legal rules would be practically disastrous.[9] A theory of principles related to the development of the German people in the 'universal history' as 'the actualization of the universal spirit'

dates back to the decision of the Constitutional Council of 16 July 1971, which established that the preamble to the 1958 Constitution and the texts to which it refers, among which the 1789 Declaration of the Rights of Man and of the Citizen, were part of the parameters of constitutional control (Decision No. 71-44 DC of 16 July 1971). In turn, when judging Article 62 of the Finance Law for 1974, on 27 December 1973, the Council based its decision for unconstitutionality directly on the 1789 Declaration (Decision No. 73-51 DC of 27 December 1973, Paragraph 2).

[5] Carbonell (ed.), 2003; 2007a.

[6] That is the case, for instance, of Karl Larenz, whose legal works stood out at the height of National Socialism. In this regard, his article titled 'Spirit of the People and Law' (*Volksgeist und Recht*) (Larenz, 1938) is noteworthy.

[7] Brunkhorst, 2002.

[8] Kelsen was expelled from his professorship at the University of Cologne in 1933 and, while persecuted by National Socialists, fled Germany in that same year. Kelsen was persecuted not only because of his Jewish origin, but also because he was 'a democrat and a pacifist' (Bastos, 2005, 53; for more details on this subject matter, see Métall, 1969, 60 ff.).

[9] In this regard, Schmitt (2014 [1933], 515) peremptorily asserted: 'In the German state of the present time, the National Socialist movement is leading. Therefore, based on its principles, one must determine what are good morals, good faith, reasonable requirements, public security and order, etc. So, each particular case of application of these concepts has to be identified on the basis of National Socialist principles and must be scrutinized under national socialist points of view.'

or 'immersion of the world spirit in itself'[10] more appropriately served the 'ends' of Nazism.

Nevertheless, the examples are not restricted to the German experience. There was also no primacy of a formalistic theory of legal and constitutional argumentation in the Brazilian military regime either. Miguel Reale, perhaps the most influential legal theorist and philosopher in the authoritarian period, adopted a value-orientated model within the Hegelian tradition, having been–based on his 'three-dimensional theory of law'–a strong critic of the so-called formalist streams.[11] In that context, he went beyond theoretical abstractions, as he rather argued substantively, in the name of 'objective realism', in favour of the authoritarianism imposed by the Military in 1964.[12] Certainly, any rigorous model of constitutional rules would be inappropriate for a political regime of 'exception', i.e. a regime in which the exceptions defined ad hoc for the maintenance of the incumbent structure of domination constitute the ' rule' . The fact that authoritarianism strayed from a model of rules becomes more evident in the Latin American experience due to a lack of ideological consistency of the regimes, which demanded a certain malleability to particularistic pressures of individuals and groups, implying a case-to-case break with the rules imposed by them, at the mercy of concrete political expediency.[13]

Care should also be taken when referring to the rhetoric of 'the beginning of history', which suggests a lack of orientation by principles-based arguments in Brazil's past legal and constitutional tradition.[14] During the Brazilian Empire (1822-1889), Pimenta Bueno referred to law as an order of 'principles'.[15] Arguments based on principles were not uncommon in the First Republic (1889-1930), during which Rui Barbosa stood out by permanently invoking principles related to constitutional and individual rights. For this reason, he is the first person in Brazilian constitutional history to whom the expressions 'constitutionalization of law' and–ironically–'neo-constitutionalism' could be applied.[16] During the military regime (1964-1985), Celso Antonio Bandeira

[10] See above pp. 30–1.

[11] Reale, 1979.

[12] Reale, 1983, 66–7, referring to Hegel and contrasting 'objective realism' with 'legal enlightenment'. See also Reale, 1965, defending the military coup and the resulting authoritarian politics.

[13] With regard to Getúlio Vargas's dictatorship (1937–1945), see Loewenstein, 1942, with some cultural bias.

[14] Barroso and Barcellos, 2005.

[15] 'Law and the obligations thereunder are the principles, the firm foundations of all sociability, legislation, progress, and human perfection' (Pimenta Bueno, 1857, 70).

[16] Rui Barbosa emphasized constitutional supremacy in the following terms: 'The judge violates the statutory law to comply with the Constitution' (Barbosa, 1932, 19–21). And he related 'individual resistance' to the general right to liberty associated with the principle of legality, as per Article 72.1 of the Brazilian Federal Constitution of 1891 (Barbosa, 1934, 205–12; see also pp. 151-3 below). In the First Republic, Barbalho (1902, 267) included both 'individual freedom and its guarantees' ('*free regime*,

de Mello, a prominent jurist, with strong influence on the doctrine of public law, although associated with the tradition of what I would call 'Brazilian democratic legal positivism', took the topic of principles seriously, presenting the first elements for a model of affirmative action in the light of the principle of equality.[17]

Indeed, the present work seeks to address a specific approach to the relationship between the constitution and statutory law in terms of the dynamic aspect of law, and between constitutional principles and rules in terms of the static aspect of law. Our focus is on the latter relationship, but since we are discussing the fascination with *constitutional* principles and their balancing between them as *ultima ratio* and panacea for constitutional problems, the two aspects are inseparable in the scope of this work. This topic has been discussed, as previously mentioned, under the label 'constitutionalization of law' and especially under the term 'neo-constitutionalism'. But it goes further, because lawyers who refuse to be labelled by these expressions and take a critical distance with regard to the corresponding theoretical or doctrinal attitudes have been highlighting the role played by principles and their balancing.[18]

It is beyond the scope of this study to make a comprehensive analysis of the 'neo-constitutionalism' in Brazil. A criticism of this doctrinal stream points out that the theoretical and practical significance of the debate on constitutional review, normative force of the constitution, and constitutional principles has developed since the early 19th century.[19] In fact, this criticism unveils the rhetorical character of peremptory assertions made by 'neo-constitutionalists', but the intended purpose of this study is not limited to such a criticism.

Ávila goes further and, based on four claims that he attributes to some authors,[20] seeks a more comprehensive critique of 'neo-constitutionalism' in general, endowing it with the following basic features in terms of focus shift: from rule to principle, as regards the normative fundament; from subsumption to balancing, referring to the methodological fundament; from general justice to particular justice, concerning the axiological fundament; from legislative (or executive) power to judicial power, as regards the organizational

preamble, and declaration of rights') and democracy among the constitutional principles of the Union, followed in this particular instance by Barbosa (1934, 10). See also Sampaio Dória, 1926, 19–20, 114 ff.

17 Bandeira de Mello, 1993.

18 Thus, e.g. V.A. Silva, 2009; Ávila, 2003 (Engl. trans. 2007) (and later with more restrictions, 2009).

19 In this regard, see Dimoulis, 2009, 214–22, criticizing Barroso, 2007a. In this context, Dimoulis attempts to define 'neo-constitutionalism' as a sort of constitutionalism linked with legal moralism (2009, 222–4), but the very diversity of positions that develop under that label makes it difficult to bet on a comprehensive definition.

20 Carbonell, 2007b; Ferrajoli, 2003; Sanchís Pietro, 2000; Moreira, 2008.

fundament.[21] Based on this characterization, Ávila presents their respective restrictions: by emphasizing constitutional principles to detriment of rules, 'neo-constitutionalism' does not take into account the very character of the Brazilian Constitution, which is rather 'regulatory' ('composed basically of rules') than 'principled';[22] by overestimating the paradigm of balancing at the expense of subsumption, not only does it undermine the hierarchical structure of law and annihilate 'the rules and the regular exercise of the democratic principle', but, above all, it also leads to 'subjectivism, and therefore to the elimination of the hetero-limiting character of law', since it fails to offer 'intersubjectively controllable criteria for the enforcement' of balancing;[23] by giving preference to 'particular justice' over 'general justice', it promotes 'uncertainty' and 'arbitrariness';[24] finally, by favouring the judicial over the legislative (or the executive) power, it fails to properly consider both the demands of the 'rule of law in force in a complex and plural society' and the features of a 'legal order that favours democratic participation'.[25] Based on these reviews, Ávila concludes that 'neo-constitutionalism' in Brazil 'relates more to what one could provocatively call a concealed kind of "non-constitutionalism": a movement or an ideology that loudly proclaims the overvaluation of the constitution while silently promoting its devaluation'.[26]

Even though such a criticism points to relevant theoretical and practical problems of a principle-overestimating model of constitutional interpretation-application, it deserves further scrutiny. Initially, it should be noted that this criticism may lead to 'injustices', insofar as some authors of a stream composed of various trends in constitutional theory and doctrine are strategically chosen in order to peremptorily assign some of their assertions to the reception of this stream in Brazil, as if there were an accurate unity in the neo-constitutional doctrine and in its corresponding reception in Brazil. For example, authors classified by Carbonell as belonging to the so-called neo-constitutionalism(s) might not accept any of the peremptory assertions that Ávila attributes to this vast current.[27] Authors who call themselves 'neo-constitutionalists' could also reject any of these assertions.[28] So the objections to some authors (three from

[21] Ávila, 2009.
[22] Ávila, 2009, 3, 5, 18.
[23] Ávila, 2009, 7–10.
[24] Ávila, 2009, 15, 18.
[25] Ávila, 2009, 16, 18.
[26] Ávila, 2009, 19.
[27] Carbonell (ed. 2003) included in the first book that he edited on the topic an article by Alexy, who would hardly agree with Carbonell's peremptory assertions, which are the object of Ávila's criticism.
[28] See e.g. Barcellos, 2005, 190, 193, pointing to the precedence of rules over principles.

other country and one from Brazil) cannot serve as a model for criticism of an entire stream of Brazil's recent constitutional doctrine.

However, this issue is secondary for the purpose of this study. In turn, the foundations of Ávila's criticism are relevant. With regard to what matters directly to this work—the relationship between constitutional principles and rules—the saturated distinction between 'principled constitution' and 'regulatory constitution' does not seem appropriate as a parameter to criticize a constitutional theory or doctrine that favours constitutional principles over rules. This distinction is very restricted to the constitutional text.[29] The intention here is not to deny the significance of constitutional texts, since interpretation is the creation of texts based on texts[30] and cannot 'destroy the uniting function of the text'.[31] Nevertheless, it is not textualization per se that is relevant to law and rights but the norms attributed to the text. Strictly speaking, texts alone (signifiers) are not law yet, whose formation depends on binding norms assigned to them in the interchange between the institutional instance of law-making and the hermeneutic instance of law-construing. The same constitutional text can give birth to several different constitutional doctrines and practices. Moreover, the distinction between constitutional principles and rules has meaning only in the argumentation related to complex constitutional disputes, being irrelevant in routine applications and the everyday observance of constitutional norms.[32] Thus, the criticism of a principle-overestimating constitutional doctrine cannot be attached to and based on a classic difference of a highly textual nature between 'principled constitution' and 'regulatory constitution', which ultimately relates to a quantitative distinction based on the number and extent of constitutional provisions.

This decisive limitation is associated with the fragility of other foundations for Ávila's criticism to the so-called neo-constitutionalism. The assertion that the paradigm of balancing (to the detriment of subsumption) leads to subjectivism, not providing intersubjective criteria for the hetero-limiting function of law, comes from a saturated distinction, unsuitable for analysing models

[29] Moreover, it can be assumed that the notion of 'regulatory constitution' is related to the idea of 'the steering constitution' (Canotilho, 1994), which seems highly questionable in the context of a complex society.

[30] See p. 117 above.

[31] Luhmann, 1993, 364 (Engl. trans. 2004, 324). About the requirement to take seriously the text, see Alexy, 1986, 121 (Engl. trans. 2002, 83). In turn, F. Müller (1995, 99) speaks of 'binding all legal functions *to the normative text*'. On the textuality of law, see recently Ladeur, 2016. In this sense, one might argue in Derrida's terms, at least in relation to law, that 'there is nothing outside the text' (*'il n'y a rien hors du texte'*: Derrida, 1967, 233 (Engl. trans. 1997, 163)), or: 'There is no outside-text' (*'Il n'y a pas de hors-texte'*: ibid., 227 (Engl. trans. 158)).

[32] See pp. 78–9 above.

related to the constitutional concretization. Balancing and subsumption occur within complex communication processes. What goes on in the minds of judges before argumentation and interpretation (as text creation) is uncontrollable in both subsumption and balancing. What is socially and legally controllable is what is communicated. The alternative, inter-subjective control, is irrelevant in this context. The model of inter-subjectivity has appeared more like an alternative to the monological legitimation claimed by a judge as the (ideal) subject who is able to make the right decision from a privileged viewpoint. But the social and legal communication process cannot be seen as a reciprocal observation of minds in terms of an intersubjective model. In any case, decisions must be taken as communications susceptible to criticism. In neither case is it about subjectivism, but rather the conditions of possibility for criticizing decisions in the transsubjective context of communications.[33] Finally, resorting to this alternative disregards the meaning of complex communication arrangements marked by both the systemic plurality of viewpoints and the double contingency of any communication event.

Moreover, resorting to the distinction between 'general justice' and 'particular justice' in this context, suggesting a (predominant) association of the former with rules and of the latter with principles, seems problematic to me. Firstly, one cannot deny that some rules are more orientated to the concrete and the particular (especially when they are built by case-law), and nothing indicates that principles, far beyond their balancing in individual cases, cannot serve the so-called general normative requirements. Secondly, the 'general justice/particular justice' dichotomy is debatable. In this regard, there is a permanent interaction between the abstract and the concrete when it comes to meeting normative expectations. Justice relates to processing of the paradox of a decision that has to be at the same time legally consistent and socially adequate, simultaneously involving the abstract and the concrete, the general and the individual.

Finally, although criticism of the fact that 'neo-constitutionalism' places excessive emphasis on the judiciary is relevant, Ávila does that in a rather simplistic way. According to him, the legislative, bound by the democratic process, has the ability to devise rules aimed at 'stabilizing moral conflicts' and 'reducing uncertainty and arbitrariness' in a complex society,[34] whereas the judiciary is responsible for applying them. In fact, the legislative production of rules (texts)

[33] Fischer-Lescano (2013, 17 ff.) emphasizes the 'transsubjective' characteristic of the 'societal relations' in general, starting from the framework of a 'critical system's theory'. In turn, Ladeur (2014) points out the 'transsubjective' dimension of the fundamental rights.

[34] Ávila, 2009, 16.

is fundamental to reducing the complexity and stabilizing normative expectations in modern society. This is a result of the positivization of law.[35] However, the introduction of legal rules by the legislative power is only a stage in the process of selecting norms before a multitude of conflicting normative expectations present in society. The introduction of a legal rule by the legislative process could create even more conflicts than the ones that already existed before the law in question comes into force. The issue of different understandings of the same legal rule—its meaning, its scope of validity and application, etc.—requires judicial activity to stabilize and reorient conflicting normative expectations around the respective legal text. And this activity can only be successful, in some cases, if one resorts to suitable principles in order to resolve the corresponding legal-constitutional controversy. Therefore, the legislative activity and rules as well as the judicial activity and principles play a key role and perform decisive functions in stabilizing normative expectations within a hyper-complex and conflictual society. This stabilization depends on how the circular-reflexive relationship develops between legislators (especially the constitutional legislators) and judges or courts (particularly the constitutional judges or courts) under the dynamic aspect of law and between principles and rules under the static aspect of law.

For the purpose of this work, a more comprehensive analysis of trends seems to be more appropriate for a critical consideration of the adoption of principle-based models in Brazil's recent constitutional doctrine than focusing on a stream that is difficult to demarcate due to the very different theories and authors it encompasses. Towards a broader critique of the fascination with the model of principles in the constitutional doctrine of the 1990s and 2000s, it is worth considering Virgílio Afonso da Silva's critique. Overall, Silva points to a methodological syncretism that would render several formulations of the constitutional theory concerning topics such as principles and rules, weighing or balancing, proportionality and reasonableness, among others, inconsistent.[36] His critique focuses on the form of adopting catalogues of principles and methods of interpretation proposed under certain circumstances of the development of constitutional doctrine and practice in a country, especially Germany, and then transplanted to another, Brazil in this case, as if they were something universal. Thus, he emphasizes that the catalogue of principles of constitutional interpretation presented by Konrad Hesse in a textbook originally published in 1967, which according to Silva has not found broad

[35] See Chapter 3 section 2 above.

[36] V.A. Silva, 2005; 2003; 2002b.

doctrinal and judicial acceptance within the German constitutional order to which it was directed, became widespread in Brazil from the 1990s on as an intrinsic requirement for any constitutional state: the principles of integrative effect, unity of the constitution, practical concordance, functional conformity, and normative force of the constitution. Silva peremptorily states: 'A list devised by an author—Konrad Hesse—came to be seen as containing universal and indispensable principles.'[37] To this catalogue he adds the principle of maximum effectiveness that arrived in Brazil thanks to the work of José Joaquim Gomes Canotilho. In addition, Silva asserts he has nothing to say about the introduction of the principle of interpretation according to the constitution in this catalogue (also mentioned by Hesse), for he maintains that this would be a specific criterion of legal interpretation.[38]

With respect to the methods of constitutional interpretation, Silva proceeds in a similar fashion. He points to the dissemination in Brazil of a list drawn up by Böckenförde in an article on the subject, which is composed of the following types of methods: the classic hermeneutical, the topical-problematic, the scientific-realistic, and the concretizing hermeneutical method.[39] He maintains that Böckenförde intended '*only* to summarize the stage at which the discussion was at the time his article was published, rather than putting forward a set of complementary methods' and, in this regard, he draws attention to the article's subtitle: 'inventory and criticism'.[40] From that point on, Silva criticizes Brazilian jurists' inconsistency when adopting and disseminating methods presented by Böckenförde and other German constitutional scholars, especially the variant formulated by Canotilho. He then goes to associate this inconsistency with a lack of reference to the practical application and, above all, with 'methodological syncretism'.[41] Based on both this critique and the objections to the adoption of Hesse's catalogue of principles, Silva programmatically pontificates on the need for a constitutional theory to be developed that can be applied to the Brazilian Constitution, arguing such a theory would not

[37] V.A. Silva, 2005, 133.

[38] V.A. Silva, 2005, 118–33. Cf. Hesse, 1969, 28–34; Canotilho, 1998, 1096–101. The 'principle of interpretation according to the constitution' in the terms of Euro-continental tradition is akin to the 'canon of avoidance' in the two versions ('classic' and 'modern') developed in the language of the US jurisprudence (see Eskridge Jr., 2016, 309 ff.).

[39] Böckenförde, 1991 [1976], 56–80.

[40] V.A. Silva, 2005, 134. In that article, Böckenförde (1991 [1976], 80) stated critically: 'All treated methods of interpretation ultimately contribute—perhaps with the exception of F. Müller—to undermining the normativity of the constitution.'

[41] V.A. Silva, 2005, 133 ff. See Canotilho, 1998, 1084–8.

exclude methods and concepts developed in the context of other legal orders, but would require them to go through a compatibility test.[42]

These critiques are relevant because they point to the limits of the legal and constitutional debate established in Brazil since the promulgation of the 1988 Constitution, especially when it comes to the frequent invocation of principles and their balancing. They 'denounce' not only the lack of doctrinal, theoretical, and methodological accuracy in that debate but also that it has been unable to establish a solid connection with the Brazilian constitutional order and its corresponding legal practice. On the one hand, there is inconsistency; on the other hand, there is what is controversially called 'misplaced ideas' in Brazilian social theory.[43] Yet, it seems to me that Silva's direct and peremptory critiques come with a dash of simplification and become entangled in the very deficiencies he seeks to criticize.

My initial point refers to the tendency to attribute supposed failures to the way Brazilian legal scholars and courts have received ideas or concepts from a specific author (almost always a German jurist), without carefully ascertaining whether such failures appears in the original formulation. An obvious example is the reference to interpretation according to the constitution, which could not be the subject of an article on constitutional interpretation, as that would be a criterion for statutory interpretation.[44] Without going into this discussion here, which is beyond the scope of this work, it is worth reminding that although Hesse did not include this 'principle' in the catalogue he initially presented in his textbook, he regarded it then as a 'principle of interpretation' that had appeared in the 'more recent development of constitutional law' and confirmed the 'mutual reference between constitution and statutory law' with the following assertion: 'The interpretation according to the constitution not only raises the question of the content of the statutory law to be reviewed, but also the question of the content of the constitution based on which the law must be scrutinized. It therefore requires both statutory and constitutional interpretation.'[45] Silva suggests that the inclusion of the topic of interpretation according

[42] V.A. Silva, 2005, 143. Also in that article, Böckenförde (1991 [1976], 81) spoke precisely of the 'need for a (binding) theory of the constitution'.

[43] Schwarz, 2000 [1977] (Engl. trans. 1992). This formulation is susceptible to criticism because ideas gain new meaning and perform other functions in contexts while moving or migrating. From this perspective, recently Schwarz (2012), instead of corroborating as he suggests, strictly speaking has revised his original thesis. However, it seems to me that the concept of 'misplaced ideas' must be definitively ruled out. Otherwise, it is appropriate to talk about ideas in another place (the legal-political unity to which they have moved) and at the same time, paradoxically, in the same place (world society). In this regard, see Neves, 2015.

[44] V.A. Silva, 2005, 132–3.

[45] Hesse, 1969, 31, 34.

to the constitution in the catalogue of principles in Brazil is due to an improper reception of Hesse's formulation, but if there had been a failure or inaccuracy, it would already be found in Hesse's work.

Another aspect to be considered is Silva's generalized critique of 'methodological syncretism' in Brazil, without carefully addressing the contribution of authors who are not part of his strict theoretical universe. An example is his critique of the inadequate overlap, without proper conceptual filtering, between Friedrich Müller's 'structuring theory' and Robert Alexy's legal theory of principles. It is definitely important to point to theoretically and methodologically impossible reconciliations of those two models, especially if both are adopted without restrictions. This problem relates to an old tradition of legal doctrine and theory in Brazil, including authors who stand out in the national debate.[46] However, care is required when referring to the position of a certain author so as to characterize it, under a specific aspect, as contrary to that of another author. Silva asserts that Müller maintains a concept of legal norm unsusceptible to collision and therefore to balancing, in order to point out the contradiction between Müller's theory and Alexy's.[47] He is correct when he states that Müller's legal norm is not subject to balancing. But Müller's legal norm only appears at the end of the concretizing process.[48] Thus, it corresponds, according to Alexy's model, to the legal rule construed as a definitive reason for the judicial decision after balancing.[49] Also according to Alexy, no (complete) rule as a definitive reason is susceptible to balancing. In this specific sense, nothing would be problematic between the two theories. Given the different theoretical assumptions, the difference would lie in the meaning of balancing before the end of the concretization or argumentation chain, respectively: for Müller, during concretization, balancing appears as a potentially irrational factor in the process of constructing the legal norm as the immediate reason for the ought-judgment of a case;[50] for Alexy, balancing—in the case of principles and incomplete rules—is the decisive rational element in argumentation aimed at building the (complete) rule as a definitive reason for the concrete solution to the case. There are still problems on both sides, and the

[46] For example, in reference works, Ferraz Jr. (1980; 1988) conflates Theodor Viehweg's Topic, Niklas Luhmann's systems theory, and Hannah Arendt's theory of action, as well as decision technique models in vogue at the time, among other perspectives, not making any effort to filter them, as if they were all compatible.

[47] V.A. Silva, 2005, 135–6.

[48] See pp. 14–15 above. In a way, V.A. Silva (2005, 137) admits this by maintaining that 'after this arduous task' of 'delimitating the field of normative operation' (and it should be added: the 'the norm program'), 'there is no room for collisions', but he mixes up levels.

[49] See pp. 56–7 above.

[50] Cf. F. Müller, 1995, 62–3, 67–8; 1994, 208 ff.; 1990a, 21 ff.

following questions persist: before the end of the concretizing process, would there be no legal norm to bind judges (for Müller)? Is it possible to speak of complete rules as definitive reasons before the argumentation process is completed in complex constitutional controversies (for Alexy)? But the answer to those questions does not lie in the attempt to reconcile both theories, nor in the unconditional adoption of one of them, but in reflexions that seek theoretical alternatives to these models.[51]

Although I have expanded on the shortcoming of a peremptory critique of 'methodological syncretism' in the Brazilian constitutional doctrine, this is a secondary issue for this study. It is more important to consider that Silva's objections to Brazilian authors in this context (concerning the local and the universal)[52] applies in part to him as well. First of all, it should be noted that Alexy's theory of constitutional rights, based on which his model of constitutional principles was more broadly presented, developed from the doctrinal reconstruction of the German Federal Constitutional Court's case-law until the beginning of the 1980s. Even in Germany there are indications that this case-law is gradually being overcome in more recent times.[53] Moreover, the model of proportionality, in the specific form it was articulated both conceptually and terminologically in Germany, Austria, and Switzerland,[54] finds no correspondence in other constitutional states with a strong legal tradition. It is sufficient to mention French and American constitutional experiences as examples.[55] This does not mean that the underlying questions and solutions (consideration of how suitable and necessary measures are, as well as the hypertrophy of one principle to the detriment of another) have no connection with other concepts nor are they under the cover of other—more or less accurate—terminologies. Concepts and terminology may vary, but what is most important is not the

[51] See above pp. 14–16, Chapter 2 section 3 and p. 98, where I provide answers to these questions.

[52] V.A. Silva, 2005, 118–21.

[53] Cf. Kahl, 2004, who, with a critical position in relation to this doctrinal and judicial transformation, stresses that a consensus had already been reached in the 1st Chamber (*Senat*) of the German Federal Constitutional Court to avoid the balancing (180). Against Kahl's critiques, see Hoffmann-Riem, 2004, maintaining that, apart from having the form of subjective rights, constitutional rights also contain objective determinations for the guarantee of freedom (231).

[54] In these terms, it is the typical object of the exercises (*Übungen*), i.e. classes devoted to case studies in Germany, Switzerland, and Austria. For the reception in Brazil, see Mendes, 1999; 2000; 2011; Guerra Filho, 2001; 2005; 2008; Steinmetz, 2001; Martins, 2003; Dimoulis and Martins, 2007, 176 ff.

[55] As regards the United States, see Hamilton and Schoenbrod, 1999; Zoller, 2003; Thomas, 2007; Yowell, 2014 (he points out the existence of similarities between the US approach and the German model (101 ff.)). Regarding France, see Bousta, 2007; Goesel-Le Bihan, 2007, esp. 287 ff.; 2001. However, in the judgment of 21 February 2008, the French Constitutional Council expressly used the three components of proportionality as a reason for its decision (Decision 2008-562 DC of 21 February 2008). On this decision, see Bousta, 2008; Conseil Constitutionnel, 2008. For an overview of proportionality in comparative law, see Beatty, 2004, 159 ff. With regard to 'global constitutionalism', see Sweet Stone and Mathew, 2008; for a historical overview in comparative perspective, see Barak, 2012a, 175 ff.

choice between either one or the other model, but rather the question of whether a legally consistent and socially adequate model will develop in the corresponding constitutional order, in the reciprocal relationship between constitutional doctrine and constitutional practice. Whether they can be satisfactorily transplanted to another legal and constitutional order depends on several factors of historical, political, legal, and social nature. Discussing, for instance, whether the reasonableness, in the sense of a suitable relationship between means and ends, corresponds to the proportionality as seen in German case-law and legal doctrine, in order to conclude that the reasonableness corresponds only to the first criterion of proportionality,[56] falls too short for a program of constructing a constitutional theory that suits the Brazilian Constitution. Although it helps prevent certain conceptual inconsistencies in Brazilian constitutional doctrine and practice, the trend in this direction is to turn the constitutional debate into a terminological discussion about who is using more accurately a model that is valid within another legal order. In this sense, constitutional jurists on the side of the receiving legal order may become censors of the right use of the terminology built and developed in a theoretical model based on the doctrinal reconstruction of the constitutional practice of a foreign legal order. In brief: instead of using this model to 'control' the Brazilian constitutional theory, doctrine, and practice, one should reflect upon the theoretical and practical shortcomings that hinder the development of constitutional law towards making legally consistent and socially appropriate decisions in Brazil; based on this reflexion, conditions can be met to foster the rise of a constitutional theory (or theories) that, while starting with the doctrinal reconstruction of the constitutional practice, can contribute decisively to the improvement of constitutional adjudication.

From this perspective, without denying the importance of Dimoulis's, Ávila's, and Silva's critiques, I intend to present a brief reflection on the overestimation of principles that has quickly spread in Brazil. It seems to me that this model is *over*-adequate to the social and political reality. What do I mean by this? In a legal system differentiated from politics, economics, and other social spheres, law and constitution (in the legal sense) maintain some 'distance from reality'.[57] This relates to the autonomy of law in the face of other social variables. When law and constitution are immediately subordinate to the particularities of several social factors, legal rules and principles lose their practical significance for guaranteeing rights and controlling power: there is

[56] V.A. Silva, 2002b, 32–3. See note 3 in Chapter 3 above.
[57] Grimm, 1991, 15.

either autocracy (authoritarianism and totalitarianism) or—although the textual arrangement of some constitutions corresponds to the constitutional state model—diffuse blockages (economic, political, relational, familial, etc.) that hamper a satisfactory constitutional concretization and realization. Brazilian constitutional history is marked by this problem of low capacity to ensure and improve a constitutionally consistent reproduction of law. Both in the past and in the present, based on several differing theoretical assumptions, this problem has been pointed out by Brazilian scholars.[58] Discussing this sociological backdrop is out of the scope of this work,[59] but this issue affects legal-constitutional practice and doctrine. Legal consistency (legality, constitutionality) is ensured in the reciprocal relationship between legal practice and the doctrine or the theory of law.[60] If there are structural legal inconsistencies in practice, the legal reflexion (doctrine and theory of law) gets weakened. But there are two alternatives: to act reactively, reproducing and contributing to the maintenance of an inconsistent legal practice, one that is open to the concrete pressures of several social particularisms; or to offer a solid conceptual apparatus in order to bolster changes in the legal practice. Inconsistent practices reject the rules, which in turn can reach a point of definitiveness at which deviations become manifest. Principles, on the contrary, as reflexivity structures that never in themselves achieve definitiveness, can be more easily articulated to cover solutions that undermine the consistency of the legal system in favour of particularistic interests that push for a solution of a case. In other words, principles are more prone to abuses during the concretization process, as they are linked primarily with the moment of cognitive openness of law.[61] When they work in a strictly consistent constitutional state (self-reference), they play a key role in adjusting law to society (external reference). However, if the social context and the corresponding legal practice are heavily marked by illegalities and unconstitutionalities systematically practised by public officials, a principle-overestimating doctrine can be both a factor for and a result of the abuse of principles in the legal practice.[62] This situation gains strength with the

[58] For instance: 'Constitutions made not to be fulfilled, laws that exist to be violated' (Buarque de Hollanda, 1988 [1933], 136–7); 'The root is the same: the creation of a false world that is more efficient than the real world' (Faoro, 1976, 175); 'the discrepancy between norm and reality . . . fiction becoming reality, reality becoming fiction' (J.M. Carvalho, 2011, 381 and 419) However, Buarque de Hollanda, Faoro, and Carvalho are overburdened with culturalist assumptions according to a methodological nationalism with that I disagree completely (see reference of the next footnote).

[59] Comprehensively, see Neves, 1992; 2018.

[60] See Neves, 1992, 207 ff.; Luhmann, 1974, 22, 59; 1981, 438 ff.

[61] One can also speak of *normative* openness when it comes to the relationship with other normative orders within transconstitutionalism (Neves, 2009, 126–7 (Engl. trans. 2013, 80–1)).

[62] Regarding abuse of principles from another theoretical perspective, see Kellog, 2010.

introduction of another ingredient: excessive balancing. The remedies against excessive legal consistency that follows the regime of rules become poisons (or hallucinogens) in the context of a legally inconsistent practice that operates at the mercy of various social pressures.

In Brazil, this fascination with principles suggests their intrinsic superiority in relation to rules. Underlying this understanding is the idea that constitutional rules (complete, i.e. when the issues of exceptions and occasional balancing have already been overcome) can be averted by constitutional principles due to the justice that is inherent in the decisions based on them. But such a model implies a fundamental denial of one aspect of the legal system that enables the processing of 'just' decisions: consistency. Averting the rules every time a principle is rhetorically invoked in the name of justice, in a complex society with several ways to interpret principles, helps rather accommodate concrete and particular interests at the expense of the normative force of the constitution. Therefore, it is worth quoting a theorist of principles that is one of the most cited by the Brazilian principle-overestimating legal scholars:

> This raises the issue of the relative status of the two levels. And the answer can only be that from the perspective of the binding nature of the Constitution, the level of rules takes precedence ... So decisions made at the level of rules take precedence over other alternative decisions which the level of principle merely makes possible.[63]

Although Alexy admits exceptions, using as an example a case in which for him a principle prevailed over a rule in a judgment of the German Federal Constitutional Court, it should be noted that it was 'a case which does not correspond to the precedence of the level of rules over the level of principles as *defined by the text of constitutional provisions*'.[64] In fact, the question concerned the relationship between text and norm. It was not about balancing, but rather a simple 'broad interpretation' (of the provision, but restrictive of the right) in the classic sense. Therefore, once a rule (complete, no longer subject to balancing) is defined beyond its wording, it takes precedence over the principles that are formally at the same hierarchical level. Were it always possible to resort to constitutional principles in the name of justice in order to avert constitutional rules, we would reach a model in which the indirect criterion to solve a

[63] Alexy, 1986, 121–2 (Engl. trans. 2002, 83).

[64] Alexy, 1986, 122 (Engl. trans. 2002, 84) (emphasis added). It concerns the 'Pharmacists Judgment' (*Apothekenurteil*): BVerfGE 7, 377 (401).

case would always be able to remove ad hoc the direct and definitive criterion. Such a model would lead to a lack of consistency in the legal order, socially diluted in the light of a principle-overestimating substantive legal reasoning, which would be catastrophic in a complex society. In the Brazilian context, the rhetorical invocation of principles to ward off rules is (as stated above) over-adequate to society but goes against the development of a solid constitutional state and the normative force of the constitution.

In a different sense, resorting to a certain principle and turning it into a simplifying element of constitutional interpretation also seem problematic. It is true that for the world society human rights—strictly referring to the protection against mass deportation, torture, genocide, etc.—relate to severe and shocking offenses to human dignity.[65] Nevertheless, not all constitutional principles are related to human dignity, including some principles concerning constitutional rights. Indeed, in absolute terms, 'without assigning the fundamental rights to the human person, ... her/his dignity will be denied'.[66] Notwithstanding, the constitution includes functional requirements in its principles in the form of fundamental rights, which can hardly be linked with the dignity of the human person directly.[67] For instance, it is hard to find a strong correlation between the principle of free enterprise and the dignity of the human person. The question presents itself rather rhetorically in a paradoxical way: does human dignity prevail over free enterprise or does it exist despite free enterprise? In other words, not only constitutional principles but especially constitutional rules may occasionally imply restrictions to the constitutional principle of human dignity. The simplification of the constitutional order in the sense of bringing it back to an ultimate, widely open principle tends to a moralism incompatible with the functioning of law in a complex society, in which human dignity is subject to the most diverse readings and understandings (is not imprisonment, considering aspects of general prevention in criminal law, a restriction to human dignity?). The very question of intra-principles collisions in the face of multiple understandings of human dignity, in the context of concrete constitutional disputes, renders inappropriate a model of absolutizing a principle. In Brazil, the rhetorical invocation of human dignity is used to avert accurate

[65] Luhmann, 1993, 574 ff. (Engl. trans. 2004, 482 ff.).

[66] Sarlet, 2004, 84.

[67] Even from a deontological perspective, Kumm and Walen (2014) argue, based on a few typical cases, that human dignity can be subject to balancing and outweighed in cases in which the claimant does not make 'non-restricting claims' and thus cannot insist 'on a nearly absolute right not to be required to make himself an instrument for the use of others (a mean to another's end)'; they assert finally that 'human dignity is not about rule-like absolutes' and 'respect for human dignity requires balancing' (88–9).

constitutional rules in the name of the justice 'inherent' in this principle. This practice can, although this may seem strange, lead precisely to the opposite outcome: the satisfaction of particularistic interests that are incompatible with the limits established by the legal order for the corresponding activities.

The 'compulsion to balancing', which is a commonplace in the new Brazilian constitutional landscape, is more problematic and much more present than tendencies to absolutizing principles to the detriment of more specific principles and rules.[68] Without a doubt, not only in politics but also in the legal sphere and especially in the field of judicial application of the constitution, there are situations in which the need for balancing, in particular among principles, is indispensable.[69] But an 'unlimited balancing' from the viewpoint of constitutional adjudication has devastating effects on the relationship of autonomy and reciprocal conditioning between politics and law in the constitutional state. It leads to both the judicialization of politics and the politicization of law. These expressions must be clarified. The constitution in the modern sense, as a structural coupling between politics and law (constitutional courts themselves are part of this coupling),[70] always has two dimensions: 'constitution as politicization of law' and 'constitution as juridification of politics'.[71] It means the constitution establishes a reciprocal relationship between democracy and the rule of law. However, by judicialization of politics and politicization of law I mean an excess, a hypertrophy, to the detriment of democracy and the rule of law, respectively. In these terms, the autonomy and functioning of both systems are compromised. The political game between government and opposition as well as the circular legitimating relationship among people, the public, administration (in the broad sense), and politics (in the narrow sense)[72] are affected by an excess of judicial intervention, what means at the same time the politicization of law. The judicial branch is strictly orientated to provide politically legitimizing answers by strongly binding itself to the difference between government and opposition. This situation could be related to broader structural problems of the constitutional state.[73] However, it can also be associated, in certain contexts, with the political 'corruption' of the judiciary. Thus, the operational boundaries between law and politics are diluted. Judicial decisions are made

[68] This does not mean that there are no works worth reading in Brazilian legal literature. See, among others, Torres, 2000; Sarmento, 2001; 2000; Barcellos, 2005; Clève and Freire, 2003, esp. 241 ff.

[69] With a different view, Martins (2003, 36–7) affirms the purely political character of balancing in the narrow sense, and therefore of proportionality in the strict sense. Similarly, see Schlink, 2001, 458 ff.; 1976, esp. 152–3; Poscher, 2003, esp. 96.

[70] Luhmann, 2000a, 398.

[71] Möllers, 2003, 3–18.

[72] Luhmann, 2000b, 253 ff.

[73] In Germany, this issue had already been addressed by Maunz, 1959, 220 ff.

primarily based on the 'government/opposition' distinction or on political criteria, especially in constitutional matters. In the Brazilian context, this is often related to particularistic and diffuse connections of members of the judicial branch with politicians. In turn, this situation is associated with the economic 'corruption' of the state as a political and legal organization.

In these circumstances, it could be argued that the balancing would offer elements of legal rationality to politics and of political rationality to law. However, with the 'balancing without limits' or the 'compulsion to balancing', political rationality becomes entirely irrational for the legal system of the rule-of-law State, and legal rationality becomes irrational to the political system of the democratic State. An ad hoc balancing ends up developing in this context without a long-term perspective and dependent on the specific constellation of interests involved in each case. Rather than being an exception, acting as an argumentation technique to reduce the 'surprise value' of court decisions in overcomplex constitutional disputes, balancing may under these conditions be subverted in the midst of accommodation of interests circulating at the margin of the rule of law and democracy under the rhetorical cover of principles.

In short, apart from entailing a simplifying model, the rhetorical invocation of principles as the new panacea for Brazilian constitutional problems—whether in the form of absolute principles or as a compulsion to balancing—can serve to strategically conceal practices oriented to satisfy interests averse to legality and constitutionality, promoting thus the continuous erosion of the normative force of the constitution. Rather than emphasizing the debate (which is often sterile) on the difference between principles and rules, the construction of a theory of constitutional norms that serves a legally consistent and socially adequate concretization of the corresponding principles, rules, and normative hybrids in the Brazilian context is required.

2. ... To the Confusing Legal-Constitutional Practice

The doctrinal fascination relates to a confusing legal-constitutional practice concerning the application of constitutional principles and their balancing. It has become commonplace to refer to the weighing or balancing of values, goods, and principles, and also to proportionality. In this regard, the recent precedents actually point to a transformation, given the more and more frequent invocation of principles combined with the use of balancing and proportionality or reasonableness has increased. This is not a purely quantitative matter; it also has to do with the legal and social significance of the cases. In the aforementioned *Ellwanger* case, the absoluteness of freedom of speech was denied in order to affirm the precedence of the principle of human dignity, according to a model of balancing.[74] It is interesting to note in this regard that, in the judgment of Claim of Non-Compliance with a Fundamental Precept (ADPF) No. 130, the opposite view prevailed, namely, that freedom of speech is not a principle and therefore is not subject to balancing.[75] In the aforementioned Claim of Non-Compliance with a Fundamental Precept (ADPF) No. 101 (import of used tyres), the issue was dealt with expressly in terms of the balancing between economic freedom and right to health and to an ecologically balanced environment, with the latter right prevailing, save some businesses conducted according to Mercosur rules.[76] In the judgment of the Extraordinaire Appeal No. 511.961 (degree in journalism required for the professional practice of journalist), the Supreme Federal Court—when interpreting Article 5.XIII of the Brazilian Constitution (freedom of profession)—considered that its formulation results in a qualified legal reservation, pointing to the 'immanent issue of reasonableness and proportionality of restrictive laws'.[77] In regard to the Extraordinary Appeal No. 197.917, not only the principles of reasonableness and equality were invoked, but also the 'postulates of morality, impersonality and economy of administrative acts (BFC, Article 37)', so as to contrast them with municipal autonomy.[78] In the judgment of Extraordinary Appeal No. 201.819, which dealt with the question of the effect of constitutional rights on private affairs, the guarantee of due process took precedence over the private autonomy of associations.[79] In addition, it is worth mentioning the aforesaid Direct Action of Unconstitutionality No. 3.510/DF, concerning research using embryonic stem cells, in which reference to principles proliferated: 'the right to "family planning" based on the equally constitutional principles of "dignity of the human person" and "responsible parenthood" '; 'freedom, security, welfare, development, equality, and justice'; 'the constitutional combination of state secularism and the primacy of private autonomy'; 'the right to health as a fundamental corollary of the right to a dignified life'; 'freedom of scientific expression and the Biosafety Law as materialization of this freedom'.[80]

[74] HC 82.424/RS, judgment 17 November 2003, TP, DJ 19 March 2004.

[75] ADPF 130/DF, judgment 30 April 2009, TP, DJe 6 November 2009.

[76] ADPF 101/DF, judgment 24 June 2009, TP, DJe 4 June 2012. The exception for the Mercosur is restricted to remoulded tyres (Item 7 of the judgment summary).

[77] RE 511.961/SP, judgment 17 June 2009, TP, DJe 13 November 2009.

[78] RE 197.917, judgment 24 March 2004, TP, DJ 7 May 2004.

[79] RE 201.819/RJ, judgment 11 October 2005, 2nd T, DJ 27 October 2006.

[80] STF, ADI 3.510/DF, judgment 29 May 2008, TP, DJ 5 June 2008. See above p. 111.

This is obviously not the proper place to present or analyse the most recent constitutional precedents of the Brazilian Supreme Federal Court, even if limited to the most important cases or those with stronger legal impact. I will return to some cases later, since a brief consideration of certain aspects of them can be relevant to empirically support the thesis I am about to reveal.

In Brazil's constitutional case-law, with regard to managing constitutional principles, the proportionality technique, and the balancing model, as well as the use of other argumentation strategies, a persistent problem lies in the fact that the decisions and arguments used to substantiate them tend to be limited to the sub judice case, but do not provide criteria to reduce the 'surprise value' of decisions in a future case in which the same legal identity of the underlying facts is present. Thus, the history begins again with each case, at the mercy of methodological and doctrinal novelties. Precedents to guide future judgments are not built up. In this regard, there is often a lack of clarity when it comes to know the real reason for the decision. It is true that this issue is associated with the very institutional organization of the decision-making procedure in the Supreme Federal Court. Justices present their vote (usually very lengthy) separately, adducing various different arguments and reasons. It is not uncommon that they reach the same results with highly different reasons. The final decision becomes inconsistent in relevant cases: the fact that the operative part of the judgment is agreed upon by the majority or unanimity says nothing about its reasons, since in some cases the arguments adduced by each Justice are incompatible with arguments presented by other Justices. How can one be guided in future cases based on a confusing judgment and occasionally contradictory in its reasons? But the question is not only about this form of voting and writing the decision (which is usually done by the rapporteur or, when he is defeated, by the reviser). There is also little clarity and consistency in the position of the court as a whole and of some judges, with variations from case to case. The case-law, including the consolidated precedents, can obviously be overruled, but that requires some argumentative overburden and transparency in particular, making this shift in direction clear. The malleability with which mitigations are frequent and the 'exception' can become the 'rule' is harmful to the normative force of the constitution and the constitutional self-consistency of law. Such a malleability in certain hyper-politicized situations can serve to accommodate the constitution to the specific interests of the occasional power holder, or even the opposition.

In this respect, it is worth introducing a distinction, reconstructed by Bernstorff based on the American and German debates, between the argumentation style guided by balancing and the categorical argumentation style, which is independent of balancing.[81] Between these two extremes there is, according to him, a continuum of argumentative forms. Along this continuum, he distinguishes 'between ad hoc balancing as the extreme form of argumentation style guided by balancing, on the one hand, and the forms of balancing determined by criteria and definitional balancing, which can also be used, at least potentially, in the categorical style'.[82] Concerning this matter, Bernstorff explains as follows:

> These forms of balancing are a particular way of justifying the establishment of a new bright-line rule for a specific scenario, which can be applied in similar cases in the future. *Definitional* balancing is used to define the scope of a particular right whereas *principled* balancing justifies why, with respect to a specific scenario, the court comes to the conclusion that the infringement of the right can be found legal or illegal. Unlike ad hoc balancing, both forms of reasoning are meant to concretise human rights entitlements beyond the individual case at hand.[83]

He then states more specifically: 'The difference between ad hoc balancing and definitional balancing lies in the degree to which criteria for other cases are generated by balancing processes through judicial standards.'[84] In these terms, to be very attached to the case (by claiming to consider all of its elements), the adoption of the arguments resulting from the ad hoc balancing is always easily contestable in other similar cases.[85] Bernstorff, based on an extensive research including the case-law of both domestic and international courts and bodies, concludes that the more balancing is limited to the consideration of each particular case, that is the more it can be characterized as typical ad hoc balancing, the smaller is the possibility of introducing argumentation forms that serve to protect the 'core' of human and fundamental rights.[86]

[81] Bernstorff (2010) critically examines the precedents of several constitutional and international courts and bodies regarding the protection of constitutional rights and human rights in view of their 'core' ('essential content' or 'core content').

[82] Bernstorff, 2010, 12; see also ibid., 2014, 76 ff. Cf. Aleinikoff, 1987, 948, who had long before warned that '*ad hoc* balancing may undermine the development of stable, knowable principles of law' (ibid.).

[83] Bernstorff, 2014, 76. On 'principled balancing', see Barak, 2012a, 370, 542 ff.; 2012b, 747.

[84] Bernstorff, 2010, 69.

[85] Bernstorff, 2010, 355. He adds (2014, 76): '*Definitional* balancing is one particular option to justify such rule—like concretizations of human rights, which can then be applied to other cases, whereas in a judicial culture of ad hoc balancing each new case would be judged predominantly on the basis of its concrete circumstances.'

[86] Bernstorff, 2010, 364. In turn, Aleinikoff went beyond the criticism of ad hoc balancing, also raising objections to definitional balancing: 'Any gain in certainty it provides comes at the price of reduced

These conceptual observations area of relevant significance in the Brazilian context. With regard to the question of principles and their balancing, there is an ad hoc argumentation style in Brazil's constitutional case-law. Moreover, if the principle-based pattern and the balancing model are adopted in a very malleable and technically inaccurate way, they act as a stimulant for a 'casuistry' with no commitment to the normative force of the constitution and the constitutional self-consistency of the legal system. Ad hoc balancing focuses on short-term or immediate effects, 'neglecting the long-term ones'.[87] In this context of malleability and immediacy, the domination of occasional particularisms can more easily invade the concretization process, undermining the constitutional order case by case. This does not mean that this problem can be attributed simply to the specific intention of judges or authorities participating in the process, nor to a subjective stance oriented to the erosion of the constitution, because it is a complex connection of actions and communications in deficient organizational and institutional structures. However, an appropriate theoretical and doctrinal reflexion on this problem can be useful to detect flaws and suggest alternative solutions, thus contributing to the development and improvement of a more consistent and adequate legal practice in constitutional matters. Just like the legal-constitutional practice conditions its doctrinal or theoretical legal reconstruction, the latter influences and is essential to the improvement of the former.

In regard to the constitutional practice in Brazil, there are four relevant cases with major legal and social impact in which the problematic aspects of the arguments that led to the decision reveal this trend to an ad hoc argumentation model marked by occasional inconsistencies and the abuse of principles. One of the cases is historic in the context of the 'Vaccine Revolt' (Habeas Corpus Appeal No. 2,244, judged on 31 January 1905), which I will take it into account to show that the abuse of principles is not entirely new in our constitutional case-law. Two of the cases were judged under the terms of the 1988 Constitution. My goal is to evince argumentative flaws both between and within them (ADPF No. 130/DF and HC 82.424/RS). Finally, I will consider ADPF No. 54 / DF (termination of pregnancy in case of an anencephalic foetus: abortion or therapeutic anticipation of delivery?), focussing on attorney Luis Roberto Barroso's petition, as well as the Attorney-General of the Republic's opinion.

coherence' (1987, 979). But this relates to the paradox of justice between legal consistency and social adequacy.

[87] See p. 112 above.

During the Brazilian Empire and the early Republic, legal norms were in place to enforce a mandatory vaccination campaign against smallpox, 'but these laws did not thrive, especially those that extended the obligation to all citizens'.[88] President Rodrigues Alves's administration (1902–1906) intended to implement a new law making vaccine against smallpox mandatory; smallpox was the third epidemic that bacteriologist and epidemiologist Osvaldo Cruz had to fight as a public health officer.[89] Law No. 1,551, 5 January 1904, was designed to 'reorganize the Union's hygiene services'. This law was regulated by Decree No. 5,156, 8 March 1904. Subsequently, vaccination was made compulsory directly under the terms of Law No. 1,261, 31 October 1904. This law led to the 'Vaccine Revolt', in which the military schools of what was then the Federal District (Rio de Janeiro) rebelled. Carvalho interprets this 'Revolt' 'as an almost unique example in Brazilian history of a successful popular movement based on the defence of citizen's right not to be treated arbitrarily by the government', maintaining that 'the reason behind the Revolt was the mandatory vaccination' and even praising the resulting interruption of the vaccination campaign. Nevertheless, he makes no direct objection to the fact that 'there is a consensus in historiography that a coup was being prepared by military officers who represented a residue of Floriano Peixoto's Jacobinism'. He only warns that 'the appeal for the regeneration of the Republic, however, was too abstract'.[90] Despite the characteristic arbitrariness of the 'Old Republic' (1899–1930) administrations in their way of implementing vaccination campaign, it is undeniable that the 'Revolt' was closely related to a primary conflict between part of the opposition (militaristic and in favour of a coup) and the government.[91]

Considering this background, we can analyse two episodes in which the issue of constitutional principles is presented in the context of the 'Vaccine Revolt': one of them is of parliamentary nature but with legal features—Rui Barbosa's speech in the Senate on 16 November 1904, addressing the revolt

[88] J.M. Carvalho, 1987, 96. For a historical-critical understanding of vaccination programs during the Empire and the early Republic, pointing to abuses in an effort to implement them, see Chalhoub, 1996.

[89] J.M. Carvalho, 1987, 95 ff. Before that, Osvaldo Cruz had faced yellow fever and the bubonic plague (Carvalho, 1987, 94).

[90] J.M. Carvalho, 1987, 127, 128, 139.

[91] Contemporaneous with and witness to the events, Barbosa (1952, 52–3) points to the political and military exploitation of the 'Revolt', considering 'the people at this time as a victim' (57). Accordingly, in a historical and critical analysis of vaccination programs in the Empire and the early Republic, Chalhoub (1996) emphasizes, in relation to the 'Vaccine Revolt', that 'for a long time, there had already been a suspicion towards the actions of hygiene officials—always supported by the police apparatus—who were promoting disinfection, evictions, and demolitions of slums and poor housing in general, isolating the sick and driving them to the feared hospitals, and—historiography could have added—suppressing popular healing practices' (101). In turn, Sevcenko (1984) stresses that the 'immediate pretext [of the uprising] was the vaccination campaign' and, in that context, 'the health authority was essentially conflated with the police' (8, 79).

of the military schools, the army situation, and the approval of a decree authorizing the declaration of a state of siege;[92] the other is of a judicial nature—the judgment of Habeas Corpus Appeal No. 2,244 by the Brazilian Supreme Federal Court.

In his speech, Rui Barbosa attempted to explain the unconstitutionality of the vaccination campaign.[93] His argument is typically principle-based, pointing to the inadequacy of the means to the ends (reasonableness or, according to the German model, the first criterion of proportionality). On the one hand, he affirmed the intensity of a person's right to protection against state power: 'Just as law forbids human power from invading out consciousness, it also prevents it from penetrating our epidermis. One involves the moral region of thought. The other involves the physiological region the body. These two regions form the impenetrable domain of our personality.'[94] On the other hand, based on the criterion of proportionality, he questioned the suitability of the measure: 'The law could only make the vaccination mandatory in the name of general utility if the vaccine was beyond doubt harmless and beneficial.'[95] Yet, Barbosa started from an absolute concept of scientific truth, maintaining that the defence of the benefits of the vaccine was 'merely an opinion contested by other opinions', falling under the 'category of controversial hypotheses' instead of 'proven fact'.[96] He did not consider (which is understandable in his historical context) that any measure taken in public health cannot rely on an absolute guarantee, but on whatever truth is dominant in the historical context (the truth is historically 'provincial').[97] Barbosa's position was paralysing. He did not take into account data from other vaccination campaigns carried out by Osvaldo Cruz. He overlooked the misery this epidemic caused to scores of individuals among the destitute population of Rio de Janeiro, causing mass deaths. The solution that stemmed from his arguments not only impaired the interests and purposes of a public health policy, but also indirectly affected a large part of the population with respect to life itself.[98] Notwithstanding, his arguments were sustainable ad hoc. Were the vaccine beneficial, only those who were not vaccinated

[92] Barbosa, 1952.
[93] Barbosa, 1952, 47.
[94] Barbosa, 1952, 46.
[95] Barbosa, 1952, 48.
[96] Barbosa, 1952, 45; see also 49.
[97] In this sense, Habermas himself emphasizes: 'Since all real discourses that unfold in time are provincial, we cannot know whether the statements that today–even under approximate ideal conditions–are rationally acceptable will assert themselves in the future against attempts at refutation' (Habermas, 1999, 260).
[98] Note that the mandatory smallpox vaccine was introduced in France in 1903 (J.M. Carvalho, 1987, 177, note 10).

would have assumed the risk of not being immunized (the problem of children combined with the issue of contagion still remained). Apart from this particular aspect, his arguments in favour of the right to personality and individual freedom was problematic for guidance of other cases.

In this context, it is worth presenting a brief analysis of the judgment by the Supreme Court of Habeas Corpus Appeal No. 2,244. In the event, the appeal was endorsed, granting the applicant writ of preventive habeas corpus based on the reasoning that Article 172 of the Regulation approved by Decree No. 5,156, 8 March 1905, was unconstitutional because it violated the principle of separation of powers and especially Article 72.11 of the Brazilian Constitution of 1891. Art. 172 of the Regulation provided as follows: 'Once disinfection is ordered by the health authority, no one may evade it or hinder or prevent its execution, under penalty of a fine of $200 or imprisonment for eight days to one month; the sanitary inspector shall request police assistance for the sanitary operation to be accomplished immediately.'[99] According to the fact pattern, the applicant had 'received the second-time subpoena from a health inspector to vacate his residence' for the purposes of 'disinfection due to yellow fever'. Article 72.11 of the 1891 Constitution—invoked by the Supreme Court—determined: 'The home is the inviolable refuge of the individual; no one may enter it at night without the consent of the dweller, except for the purpose of aiding victims of crimes or disasters, nor during the day, *except in the cases and in the manner prescribed by law*' (emphasis added). It was a provision that included a simple reservation (in the final part) regarding the right to inviolability of the home. In spite of citing Law No. 1,151, 5 January 1904, the Supreme Court maintained that this statute did not authorize the measure and reached a decision on the grounds that, 'since regulating forced entry into citizen's house in express terms of Art. 72.11 BFC is exclusively a legislative function, the National Congress cannot sub-delegate this role to the government without offending the same Federal Constitution, which outlined the scope of each branch of government.'[100]

This excessive emphasis on the separation of powers overlooked Article 1.3 of Law No. 1,151, 5 January 1904, which provided for far more drastic measures:

[99] This provision has to be considered in conjunction with Article 163 of the same Regulation: 'The disinfection of contaminated sites and objects is free and compulsory in all cases of infectious diseases, at the discretion of the health authority.'

[100] The judgment is on the STF website in the area related to historical judgments: http://www.stf.jus.br/portal/cms/verTexto.asp?servico=sobreStfConhecaStfJulgamentoHistorico&page=rhc2244 (accessed on 19 July 2010).

> The executive is authorized to enact the Health Code according to the following bases: ... f) instituting *fines up to two thousand reis ($ 2.000)* as penalties to sanitary infractions, which may be converted into *imprisonment up to a maximum period of three months*, as well as, whether combined or not and even as a preventive measure, seizure and destruction of damaged items or items considered harmful to public health, seizure and sale of animals or objects whose existence in homes is prohibited, revocation of licences, closure and banning of buildings, works and constructions.[101]

Article 72.13 of the 1891 Constitution could be invoked by the Supreme Court: 'With the exception of flagrante delicto, the imprisonment cannot be executed before the indictment against the defendant, except in cases established by law, and with a written order issued by the competent authority.' But this provision did not restrict the legal exception to the judicial authority, as happens in the current constitutional order (Article 5.XI BFC). The Supreme Court could have applied Article 1.3.II.1 of Law No. 1,151/1904, according to which the order of a building's closing has the effect of promoting the '*voluntary or forced* evacuation of tenants within eight days, depending on the urgency' (emphasis added). But this rule referred only to tenants evacuating buildings, not the inviolability of the home for the purpose of disinfection. If we look at Article 1.3.II.2 of that Law, we can confirm its accuracy, since as it determined that the order of building's closing had the effect of making it compulsory for that building 'to be repaired or demolished by its owners within the required period', and 'if they refuse to do so, repairs or demolitions will be carried out at their expense, and in either case the building or land occupied by them will be legally mortgaged as a payment guarantee'.

Based exclusively on the principle of separation of power, the Brazilian Supreme Court not only decided by a majority opinion to grant a 'preventive writ of habeas corpus', but also declared the unconstitutionality of Article 172 of the Regulation approved by Decree No. 5,156/1905. It would be somehow reasonable if the Supreme Court argued that Law No. 1,151/1904 had offended the constitution by over-limiting the inviolability of home or the freedom of movement. The Court could have granted the preventive writ of habeas corpus without declaring the total unconstitutionality of Article 172, as seems to be Justice Pindahiba de Mattos' opinion:

[101] Emphasis added. It should be remarked that Article 1.e of Law No. 1.261, 31 December 1904, which made smallpox vaccination compulsory, relates to this provision, stating that the government should utilize the first part of it 'so as to fulfil the provisions of this law'.

> I have granted the preventive writ of habeas corpus only to protect the applicant from being arrested, for the arrest threat about which he complained does not seem justifiable to me. I do not or did not consider unconstitutional the Law and the Regulation to which the rationale for the decision refers, which I did not accept in this particular point.

In this sense, one could then assert that the unconstitutionality of the provision of the government decree and also the statutory provision was limited to arrest (freedom of locomotion), without preventing forced entry into neglected houses for disinfection aimed at combating the epidemic.[102]

The Supreme Court's decision had paralysing effects on the fight against the epidemic. Despite the abuses in the implementation of disinfection measures (that needed to be controlled by the judiciary), the solution was socially inadequate. Moreover, because the argument was ad hoc and simplified, based only on the violation of the separation of powers by the government regulation, it can be criticized for being constitutionally inconsistent. Thus, according to the decision, only the government acted against the Constitution, not the legislator, although the later issued a statute stablishing measures that were more restrictive to the individual rights in question than the measures set forth by the government decree. In the conflictual context of that time, this may indicate that the game of power between 'government and opposition' acted as a de facto obstacle for making a legally consistent and socially adequate decision.

Taking a historical leap, it seems appropriate to make some observations regarding the judgment of ADPF No. 130/DF, in which the Supreme Court decided by a majority opinion for the total incompatibility between Law No. 5,250, 9 February 1967, which regulated 'the freedom of expression of thought and the freedom of information' (Press Act), and the Constitution. The Court denies its reception by the constitutional order of 1988, and therefore its validity in the current law. The problem that arises first concerns the fact that, in the name of 'self-regulation and social regulation of the press activity', a wide range of media-related issues were left without legal regulation, thus enabling the judiciary to fill in the gaps ad hoc. In fact, the question of the authoritarian origin of this law is relevant in this case.[103] But the reception relates to

[102] It is interesting to note that Article 13(7) of the German Constitution ('Basic Law') establishes a qualified reservation according to which interferences in and restrictions of the inviolability of the home are permissible, pursuant to a law, to 'combat the danger of an epidemic' (see above pp. 66-7).

[103] In this regard, the decision contains the following grounds in relation to the Press Act: 'a) regarding its intertwining commands, at the service of the deceiving logic according to which a range of exceptions is open for each general rule that affirms freedom, so that practically everything is undone; b) regarding the unconcealable practical effect of going beyond a simple government project to achieve

possible provisions and their corresponding norms that are compatible with the democratic regime. The fact that freedom of the press is incompatible with authoritarian regimes is not a convincing argument in this case. Due process of law is also incompatible with authoritarianism, but that alone does not prevent the reception by the 1988 Brazilian Constitution of the Civil Procedure Code, approved in 1973, during the most authoritarian period of the military rule.[104] This solution would only make sense if we rhetorically invoked the self-regulation of conflict settlements in civil society. Likewise, the independence and autonomy of the judiciary are constitutional requirements incompatible with authoritarian regimes, but by no means did the judiciary declare the non-reception of the Judicature Organic Law (Complementary Law No. 35, 14 March 1979) in the name of self-regulation of the organic structure of the judiciary without any statutory demarcation. Thus, one should always check which provisions are compatible with the new order, particularly those that in the aforementioned Press Act could serve to protect citizens against the power of corporations that control the media.

In this regard, it seems worth mentioning the dissenting opinions of Justices Joaquim Barbosa, Ellen Gracie, and Gilmar Mendes, which were partly defeated because they excepted some provisions of the Press Act. Apart from denying the unconstitutionality of Article 1.1, the head provision of Article 2, Article 14, and Article 16.I (the latter allows, in part, for an even greater controversy), J. Barbosa and E. Gracie also rejected the unconstitutionality of Articles 20, 21, and 22 (libel, defamation, and slander crimes). Justice G. Mendes affirmed the constitutionality of Articles 29–36 (right of reply). This is hardly the place to start a discussion on these caveats, but one can at least dispute the constitutional correctness of judicial measures that declare the non-reception of a whole statute based only on the fact that it was issued during an authoritarian context and that its subject is directly related to the scope of protection of a fundamental right of the new constitutional order. The issue of reception has to do with the content. Indeed, it may happen that, by virtue of the interdependence among provisions, the entire content should be rejected as a block. However, such a decision should be well-grounded when it comes to laws that, beyond their unconstitutional restrictions on certain constitutional rights (in this case,

the realization of a power project that will be perpetuated in time, stifling all critical thinking in the country' (Section 10.1 of the judgment summary).

[104] But the same decision determining the non-reception of the Press Act as a whole states that not only the Civil Procedure Code, but also the Criminal Procedure Code and the Criminal Code (both having their origins in the 'New State', i.e. Getúlio Vargas's dictatorship, 1937–1945) applies to 'cases concerning the media' (Section 11 of the judgment summary).

freedom of speech or freedom of the press), also contain provisions for the protection of other constitutional rights.

Overall, this matter involves highly controversial dimensions in a social context marked by the recent dictatorial period, and it is understandable that the very constitutional adjudication has to establish positions against any step backwards in politics. But the majority decision, taken 'in accordance with the rapporteur's opinion', assigns a meaning to freedom of speech that points to ad hoc arguments that are irreconcilable with other decisions made by the Brazilian Supreme Court. It affirms a prima facie precedence of the 'block of rights that give content to the freedom of the press' over the 'block of rights to image, honour, intimacy, and privacy'. Therefore, according to the rapporteur's opinion, 'this precedence, notably in the field of press, concerns a balancing or weighing of values advanced by the constitution itself'.[105] While Justice Carlos Britto was making this argument, he resorted to Ronald Dworkin, Robert Alexy, and Virgílio Afonso da Silva in order to strip the norms protecting freedom of speech and freedom of the press of their character of principle.[106] It is not relevant to discuss here the incompatibility between this argument contained in the opinion followed by the majority and the concepts defined by the invoked authors: is freedom of speech a rule applied in an 'all-or-nothing fashion' or as a 'definitive reason'? The problematic question lies in the sustainability of the argument that prima facie (from an alleged balancing performed by the constitution itself in advance) freedom of speech will always have precedence over image, honour, intimacy, and privacy, that is the 'constitutional precedence is that which prevails in any concrete situation'.[107] The triumph of this argument leads to absurd consequences, regardless whether one starts from the model of a wide or a narrow 'scope' of the constitutional rights. It is somehow odd that an argument claiming to be categorical (irrespective of balancing) has an ad hoc character, not offering criteria to other cases in which the confrontation and the competition between aforementioned constitutional rights reappear.

This judgment brings us back in time to another: the decision of Habeas Corpus No. 82,424/RS (the *Ellwanger* case). Given the complexity of this case, I do not intend to offer a comprehensive analysis, which would require a specific study. I will briefly consider some aspects that are relevant for my critical purposes. The object of the conflict was the criminal classification of the act of

105 Opinion of Justice-Rapporteur Carlos Britto, 'Full Text of the Decision', 50.
106 Opinion of Justice-Rapporteur Carlos Britto, 'Full Text of the Decision', 62.
107 Opinion of Justice-Rapporteur Carlos Britto, 'Full Text of the Decision', 62.

publishing a book with anti-Semitic content as falling under Article 20 of Law No. 7,716, 5 January 1989, amended by Law No. 8,081, 21 September 1990, which provides for a sentence of two to five years in prison for the following crime: 'To practice, induce or incite, through the media or any form of publication, discrimination or prejudice based on race, religion, ethnicity, or national origin.'[108] Moreover, the compatibility of the statutory elements of the crime with the Article 5.XLII of the Federal Constitution (defining racism as 'a non-bailable crime, with no limitation') was discussed. First, it should be noted that in this case—unlike the formulation contained in the judgment of the Press Act, which stated the prima facie precedence of freedom of speech and the freedom of the press over the 'rights to the image, honour, intimacy, and privacy'—it was established that freedom of speech is a 'constitutional guarantee that is not deemed absolute'.[109] Next, the 'precedence of the principles of human dignity and legal equality' was affirmed, expressly being stated—in relation to freedom of speech—that 'an individual right cannot be constituted by protecting unlawful conduct, as with crimes *against the honour*'.[110] It is difficult to reconcile the reasons for this decision with those used in the judgment of the Press Act. In the latter, rights strongly linked with the principle of human dignity must cede prima facie, regardless of the concrete situation, to freedom of speech; according to the former, the balancing was admitted in the concrete case, in which freedom of speech not only ceded to human dignity in general, but also to the protection of honour in particular. These inconsistent understandings of such relevant constitutional rights and norms in cases of great legal and social significance seem to be an indication of an ad hoc reasoning model. It does not take precedents seriously and does not contribute to building up precedents that can serve to settle future cases, failing to reduce the surprise effect of the decisions in question.

Furthermore, although the decision reached in the *Ellwanger* case is sustainable from both an internal (consistency) and an external (adequacy) point of view, several principles were invoked, such as human dignity, legal equality, and non-discrimination, as opposed to freedom of speech, without an in-depth discussion on the freedom of movement and the statutory definition of the crime, which were core issues raised by the claimant. The use of balancing and proportionality models emerged without consistent reflexions, sometimes

108 This provision was amended by Law No. 9,459, 15 May 1997, to read as follows: 'To practice, induce or incite discrimination or prejudice based on race, colour, ethnicity, religion, or national origin. Penalty: imprisonment of one to three years.' See above pp. 105-6.

109 Section 13 of the Judgment summary.

110 Section 14 of the Judgment summary (emphasis added).

leading the balancing of the same principles and constitutional rights to different results.[111] This kind of attitude, which tends to escape to principle-based abstractions instead of delimitating the case, can weaken the convincing or persuasive force of the decision and the arguments. And this force is essential not only to legitimize decisions, but also to give credibility to a constitutional court.

Finally, in order to characterize the dominant constitutional atmosphere, it seems appropriate to comment on a more recent process that was still in progress when the first draft of this work was concluded, the legal and social relevance of which is striking: Claim of Non-Compliance with a Fundamental Precept (ADPF) No. 54, judged on 12 April 2012.[112] This is a famous case dealing with the legal characterization of the interruption of 'pregnancy' in the event of an anencephalic foetus. Because this process was analysed while it was still in progress, the focus will be on the pleadings of two key players for the proper functioning of constitutional jurisdiction: application by the plaintiff's attorney and the first opinion issued by the Attorney-General's Office.

In his application, the attorney and legal scholar Luís Roberto Barroso (who in 2014 became a Justice of the Federal Supreme Court), representing the National Union of Health Workers, argues based mainly on the definition of the crime of abortion in the Brazilian Criminal Code, and thus in terms of legal rules, that 'the anticipation of childbirth in cases of pregnancy with an anencephalic foetus does not characterize abortion as defined in the Criminal Code'.[113] And he rightfully adds: 'It is even possible to pose the question in terms of balancing of goods and values, but this is not technically necessary. The case is of no subsumption of the relevant factual situation under the provisions of the Criminal Code.'[114] But immediately after this statement, he takes a leap to make an abstract argument in the light of the principle of human dignity.[115] He also invokes the principles of legality, liberty, and freedom of choice.[116] Although the general principle of legality (Article 5.II BFC), which involves 'the generic constitutional provision of liberty in Brazilian law',[117] is relevant, it is too distant for a constitutional argument against the criminalization of the conduct

[111] See, for instance, Justice Gilmar Mendes's opinion, 'Full Text of the Decision', 656 ff.; Justice Marco Aurélio Mello's opinion, 'Full Text of the Decision', 895 ff.

[112] STF, ADPF 54, Judgment 12 April 2012, TP, DJe 30 April 2013.

[113] Barroso, 2004, 6 (Section 8 of the application). For a doctrinal exposition, see Barroso, 2007b.

[114] Barroso, 2004, 13 (Section 26 of the application).

[115] Barroso, 2004, 13–15 (Sections 27–30 of the application).

[116] Barroso, 2004, 15–16 (Sections 31–33 of the application).

[117] Barroso, 2004, 15 (Section 31 of the application).

in question. The Federal Constitution (Article 5.XXXIX) expressly provides a more specific rule for the case, the precept of the legality of crimes and punishments: 'there is no crime without a previous law to define it, nor a punishment without a previous legal commination'.[118] Attorney Barroso's reasoning, however, neither considered nor mentioned this provision, which is 'closer' to the case.

In addition, the Barroso's complaint resorts to an interpretation according to the constitution of the provisions of the 1940 Criminal Code that regulate abortion, especially Article 128.[119] This provision relates, however, to the causes for the exclusion of punishability; it does not address the technical classification of the case as abortion. In these terms, introducing the argument of interpretation according to the constitution can, in a way, weaken the main reason presented by Barroso: the factual situation is insufficient to be classified as crime of abortion.

Of course, the attorney's stance requires alternative strategies for convincing and persuading the judges. If there is a strong tendency to argue based on principles in a certain court, it is understandable that one uses rhetorical means that suit this context. However, it seems that the leap to an openly principle-based argument can lead the dispute to a discussion of prima facie rights, thus facilitating alternatives for the opposing party, who can also rely on other principles to be balanced by the judges. The strength of the core argument, oriented to determine the definitive reason or criterion for the decision, is thus dissipated.

In this case, the argument for not classifying the fact as a crime is promising. Let us return to Pontes de Miranda: the fact pattern is insufficient because its 'core' was not constituted for the purpose of fitting to the statutory definition of abortion.[120] Barroso argued very clearly in that direction:

> Commonly known as 'absence of brain', the anomaly imply the absence of all higher functions of the central nervous system—responsible for consciousness, cognition, relational life, communication, affection, and emotion. There are only a few lower functions that partially control breathing, the vasomotor functions, and the spinal cord.[121]

[118] It is irrelevant in this context whether the norm assigned to this provision is a rule (Alexy), a rule-like principle (Aarnio, Larenz), or a principle (the dominant legal language).

[119] Barroso, 2004, 6 and 10 (Sections 9 and 19 of the application).

[120] Regarding the sufficiency of the fact pattern, see Pontes de Miranda, 1974, vol. I, 25–7.

[121] Barroso, 2004, 4 (Paragraph 4 of the Complaint). In this passage, Barroso bases his statement on Diniz and Ribeiro, 2003, 101.

In these terms, there is no *human* foetus, since the neurological support for meaning-building units, for both the inner (consciousness) and social (communication) life, is absent *ab initio*.[122] Although temporary and partial neurological functions related to the life of the body are present, the neurological dimension allowing mental life is not. When arguing with religious people, it could be said: there is a (human) body, but there is no (human) soul. 'And God laughed . . . .'[123]

Unlike Barroso's application, the first statement issued by the Attorney-General's Office regarding the case, through the opinion of Claudio Fonteles, who was the then Attorney-General of the Republic,[124] involves an immersion into a type of principle-overestimating argument that allows for the introduction of any moral and religious valuation into the constitutional debate without any limitation. Initially, and throughout most of his opinion, based on the work of Rui Medeiros,[125] Fonteles criticizes Barroso for using an interpretation according to the constitution.[126] This doctrinal inference leads, in a sense, to a shift in the focus of the issue. Then, in general terms, Fonteles resorted to Article 5 of the Brazilian Federal Constitution ('the inviolability of the right to life'), Article 2 of the Brazilian Civil Code (protection of the unborn child's rights), Article 4.1 of the American Convention on Human Rights (protection of the right to life from the moment of conception) and the preamble to the Convention on the Rights of the Child (special protection of children who lack physical and mental maturity, before and after birth), without developing more specific arguments based on those provisions.[127] Finally, Fonteles rhetorically invoked the 'legal principle of proportionality' and balancing of goods in order to assert the precedence of the 'right to life' over 'the pregnant

[122] Regarding psychic (consciousness) and social (communication) systems, both 'constituted by the production and processing of meaning', as opposed to biological systems, see Luhmann, 1987a, esp. 64 (Engl. trans. 1995, 37).

[123] On this passage from the Talmud, Baba Meza, 59b, in which God laughs when He sees that the legal decision made based on the Torah depends on how God's 'sons' understand the matter, regardless of the interference ad hoc of God's will ('my sons have defeated me, my sons have defeated me'), see Teubner, 1989, 7 (Engl. trans. 1993, 1).

[124] Opinion No. 3,358 (Fonteles, 2004). Subsequently, on 6 July 2009, Opinion No. 6,963-PGR-DD was issued by the acting Attorney-General of the Republic Deborah Duprat Macedo de Brito Pereira endorsing the full merits of ADPF No. 54. On 12 April 2012, the Supreme Federal Court upheld the lawsuit (STF, ADPF 54, judgment 12 April 2012, TP, DJe 30 April 2013). For the purposes of the present study, it is more important to analyse the controversy that arose from former Attorney-General of the Republic Claudio Fonteles's opinion.

[125] Medeiros, 1999, 289–530 (Chapter II), esp. 300–1, 305, 308–10, 312, 314, 316–17, 494–5.

[126] Fonteles, 2004, 2–8 (Sections 4–28 of the Opinion). He departs from the following peremptory statement by Barroso: '*The ultimate goal* is the interpretation according to the constitution of the legal regulation given to abortion by under-constitutional criminal law' (Barroso, 2004, 10, Section 19; Fonteles, 2004, 2, Section 4 (b), emphasis added.

[127] Fonteles, 2004, 9–11 (Sections 30–46 of the Opinion).

woman's right not to feel pain' (to compulsorily go on with the pregnancy).[128] A model of ad hoc balancing without definitional contours is thus presented, which serves more a decision based on the particular preferences of individuals and groups rather than a normative argumentation at the constitutional level of a hyper-complex society in which evaluative preferences vary greatly from group to group.

However, the abuse of principles is patently characterized at the end of the former Attorney-General's opinion.[129] In an 'argumentative turn', he appealed to the principle of solidarity pursuant to Article 3.I of the Brazilian Constitution in order to present the following argument: the claim

> *prevents the possibility of donating organs of the anencephalic baby to so many* other babies who, despite having normal brain development, have serious impairment in the eyes, lungs, kidneys, heart, organs that are *fully healthy in an anencephalic baby*, whose untimely death frustrates the lives of other babies, who are also doomed to die, or to be blind.

Based on this bombastic assertion, Fonteles rhetorically concludes: 'The plaintiff's claim, of course, *goes against the construction of a solidary society* to which so many of us Brazilians aspire, *and being solidary is the effective way of instituting culture and life*.'[130]

Indeed, there is a tendency to turn the principle of solidarity into a panacea for solving all relevant constitutional problems and to use it, thanks to the strong rhetorical appeal that goes with it, to avert ad hoc the application of constitutional rules and principles pertinent to the case, thus concealing the most diverse particularisms. But its invocation in the former Attorney-General's opinion is somewhat nonsensical. The principle of solidarity refers basically to the question of a welfare state. But if we want to give it a broader sense, it is still inconceivable that it might exclude all other constitutional norms pertinent to a case. Organ donation is not legally mandatory in Brazil (even less in the case of stillborn babies' organs). In this respect, Article 5.II of BFC (general right to liberty) applies, to which in this context (of organ donation) a rule can be indirectly assigned as a definitive criterion for the case decision: 'In the absence of a law, no one who delivers a stillborn baby is compelled to donate its organs, with the principle of solidarity being irrelevant in this case.'

[128] Fonteles, 2004, 11 (Sections 47–53 of the Opinion).
[129] Fonteles, 2004, 11–12 (Sections 55–57 of the Opinion).
[130] Fonteles, 2004, 12 (Paragraphs 56–57, emphasis in the original).

Provided this rule is valid, much stronger is the rule that can be attributed to the same constitutional provision for protecting pregnant women with anencephalic foetuses from being compelled by the authorities to wait until the end of the pregnancy to donate the organs of the stillborn baby in the name of the principle of solidarity. Even if there was a law establishing such an obligation, its constitutionality would be difficult to support (but that is another discussion). In summary, the rhetorical invocation of the principle of solidarity by the former Attorney-General of the Republic in ADPF No. 54/DF is an extreme case of abuse of principles in Brazil's recent constitutional practice, but this occurs in a context in which principle-overestimating arguments have enormous significance. While this approach causes some fascination, it stimulates, in general, abuses of principles by ad hoc arguments immediately committed to the particularisms they tend to conceal under the rhetorical cover of the justice that is inherent in the invoked principles.

5

Final Comment

Judge Iolaus

Let us revisit our original metaphor. Just as the mythological narrative elected Iolaus to face the paradox of the Hercules versus Hydra conflict, the constitutional state requires a judge who is able to successfully tackle, in each case, the paradoxical relationship between legal-constitutional rules and principles: neither a (Herculean) Rule-Judge nor a (Hydra-like) Principle-Judge. To use the vocabulary of systems theory, it may be said: it requires a judge able to 'deparadoxize' the circular entanglement between principles and rules in more complex constitutional cases. I call that figure Judge Iolaus.

Judge Iolaus distinguishes himself from Judge Hydra in two aspects. On the one hand, he is not subject, without any direction and guidance, to the power of principles to regenerate uncontrollably in every new situation in the many-headed form in which they appear. He does not change his position ad hoc only to satisfy every new strategy in which principles are invoked. He is not impressed by principle-based rhetoric. Otherwise, he would drown in the lake of principles. On the other hand, Judge Iolaus does not operate in the same manner as Hydra. He does not regenerate, in each case, a new principle in order to cover up his actions in favour of particularistic interests linked with power, money, religion, kinship, friendship, good relations, etc. That means he does not use a principle-based rhetoric to impress those involved in legal disputes nor to conceal a legally inconsistent practice.

However, Judge Iolaus is not to be confused with Judge Hercules (in the sense defined in the introduction). Judge Iolaus does not rigidly hold on rules, preventing law from adequately addressing complex demands of society. He does not place himself in a monological position of intellectual superiority[1] when he invokes his technical-formal arguments. He does not isolate law from its social context. He is always willing to learn from the environment of the legal system. He is not a socially insensitive judge. He is aware of how limited 'his' rules are to solve complex legal disputes.

[1] In the words of Sunstein (2009, 143, 165 ff.), it is possible to say that Iolaus is a judge who does his work with 'judicial humility'.

Constitutionalism and the Paradox of Principles and Rules. Marcelo Neves, Oxford University Press. © Marcelo Neves 2021.
DOI: 10.1093/oso/9780192898746.003.0006

Judge Iolaus does not deny that in certain cases he has to resort to the balancing technique. But he knows that valuable balancing must be treated as a scarce resource: sparingly. He understands that the trivialization of balancing adversely affects constitutional principles, which he takes seriously. He also realizes that balancing has its limits, not getting thrilled by the counterfactual model of optimizing balancing. However, he admits a comparative balancing, considering the different perspectives involved while referencing principles, whereas such perspectives are derived from social systems and individuals or groups. He is also fully aware that ad hoc balancing must be avoided, since it does not lead to the construction of criteria for the solution of future legally identical or similar cases but rather to increased legal insecurity, as it does not contribute to reducing the surprise effect of subsequent decisions. By carefully using the balancing technique, he is guided by a model of definitional balancing, which in turn will orientate the solutions to future cases. For Judge Iolaus, the legal world does not begin with each case.

From another point of view, Judge Iolaus is fully aware that returning to formalism, in which rules comprehensively take over the chain of argumentation, is an under-complex solution to the most problematic constitutional controversies. Although he understands the formalist reaction to the irresponsible principle-overestimating rhetoric and to 'balancing without limits', he discards the formalist path because he perceives that, if it was followed, law would lean towards the rigidity of a crystal, which is incompatible with the flexibility required by a highly complex and contingent social context. But he has a rather special perception. An excessive attachment to balancing techniques could also lead to another type of formalism, in which balancing becomes a value on its own, disconnected from the social reality. It is therefore necessary to seek other paths beyond the formalism of rules and the substantialism of principles and their balancing.[2]

The paradoxical relationship between principles and rules is closely associated with the paradox of justice as a 'contingency formula' that motivates action and communication in the legal sphere.[3] From this perspective, justice has two dimensions: internal justice, which relates to making *legally consistent*

[2] In 1987, Aleinikoff warned that the irony of balancing lies in the fact that while it 'took blinders off judges' eyes and let them openly take into account the connections between constitutional law and the real world', and therefore had 'its merits as a way out of formalism, has itself become rigid and formulaic' (Aleinikoff, 1987, 1005). He concluded: 'Constitutional law is suffering in the age of balancing. It is time to begin the search for new liberating metaphors' (ibid.).

[3] Luhmann, 1993, 214 ff. (Engl. trans. 2004, 211 ff.). Luhmann also refers to contingency formulae in other social systems, such as scarcity in economy, legitimacy in the political system, limitationality in science, and God in religion (1997, vol. 1, 470 (Engl. trans. 2012, 282); 1993, 222 (Engl. trans. 2004, 217)).

decisions (self-reference); and external justice, related to reaching decisions that are *adequately complex for society* (external reference).[4] On the one hand, if it is unable to rely on a legally consistent solution, law loses its rationality. This implies that without a legal system primarily guided by constitutionality, and thus by the constitutional principle of legality, that is, without an 'internal constitutional justice', it is not appropriate to speak of legal rationality in a complex society. Judgments will then be subordinate to various particular factors without any legal and constitutional significance to guide behaviour and stabilize normative expectations. The rationality of law requires, therefore, constitutional consistency. On the other hand, justice as legal rationality implies the social adequacy of law. Of course, this is a difficult issue because in the environment of law there are several conflicting claims to systemic autonomy in conflict. The economic adequacy of law, for example, can have negative impacts on education, the natural environment, art and science, and vice versa. There are also several different moral values and perspectives in the fragmented life-world of today's complex global society.[5] An outcome that appears to be suitable to a group may seem inappropriate to another. And there is no single hegemonic project, neither at the level of functional systems nor on the plane of the life-world.[6] The constitutionally supported social adequacy of law cannot equal, therefore, an appropriate response to specific claims of particular contents, but rather the ability to make possible the non-destructive coexistence of various projects and perspectives, thus leading to the legitimation of constitutionally established procedures in so far as they serve to reorient expectations in the face of law, especially the expectations of those whose claims are rejected by legal decisions.

However, the relationship between internal and external justice is paradoxical. It is impossible to imagine a perfect balance between legal consistency and the social adequacy of law, namely, between internal and external constitutional justice. The justice of the legal system as a contingency formula always carries a motivating orientation of behaviours and expectations that seek this balance, which is always imperfect and defined in each case. On the one hand, a mere constitutional consistency model leads to a socially inadequate formalism. Excessive emphasis on legal and constitutional consistency

[4] Luhmann, 1993, 225–6 (Engl. trans. 2004, 219–20); 1988, 26–5; 1981, 374–418.

[5] I use the term 'life-world' to refer to the dimensions of society that are not structured in terms of functional systems, involving several different values, interests, expectations, and discourses conflicting with each other (Neves, 2000, 99 ff.).

[6] In this regard, Sonja Buckel (2007, 223) points out: 'There is no single project that could dominate the social context, but competing projects, in correspondence with the multiplicity of antagonistic differences.'

may bring about serious problems related to social inadequacy of law, which then loses its ability to reorient normative expectations and thus legitimize itself within society. On the other hand, a mere social adequacy model leads to legally inconsistent realism. In the absence of values, morals, and interests shared congruently in today's hyper-complex society, excessive emphasis on social adequacy contributes to the subordination of law to particular projects with an absolute hegemony claim. In this regard, although the equilibrium between internal and external constitutional justice is always defective, since it can never be fully achieved and depends on the experience of each case, this equilibrium helps to guide those involved in the communications network of the legal system.[7]

In this sense, justice constitutes a paradox. Every contingency formula motivates action and communication while being an experience with something that is missing.[8] For example, legitimacy in democratic politics always involves an opposition that requires changes; scarcity implies values that motivate economic players; God embodies a mystery with the unknowable, which is the basis for religious action and communication; the absence of the beloved is the moment in which love is confirmed, motivating love actions or communications. Justice is also something that is always missing, implying a permanent quest for equilibrium between legal consistency and the social adequacy of legal decisions. Such a paradox can be processed and solved in concrete cases, but it can never be completely transcended because it is a condition for the very existence of functionally differentiated law: transcending the paradox of justice as a contingency formula would mean the end of law as an autonomous social system, leading to a regressive dedifferentiation or giving rise to a 'moral paradise' in which justice is fully realized, just as the end of scarcity as a contingency formula in economy would lead to a 'paradise of abundance', namely the end of the economy.[9]

Judge Iolaus faces the paradox of justice seeking to 'overcome' it in every controversial constitutional case, although he does not make the Herculean claim to eliminate it once and for all.[10] He does not fall unilaterally into the

[7] In the last two paragraphs I resumed arguments already developed in a previous work (Neves, 2009, 63–6 (Engl. trans. 2013, 43–4)).

[8] Luhmann (1993, 220 (Engl. trans. 2004, 216)), by associating the contingency formula to 'the dimension determinacy/indeterminacy', states in turn that he does not refer to 'the actually given (perceived, defined) facts but to other possibilities of dealing with them'.

[9] Neves, 2009, 66 (Engl. trans. 2013, 44).

[10] Of course, paradoxes, which are fundamental to develop communications and to reproduce social systems, are not overcome in a definitive way (cf. e.g. Luhmann, 1997, vol. 2, 969–70 (Engl. trans. 2013, 233)), but the requirement for a legally consistent and socially adequate decision implies the requirement of deparadoxizing justice by legal criteria and programs directed at solving each case.

formalist position of the jurisprudence of concepts, nor does he fall into the realistic approach of the jurisprudence of interests.[11] He understands that, within the chain of legal argumentation, constitutional rules relate primarily to legal concepts and formal arguments, whereas principles process primarily interests and other social variables, being predominantly linked with substantive argumentation. He then seeks a balance between constitutional principles and rules in order to ensure the legal-conceptual consistency and the social adequacy of law. He is aware that this balance is always unstable and contingent because it continually implies openness to other possibilities in future cases. Yet, he attempts to establish definitional criteria to reduce the 'surprise value' of future decisions.

Judge Iolaus can go beyond justice as a contingency formula of the legal system to address constitutional principles and rules as a 'transcendence formula' of law and society.[12] From this perspective, he takes the stance of an observer of society as a whole (being aware that this is a partial position) in order to provide solutions that help avoid the expansion and imperialism of a particular systemic rationality or logic to the detriment of others, therefore preventing society from becoming subject to the empire of money, technology, science, power, religion, and law itself (juridification of society). In this sense, he rejects the absolutizing of rules and principles alike.

One may suppose that Judge Iolaus is just another regulative ideal, but I do not think he is. If we think of paradoxical limits for justice as a contingency (or transcendence) formula, it may be affirmed, to use Derrida's terms, that Judge Iolaus is faced with 'an experience of the impossible'.[13] It follows that in the search for balance between constitutional rules and principles, Judge Iolaus himself is an experience *with the* impossible. However, in order to emphasize the contingency, it is more plausible to conclude that *Judge Iolaus is an experience with the improbable.*

[11] According to Luhmann (1990b, 10), the legal system processes its self-reference by concepts and works on its external reference by interests.

[12] Teubner, 2008 (Engl. trans. 2009).

[13] 'Justice is an experience of the impossible' (Derrida, 1990, 947).

Bibliography

Aarnio, Aulis (1987), *The Rational as Reasonable: A Treatise on Legal Justification* (Dordrecht: Reidel).

Aarnio, Aulis (1990), 'Taking Rules Seriously', in W. Maihofer and G. Sprenger (eds), *Law and the States in the Modern Times: Proceedings of the 14th IVR World Congress in Edinburgh, August 1989* (*ARSP*, *Beiheft* 42, Stuttgart: Franz Steiner), 180–92.

Aarnio, Aulis (1997), *Reason and Authority: A Treatise on the Dynamic Paradigm of Legal Dogmatics* (Aldershot: Ashgate).

Aarnio, Aulis (2011), *Essays on the Doctrinal Study of Law* (Dordrecht: Springer).

Abbagnano, Nicola (1961), *Dizionario di filosofia* (Turin: Unione Tipografico-Editrice Torinese).

Adorno, Theodor W. and Horkheimer, Max (1969), *Dialektik der Aufklärung: Philosophische Fragmente* [1947] (Frankfurt am Main: Fischer).

Alcántara, Manuel and Crespo, Ismael (eds) (1995), *Los Límites de la Consolidación Democrática en América Latina* (Salamanca: Universidad de Salamanca).

Alchourrón, Carlos (1996), 'On Law and Logic', 9 *Ratio Juris*, 331–48.

Aleinikoff, Alexander (1987), 'Constitutional Law in the Age of Balancing', 96 *Yale Law Journal*, 943–1005.

Alexy, Robert (1979), 'Zum Begriff des Rechtsprinzips', in W. Krawietz, K. Opałek, A. Peczenik, and A. Schramm (eds), *Argumentation und Hermeneutik in der Jurisprudenz* (Berlin: Dunker und Humblot), 59–87.

Alexy, Robert (1983), *Theorie der Juristischen Argumentation: Die Theorie des rationalen Diskurses als Theorie der juristischen Begründung* (Frankfurt am Main: Suhrkamp) (Engl. trans. (1989): *A Theory of Legal Argumentation: The Theory of Rational Discourse as Theory of Legal Justification* (Oxford: Oxford University Press)).

Alexy, Robert (1985), 'Rechtsregeln und Rechtsprinzipien', in N. MacCormick, S. Panou, and L.L. Vallauri (eds), *Conditions of Validity and Cognition in Modern Legal Thought* (*ARSP*, Beiheft 25, Stuttgart: Steiner), 13–29.

Alexy, Robert (1986), *Theorie der Grundrechte* (Frankfurt am Main: Suhrkamp) (Engl. trans. (2002): *A Theory of Constitutional Rights* (Oxford: Oxford University Press)).

Alexy, Robert (1995), *Recht, Vernunft, Diskurs: Studien zur Rechtsphilosophie* (Frankfurt am Main: Suhrkamp).

Alexy, Robert (1997), 'Theorie der Grundfreiheiten', in Philosophische Gesellschaft Bad Homburg and Wilfried Hinsch (eds), *Zur Idee des politischen Liberalismus: John Rawls in der Diskussion* (Frankfurt am Main: Suhrkamp), 263–303.

Alexy, Robert (1998), 'Die Institutionalisierung der Menschenrechte im demokratischen Verfassungsstaat', in S. Gosepath and G. Lohmann (eds), *Philosophie der Menschenrechte* (Frankfurt am Main: Suhrkamp), 244–64.

Alexy, Robert (2000), 'Zur Struktur der Rechtsprinzipien', in B. Schilcher, P. Koller, and B.-C. Funk (eds), *Regeln, Prinzipien und Elemente im System des Rechts* (Vienna: Verlag Österreich), 31–52 (Engl. transl. (partial): 'On the Structure of Legal Principles', 13 *Ratio Juris*, 294–304).

Alexy, Robert (2002), 'Postscript', in R. Alexy, *A Theory of Constitutional Rights*, trans. Julian Rivers (Oxford: Oxford University Press), 388–425.

Alexy, Robert (2003a), *On Balancing and Sumbsumption: A Structural Comparison*, 16 *Ratio Juris*, 433–49.

Alexy, Robert (2003b), 'Die Gewichtsformel', in J. Jickeli, P. Kreutz, and D. Reuter (eds), *Gedächtnisschrift für Jürgen Sonnenschein* (Berlin: De Gruyter), 771–92.

Apel, Karl-Otto (1987), 'Interview to Florian Rötzer', in F. Rötzer (ed.), *Denken, das an der Zeit ist* (Frankfurt am Main: Suhrkamp), 52–75.

Aristotle (2003), *Metaphysics*, Books I–IX, Engl. trans. by H. Tredennick, bilingual edition Ancient-Greek/English (Cambridge, MA: Harvard University Press (new impression of the 1933 edition).

Aristotle (2005), *Physics*, Books I–IV, Engl. trans. by P.H. Wicksteed and F.M. Cornford, bilingual edition Ancient Greek/English (Cambridge, MA: Harvard University Press (new impression of the 1957 edition).

Atienza, Manuel and Manero, Juan Ruiz (1998), *A Theory of Legal Sentences* (Dordrecht: Kluwer).

Atlan, Henri (1979), *Entre le cristal et la fumée: Essai sur l'organisation du vivant* (Paris: Seuil).

Atria, Fernando (2001), *On Law and Legal Reasoning* (Oxford: Hart).

Ávila, Humberto (2003), *Teoria dos princípios: da definição à aplicação dos princípios jurídicos*, 2nd edn (São Paulo: Malheiros) (Engl. trans. (2007): *Theory of Legal Principles* (Dordrecht: Springer)).

Ávila, Humberto (2009), '"Neoconstitucionalismo": entre a "ciência do direito" e o "direito da ciência"', 17 *Revista Eletrônica de Direito do Estado*, 19 pages (available at: http// direitodoestado.com.br/rede.asp).

Baker, G.P. (1977), 'Defeasibility and Responsibility', in P.M.S. Hacker and J. Raz (eds), *Law, Morality, and Society: Essays in Honour of H.L.A. Hart* (Oxford: Clarendon Press), 26–57.

Balkin, Jack M. (2009), 'Framework Originalism and the Living Constitution', 103 *Northwestern University Law Review*, 549–614.

Bandeira de Mello, Celso Antônio (1993), *Conteúdo jurídico do princípio da igualdade*, 3rd edn (São Paulo: Malheiros).

Bandeira de Mello, Celso Antônio (2003), *Curso de direito administrativo*, 15th edn (São Paulo: Malheiros).

Bandeira de Mello, Celso Antônio (2006), *Discricionariedade e controle jurisdicional*, 2nd edn, 7th impression (São Paulo: Malheiros).

Barak, Aharon (2012a), *Proportionality: Constitutional Rights and their Limitations*, trans. from the Hebrew by D. Kalir (Cambridge: Cambridge University Press).

Barak, Aharon (2012b), 'Proportionality (2)', in M. Rosenfeld and A. Sajó (eds), *The Oxford Handbook of Comparative Constitutional Law* (Oxford: Oxford University Press), 738–55.

Barbalho U.C., João (1902), *Constituição Federal Brasileira: comentários* (Rio de Janeiro: Litho-Typographia (facsimile impression: Brasília: Senado Federal, 1992)).

Barber, Benjamin R. (1977), 'Die Rechtfertigung der Gerechtigkeit: Probleme der Psychologie, der Politik und der Messung bei Rawls', in O. Höffe (ed.), *Über John Rawls' Theorie der Gerechtigkeit* (Frankfurt am Main: Suhrkamp), 224–58.

Barbosa, Ruy (1932/1934), *Comentários à Constituição Federal Brasileira*, H. Pires (ed.) (São Paulo: Livraria Academica/Saraiva, vol. 1: 1932; vol. II: 1934).

Barbosa, Ruy (1952), 'Revolta das Escolas Militares—Situação do Exército (sessão de 16 de novembro de 1905)', in *Obras completas de Rui Barbosa* (Rio de Janeiro: Ministério da Educação e Saúde), vol. XXXI.1, 41–90.

Barcellos, Ana Paula de (2005), *Ponderação, racionalidade e atividade jurisdicional* (Rio de Janeiro: Renovar).

Barroso, Luís Roberto (1996), *Interpretação e aplicação da Constituição* (São Paulo: Saraiva).

Barroso, Luís Roberto (2004), Petição Inicial da Arguição de Descumprimento de Preceito Fundamental n.º 54, 16 de junho de 2004. Available at: http://www.stf.jus.br/portal/peticaoInicial/verPeticaoInicial.asp?base= ADPF&s1=54&processo=54.

Barroso, Luís Roberto (2006), 'Neoconstitucionalismo e transformações do direito constitucional', in M.M. Barreto Lima and P.A. Menezes de Albuquerque (eds), *Democracia, direito e política: estudos em homenagem a Friedrich Müller* (Florianópolis: Conceito Editorial), 481–92.

Barroso, Luís Roberto (2007a), 'Neoconstitucionalismo e constitucionalização do direito (O triunfo tardio do direito constitucional no Brasil)', in C. Pereira de Souza and D. Sarmento (eds), *A constitucionalização do direito: fundamentos teóricos e aplicações específicas* (Rio de Janeiro: Lumen Juris), 203–49.

Barroso, Luís Roberto (2007b), 'Gestação de fetos anencefálicos e pesquisas com células-tronco: dois temas acerca da vida e da dignidade na Constituição', 7 *Revista Latino-Americana de Estudos Constitucionais* (Belo Horizonte), 571–606.

Barroso, Luís Roberto (2010), *Curso de direito constitucional contemporâneo: os conceitos fundamentais e a construção do novo modelo*, 2nd edn (São Paulo: Saraiva).

Barroso, Luís Roberto and Barcellos, Ana Paula de (2005), 'O começo da história: a nova interpretação constitucional e o papel dos princípios no direito brasileiro', in Virgílio Afonso da Silva (ed.), *Interpretação constitucional* (São Paulo: Malheiros), 271–316.

Barthes, Roland (1964), 'Éléments de sémiologie', 4 *Communications*, 91–135.

Bastos, Aurélio Wander (2005), *Hans Kelsen: Resumo biográfico*—1881–1973, 2nd edn (Rio de Janeiro: Instituto Brasileiro de Pesquisa Jurídica).

Beatty, David M. (2004), *The Ultimate Rule of Law* (Oxford: Oxford University Press).

Benjamin, Walter (1965), 'Zur Kritik der Gewalt', in Walter Benjamin, *Zur Kritik der Gewalt und andere Aufsätze* (Frankfurt am Main: Suhrkamp), 29–65.

Bergel, Jean-Louis (1999), *Thérie Générale du Droit* (Paris: Dalloz).

Bernstorff, Jochen von (2010), *Kerngehalte im Grund- und Menschenrechtsschutz: Eine vergleichendeStudiezurEinschränkbarkeitnationalerundvölkerrechtlicherFreiheitsgarantien* (professorial dissertation (*Habilitation*) at Johann Wolfgang Goethe University, Frankfurt am Main).

Bernstorff, Jochen von (2014), 'Proportionality Without Balancing: Why Judicial Ad Hoc Balancing is Unnecessary and Potentially Detrimental to the Realization of Individual and Collective Self-Determination', in L. Lazarus, C. McCrudden, and N. Bowles (eds), *Reasoning Rights: Comparative Judicial Engagement* (Portland, OR: Hart), 63–86.

Betti, Emilio (1949), *Interpretazione della legge e degli atti giuridici (teoria generale e dogmatica)* (Milan: Giuffrè).

Betti, Emilio (1955), *Teoria Generale della Interpretazione* (Milan: Giuffrè), vol. II.

Blankenburg, Erhard (1977), 'Über die Unwirksamkeit von Gesetzen', 63 *Archiv für Rechts- und Sozialphilosophie*, 31–58.

Bobbio, Norberto (1958), *Teoria della Norma Giuridica*, (Turin: Giappichelli).

Bobbio, Norberto (1960), *Teoria dell'Ordinamento Giuridico* (Turin: Giappichelli).

Böckenförde, Wolfgang (1991), 'Methoden der Verfassungsinterpretation – Bestandaufnahme und Kritik', in W. Böckenförde, *Staat, Verfassung, Demokratie: Studien zur Verfassungstheorie und zum Verfassungsrecht* (Frankfurt am Main: Suhrkamp), 53–89 (first published in *Neue Juristische Wochenschrift–NJW*, 1976).

Böckenförde, Wolfgang (2003), 'Schutzbereich, Eingriff, verfassungsimmanente Schranken. Zur Kritik gegenwärtiger Grundrechtsdogmatik', 42 *Der Staat*, 165–92.

Borowski, Martin (1998), 'Prinzipien als Grundrechtsnormen', 53 *Zeitschrift für öffentliches Recht*, 307–35.

Borowski, Martin (2007), *Grundrechte als Prinzipien*, 2nd edn (Baden-Baden: Nomos).

Bousta, Rhita (2007), 'La "spécificité" du contrôle constitutionnel français de proportionnalité', 4 *Revue Internationale de Droit Comparé*, 859–78.

Bousta, Rhita (2008) 'Une avancée "a minima" (À propos de la décision n.° 2008-562 DC du 21 février 2008)', 121 *Les Petites Affiches*, 17 June 2008, 7–12.

Brugger, Winfried (2000), 'May Government Ever Use Torture? Two Responses from German Law', 48 *American Journal of Comparative Law*, 661–78.

Brunkhorst, Hauke (2002), 'Die unheroische Demokratie – Sozialphilosophische Kontexte der Weimarer Staatsdiskussion', in A. Waschkuhn and A. Thumfarth (eds), *Politisch-kulturelle Zugänge zur Weimarer Staatsdiskussion* (Baden-Baden: Nomos), 81–97.

Buarque de Hollanda, Sérgio (1988), *Raízes do Brasil*, 20th edn (Rio de Janeiro: José Olympio) (1st edn 1936).

Buckel, Sonja (2007), *Subjektivierung und Kohäsion: Zur Rekonstruktion einer materialistischen Theorie des Rechts* (Frankfurt am Main: Velbrück).

Bydlinski, Franz (1996), *System und Prinzipien des Privatrechts* (Vienna: Springer).

Canaris, Claus-Wilhelm (1983), *Systemdenken und Systembegriff in der Jurisprudenz*, 2nd edn (Berlin: Duncker und Humblot).

Canotilho, J.J. Gomes (1994), *Constituição dirigente e vinculação do legislador: contributo para a compreensão das normas constitucionais programáticas* (Coimbra: Coimbra Editora).

Canotilho, J.J. Gomes (1998), *Direito constitucional e teoria da Constituição*, 2nd edn (Coimbra: Almedina).

Carbonell, Miguel (ed.) (2003), *Neoconstitucionalismo(s)* (Madrid: Trotta).

Carbonell, Miguel (ed.) (2007a), *Teoría del neoconstitucionalismo: ensayos escogidos* (Madrid: Trotta).

Carbonell, Miguel (2007b), 'Presentación: el neoconstitucionalismo en su laberinto', in M. Carbonell (ed.), 2007a, 9–12.

Cardozo, Benjamin N. (1991), *The Nature of the Judicial Process* [1921] (New Haven, CT: Yale University Press).

Carnap, Rudolf (1948), *Introduction to Semantics* (Cambridge, MA: Harvard University Press).

Carrió, Genaro R. (1970), *Principios Jurídicos y Positivismo Jurídico* (Buenos Aires: Abeledo-Perrot).

Carrió, Genaro R. (1986), *Notas sobre derecho y lenguaje*, 3rd edn (Buenos Aires: Abeledo-Perrot).

Carvalho, José Murilo de (1987), *Os bestializados: o Rio de Janeiro e a República que não foi*, 3rd edn (São Paulo: Companhia das Letras).

Carvalho, José Murilo de (2011), *A construção da ordem/Teatro de sombras*, 6th edn (Rio de Janeiro: Editora UFRJ/Relume Dumará).

Carvalho, Paulo de Barros (2008), *Direito tributário: linguagem e método* (São Paulo: Noeses).

Chalhoub, Sidney (1996), *Cidade febril: cortiços e epidemias na Corte imperial* (São Paulo: Companhia das Letras).

Chang, Ruth (1997), 'Introduction', in R. Chang (ed.), *Incommensurability, Incomparability, and Practical Reason* (Cambridge, MA: Harvard University Press), 1–34.

Chang, Ruth (2001), 'Against Constitutive Incommensurability or Buying and Selling Friends', 11 *Social, Political, and Legal Philosophy*, 33–60.

Chang, Ruth (2002a), 'Possibility of Parity', 112 *Ethics* 4 (July), 659–88.

Chang, Ruth (2002b), *Making Comparisons Count* (London: Routledge).

Chang, Ruth (2004), 'All Things Considered', 18 *Philosophical Perspectives*, 1–22.

Chang, Ruth (2016), 'Comparativism: The Grounds of Rational Choice' in E. Lord and B. McGuire (eds), *Weighing Reasons* (Oxford: Oxford University Press), 213–40.

Christensen, Ralph (1989), 'Der Richter als Mund des sprechenden Textes. Zur Kritik des gesetzespositivistischen Textmodells' in F. Müller (ed.), *Untersuchungen zur Rechtslinguistik: Interdisziplinäre Studien zu praktischer Semantik und strukturierender Rechtslehre in Grundfragen der juristischen Methodik* (Berlin: Duncker und Humblot), 47–91.

Christensen, Ralph and Fischer-Lescano, Andreas (2007), *Das Ganze des Rechts. Vom hierarchischen zum reflexiven Verständnis deutscher und europäischer Grundrechte* (Berlin: Duncker und Humblot).

Christodoulidis, Emilios (2013), 'The European Court of Justice and "Total Market" Thinking', 14(10) *German Law Journal*, 171–86.

Clérico, Laura (2001), *Die Struktur der Verhältnismäßigkeit* (Baden-Baden: Nomos).

Clève, Clèmerson Merlin and Freire, Alexandre Reis Siqueira (2003), 'Algumas notas sobre colisão de direitos fundamentais', in E.R. Grau and S. Sérvulo da Cunha (eds), *Estudos de direito constitucional em homenagem a José Afonso da Silva* (São Paulo: Malheiros), 231–43.

Comparato, Fábio Konder (1993), 'Igualdade, desigualdades', 1 *Revista Trimestral de Direito Público* (São Paulo), 69–78.

Condillac, Étienne Bonnot de (1831), *La logique ou les premiers développements de l'art de penser* (Paris: L'Imprimerie D'Auguste Delalain).

Conseil Constitutionnel (2008), 'Loi relative à la rétention de sûreté et à la déclaration d'irresponsabilité pénal por cause de trouble mental', 24 *Les Cahiers du Conseil Constitutionnel*, 19–24.

Copi, Irving M. (1961), *Introduction to Logic*, 2nd edn (New York, NY: Macmillan).

Costa Neto, João (2015), 'Rights as trumps and balancing: reconciling the irreconcilable?', 21 *Revista Direito GV* (São Paulo), 159–87.

Crisafulli, Vezio (1939), *I principi costituzionali dell'interpretazione ed applicazione delle leggi* (Padua: CEDAM).

Crisafulli, Vezio (1952), *La costituzione e le sue disposizioni di principi* (Milan: Giuffrè).

Davidson, Donald (1982), 'Rational Animals', 36 *Dialectica* 4, 318–27.

Davidson, Donald (1991), 'Three Varieties of Knowledge', in A.P. Griffiths (ed.), *A. J. Ayer Memorial Essays* (*Royal Institute of Philosophy Supplement* 30) (Cambridge: Cambridge University Press), 153–66.

Del Vecchio, Giorgio (1921), *Sui principi generali del diritto* (Modena: Società Tipográfica Modenese).

Derrida, Jacques (1967), *De la grammatologie* (Paris: Les Éditions de Minuit) (Engl. trans. (1997): *Of Grammatology* (Baltimore, MD: The Johns Hopkins University Press).

Derrida, Jacques (1990), '*Force de loi—Le "Fondement mystique de l'autorité"*'/ 'Force of Law: The "Mystical Foundation of Authority"', 11 *Cardozo Law Review*, 919–1045.

Dicey, A.V. (1982), *Introduction to the Study of the Law of the Constitution*, Indianapolis, IN: Liberty Classics (reprint of the 8th edn, London: Macmillan, 1915).

Dimoulis, Dimitri (2009), 'Neoconstitucionalismo e moralismo jurídico', in D. Sarmento (ed.), *Filosofia e teoria constitucional contemporânea* (Rio de Janeiro: Lumen Juris), 213–27.

Dimoulis, Dimitri and Martins, Leonardo (2007), *Teoria geral dos direitos fundamentais* (São Paulo: Revista dos Tribunais).

Diniz, Débora and Ribeiro, Diaulas Costa (2003), *Aborto por anomalia fetal* (Brasília: Letras Livres).

Dworkin, Ronald (1978), *Taking Rights Seriously*, 2nd impression (corrected) with appendix (London: Duckworth) (1st impression 1977).

Dworkin, Ronald (1985), *A Matter of Principle* (Cambridge, MA: Harvard University Press).

Dworkin, Ronald (1986), *Law's Empire* (Cambridge, MA: Harvard University Press).

Dworkin, Ronald (2000), *Sovereign Virtue: Theory and Practice of Equality* (Cambridge, MA: Harvard University Press).

Dworkin, Ronald (2006a), *Justice in Robes* (Cambridge, MA: Harvard University Press).

Dworkin, Ronald (2006b), *Is Democracy Possible? Principles for a New Political Debate* (Princeton, NJ: Princeton University Press).

Dworkin, Ronald (2011), *Justice for Hedgehogs* (Cambridge, MA: Harvard University Press).

Eckhoff, Torstein and Sundby, Nils Kristian (1988), *Rechtssysteme: Eine systemtheoretische Einführung in die Rechtstheorie* (Berlin: Duncker und Humblot).

Eco, Umberto (1975), *Trattato di semiotica generale*, 12th edn (Milan: Bompiani).

Eder, Klaus (1980), *Die Entstehung staatlich organisierter Gesellschaften: Ein Beitrag zu einer Theorie sozialer Evolution* (Frankfurt am Main: Suhrkamp).

Ely, John Hart (1980), *Democracy and Distrust: A Theory of Judicial Review* (Cambridge, MA: Harvard University Press).

Endicott, Timothy A.O. (2000), *Vagueness in Law* (Oxford: Oxford University Press).

Engisch, Karl (1983), *Einführung in das juristische Denken*, 8th edn (Stuttgart: Kohlhammer) (1st edn 1956).

Eskridge Jr., William N. (2016), *Interpreting Law. A Primer on How to Read Statutes and the Constitution* (St. Paul, MN: Foundation Press).

Esser, Josef (1956), *Grundsatz und Norm in der richterlichen Fortbildung des Privatrechts* (Tübingen: Mohr).

Faoro, Raymundo (1976), *Machado de Assis: a pirâmide e o trapézio*, 2nd edn (São Paulo: Editora Nacional/Secretaria de Cultura, Ciência e Tecnologia do Estado de São Paulo).

Favoreu, Louis (1996), 'La Constitutionalisation du droit', in J.-B. Auby et al. (eds), *L'unité du droit: mélange en hommage à Roland Drago* (Paris: Economica), 25–42.

Ferrajoli, Luigi (2003), 'Pasado y futuro del Estado de derecho', in Miguel Carbonell (ed.), *Neoconstitucionalismo(s)* (Madrid: Trotta), 13–30.

Ferraz Jr., Tércio Sampaio (1980), *Função social da dogmática jurídica* (São Paulo: Revista dos Tribunais).

Ferraz Jr., Tércio Sampaio (1988), *Introdução ao estudo do direito—técnica, decisão, dominação* (São Paulo: Atlas).

Fischer-Lescano, Andreas (2013), 'Systemtheorie als kritische Gesellschaftstheorie', in A. Fischer-Lescano (ed.), *Kritische Systemtheorie: Zur Evolution einer normativen Theorie* (Bielefeld: Transcript Verlag), 13–39.

Fischer-Lescano, Andreas and Teubner, Gunther (2006), *Regime-Kollisionen: Zur Fragmentierung des globalen Rechts* (Frankfurt am Main: Suhrkamp).

Foerster, Heinz von (1993), 'Die Gesetze der Form', in D. Baecker (ed.), *Kalkül der Form* (Frankfurt am Main: Suhrkamp), 9–11.

Fonteles, Cláudio (2004), Parecer no. 3358, do Procurador-Geral da República, na Arguição de Descumprimento de Preceito Fundamental n.º 54, de 18/08/2004. Available at: http://redir.stf.jus.br/estfvisualizadorpub/jsp/consultarprocessoeletronico/ConsultarProcessoEletronico.jsf?seqobjetoincidente=2226954.

Gadamer, Hans-Georg (1990), *Wahrheit und Methode: Grundzüge einer philosophischen Hermeneutik*, 6th edn (Tübingen: Mohr) (1st edn 1960).

Goesel-Le Bihan, Valérie (2001), 'Le contrôle exercé par le Conseil constitutionnel: défense et illustration d'une théorie générale', 45 *Revue Française de Droit Constitutionnel*, 67–83.

Goesel-Le Bihan, Valérie (2007), 'Le contrôle de proportionnalité dans la jurisprudence du Conseil constitutionnel: figures récentes', 70 *Revue Française de Droit Constitutionnel*, 269–95.

Grau, Eros (1996), *La Doppia Destrutturazione del Diritto: una teoria brasiliana sull'interpretazione* (Milan: Unicopli) (Ital. trans. E. Albesano).

Grau, Eros (2009), *Ensaio e discurso sobre a interpretação/aplicação do direito*, 5th edn (São Paulo: Malheiros).

Grimal, Pierre (1951), *Dictionnaire de la mythologie Grecque et romaine* (Paris: Presses Universitaire de France).

Grimm, Dieter (1991), *Die Zukunft der Verfassung* (Frankfurt am Main: Suhrkamp).

Guastini, Riccardo (1992), *Dalle fonti alle norme*, 2nd edn (Turin: Giappichelli).

Guastini, Riccardo (1993), *Le Fonti del diritto e l'interpretazione* (Milan: Giuffrè).

Guastini, Riccardo (1995a), *Il giudice e la legge* (Turin: Giappichelli).

Guastini, Riccardo (1995b), 'Grounds of Unconstitutionality: The Italian Case', 17 *Cardozo Law Review*, 253–67.

Guastini, Riccardo (1998a), *Teoria e Dogmatica delle Fonti* (Milan: Giuffrè).

Guastini, Riccardo (1998b), '"La costituzionalizzazione" dell'ordinamento italiano', 1 *Ragion Pratica* (Milan: Anabasi), 185–206.

Guastini, Riccardo (2010), *Le fonti del diritto: Fondamenti teorici* (Milan: Giuffrè).

Guerra Filho, Willis Santiago (2001), 'Princípio da proporcionalidade e teoria do direito', in E.R. Grau and W.S. Guerra Filho (eds), *Direito constitucional: estudos em homenagem a Paulo Bonavides* (São Paulo: Malheiros), 268–83.

Guerra Filho, Willis Santiago (2005), 'Princípio da proporcionalidade e devido processo legal', in V.A. da Silva (ed.), *Interpretação constitucional* (São Paulo: Malheiros), 255–69.

Guerra Filho, Willis Santiago (2008), 'Sobre o princípio da proporcionalidade', in G. S. Leite (ed.), *Dos princípios constitucionais: considerações em torno das normas principiológicas da Constituição*, 2nd edn (São Paulo: Método), 225–42.

Günther, Klaus (1988), *Der Sinn für Angemessenheit: Anwendungsdiskurse in Moral und Recht*. Frankfurt am Main: Suhrkamp (Engl. trans. (1993): *The Sense of Appropriateness: Application Discourses in Morality and Law*. Albany, NY: State University of New York Press)).

Gusfield, Joseph R. (1986), *Symbolic Crusade: Status Politics and the American Temperance Movement*, 2nd edn (Urbana, IL: University of Illinois Press).

Haba, Enrique P. (1996), 'Standortbestimmung zeitgenössischer Rechtstheorie—Rawls, Dworkin, Habermas und andere Mitglieder der "Heiligen (Rede-) Familie"', in W. Krawietz and G. Preyer (eds), *System der Rechte, demokratischer Rechtsstaat und Diskurstheorie des Rechts nach Jürgen Habermas: Habermas-Sonderheft* (27 *Rechtstheorie* 3) (Berlin: Duncker und Humblot), 277–327.

Haba, Enrique P. (2001), 'Rehabilitación del no-saber en la actual teoría del derecho. El *Bluff* Dworkin', 24 *Doxa—Cuadernos de Filosofía del Derecho*, 165–201.

Häberle, Peter (1962), *Die Wesensgehaltsgarantie des Artikel* 19 *Abs.* 2: *zugleich ein Beitrag zum institutionellen Verständnis der Grundrechte und zur Lehre vom Gesetzesvorbehalt* (Karlsruhe: Müller).

Häberle, Peter (1980), 'Die offene Gesellschaft der Verfassungsinterpreten: Ein Beitrag zur pluralistischen und "prozessualen" Verfassungsinterpretation', in P. Häberle, *Die Verfassung des Pluralismus: Studien zur Verfassungstheorie der offenen Gesellschaft* (Königstein: Athenäum), 79–105 (first published in *Juristische Zeitung*, 1975, 297–305).

Habermas, Jürgen (1971), *Theorie und Praxis: Sozialphilosophische Studien* (Frankfurt am Main: Suhrkamp) (Engl. trans. (1974): *Theory and Practice* (Boston, MA: Beacon Press)).

Habermas, Jürgen (1982a), *Theorie des kommunikativen Handelns*, 2nd edn (Frankfurt am Main: Suhrkamp), 2 vols (Engl trans (1984-1987): *The Theory of Communicative Action* (Boston, MA: Beacon Press, vol. 1, 1984; vol. 2, 1987)).

Habermas, Jürgen (1982b), *Zur Rekonstruktion des Historischen Materialismus*, 3rd edn (Frankfurt am Main: Suhrkamp).

Habermas, Jürgen (1983), *Moralbewußtsein und kommunikatives Handeln* (Frankfurt am Main: Suhrkamp) (Engl. trans. (1990): *Moral Consciousness and Communicative Action* (Cambridge, MA: MIT)).

Habermas, Jürgen (1986), *Vorstudien und Ergänzungen zur Theorie des Kommunikativen Handelns*, 2nd edn (Frankfurt am Main: Suhrkamp).

Habermas, Jürgen (1987), 'Wie ist Legitimität durch Legalität möglich?' 20 *Kritische Justiz*, 1–16.

Habermas, Jürgen (1988), 'Law and Morality' (The Tanner Lectures on Human Values, delivered at Harvard University, 1–2 October 1986), in Sterling M. McMurrin (ed.), *The Tanner Lectures on Human Values*, vol. 8 (Salt Lake City, UT: University of Utah Press), 217–79 (transl. Kenneth Baynes).

Habermas, Jürgen (1991), *Erläuterung zur Diskursethik* (Frankfurt am Main: Suhrkamp).

Habermas, Jürgen (1992), *Faktizität und Geltung: Beiträge zur Diskurstheorie des Rechts und des demokratischen Rechtsstaats* (Frankfurt am Main: Suhrkamp) (Engl trans (1996): *Between Facts and Norms. Contribution to a Discourse Theory of Law and Democracy* (Cambridge, MA: MIT Press)).

Habermas, Jürgen (1996), 'Reply to Symposium Participants, Benjamin N. Cardozo School of Law', 17 *Cardozo Law Review*, 1477–557.

Habermas, Jürgen (1999), *Wahrheit und Rechtfertigung: Philosophische Aufsätze* (Frankfurt am Main: Suhrkamp).

Habermas, Jürgen (2001), *Die Zukunft der menschlichen Natur. Auf dem Weg zu einer liberalen Eugenik* (Frankfurt am Main: Suhrkamp) (Engl. trans. (2003): *The Future of Human Nature* (Cambridge: Polity Press)).

Hage, Jaap C. (1997), *Reasoning with Rules: An Essay on Legal Reasoning and Its Underlying Logic* (Dordrecht: Kluwer).

Hage, Jaap C. (2005), *Studies in Legal Logic* (Dordrecht: Springer).

Hage, Jaap C. and Peczenik, Alexander (2000), 'Law, Morals and Defeasibility', 13 *Ratio Juris*, 305–25.

Hamilton, Marci A. and Schoenbrod, David (1999), 'The Reaffirmation of Proportionality Analysis under Section 5 of the Fourteenth Amendment', 21 *Cardozo Law Review*, 469–92.

Hart, H.L.A. (1949), 'The Ascription of Responsibility and Rights', 49 *Proceedings of the Aristotelian Society*, 171–94.

Hart, H.L.A. (1973), 'Rawls on Liberty and its Priority', 40 *Chicago Law Review*, 534–55.

Hart, H.L.A. (1976), 'Law in the Perspective of Philosophy: 1776-1976', 51 *New York University Law Review*, 538–51.

Hart, H.L.A. (1994), *The Concept of Law*, 2nd edn (Oxford: Clarendon Press).

Hartwig, Matthias (2005), 'Much Ado About Human Rights: The Federal Constitutional Court Confronts the European Court of Human Rights', VI *German Law Journal*, 5, 869–94.

Hauriou, Maurice (1927), *Principios de derecho público y constitucional* 2nd edn (Madrid: Reus) (Spanish trans. C.R. del Castillo).

Hauriou, Maurice (1929), *Précis de droit constitutionnel* (Paris: Recueil Sirey).

Haverkate, Görg (1983), *Rechtsfragen des Leistungsstaates. Verhältnismäßigkeitsgebot und Freiheitsschutz im leistenden Staatshandeln* (Tübingen: Mohr).

Hedigan, John (2007), 'The Princess, the Press and Privacy: Observations on Caroline von Hannover *v.* Germany', in *Liber Amicorum Luzius Wildhaber: Humans Rights—Strasbourg Views / Droit de l'homme—Regards de Strasbourg* (Arlington, VA: Engel), 193–205.

Hegel, G.W.F. (1986), *Grundlinien der Philosophie des Rechts oder Naturrecht und Staatswissenschaft im Grundrisse: mit Hegels eigenhändigen Notizen und den mündlichen Zusätzen* (*Werke* 7) (Frankfurt am Main: Suhrkamp) (1st edn Berlin, 1821) (Engl trans (1991): *Elements of the Philosophy of Right* (Cambridge: Cambridge University Press)).

Hesse, Konrad (1969), *Grundzüge des Verfassungsrechts der Bundesrepublik Deutschland*, 3rd edn (Karlsruhe: Müller) (1st edn 1967).

Hirschberg, Lothar (1981), *Der Grundsatz der Verhältnismäßigkeit* (Göttingen: Schwartz).

Hobbes, Thomas (1991), *Leviathan*, R. Tuck (ed.) (Cambridge: Cambridge University Press) (1st edn London, 1651).

Höffe, Otfried (1977), 'Kritische Einführung in Rawls' Theorie der Gerechtigkeit', in O. Höffe (ed.), *Über John Rawls' Theorie der Gerechtigkeit* (Frankfurt am Main: Suhrkamp), 11–40.

Hoffmann-Riem, Wolfgang (2004), 'Grundrechtsanwendung unter Rationalitätsanspruch: Eine Erwiderung auf Kahls Kritik an neueren Ansätzen in Grundrechtsdogmatik', 43 *Der Staat*, 203–33.

Hoffmeister, Frank (2006), 'Germany: Status of European Convention on Human Rights in Domestic Law', 4 *International Journal of Constitutional Law*, 722–31.

Hofmann, Rainer (2004) 'The German Federal Constitutional Court and Public International Law: New Decisions, New Approaches?' 47 *German Yearbook of International Law*, 9–38.

Hofstadter, Douglas R. (1979), *Gödel, Escher, Bach: An Eternal Golden Braid* (Hassocks: The Harvester Press).

Holländer, Pavel (2007), 'Verhältnismäßigkeitsgrundsatz: Variabilität seiner Struktur', in Jan-Reinard Sieckmann (ed.), *Die Prinzipientheorie der Grundrechte: Studien zur Grundrechtstheorie Robert Alexys* (Baden-Baden: Nomos), 179–95.

Isensee, Josef (1992), 'Verfassungsrecht als "politisches Rechts"', in J. Isensee and P. Kirchhof (eds), *Handbuch des Staatsrechts der Bundesrepublik Deutschland* (Heidelberg: Müller), vol. VII, 103–63.

Ivainer, Théodore (1988), *L'interprétation des faits en droit: essai de mise en perspective cybernétique des 'lumières du magistrat'* (Paris: Librairie Générale de Droit et de Jurisprudence).

Jackson, Vicki C. (2004), 'Being Proportional about Proportionality' (review of David M. Beatty's book *The Ultimate Rule of Law*), 21 *Constitutional Commentary*, 803–59.

Jackson, Vicki C. (2005), 'Constitutional Comparisons: Convergence, Resistance, Engagement', 119 *Harvard Law Review*, 109–28.

Jackson, Wicki C. and Tushnet, Mark (eds) (2018), *Proportionality: New Frontiers, New Challenges* (Cambridge: Cambridge University Press).

Jakab, András (2006), 'Prinzipien', 37 *Rechtstheorie*, 49–65.

Jarass, Hans (1998), 'Die Konstitutionalisierung des Rechts, insbes. durch die Grundrechte', in R. Scholz et al. (eds), *Realitätsprägung durch Verfassungsrecht: Kolloquium aus Anlass des* 80. *Geburtstages von Peter Lerche* (Berlin: Duncker und Humblot), 75–87.

Jeand'Heur, Bernd (1989), 'Gemeinsame Probleme der Sprach- und Rechtswissenschaft aus der Sicht der Strukturierenden Rechtslehre', in F. Müller (ed.), *Untersuchungen zur Rechtslinguistik: Interdisziplinäre Studien zu praktischer Semantik und strukturierender Rechtslehre in Grundfragen der juristischen Methodik* (Berlin: Duncker und Humblot), 17–26.

Jestaedt, Matthias (1999), *Grundrechtsentfaltung im Gesetz: Studien zur Interdependenz von Grundrechtsdogmatik und Rechtsgewinnungstheorie* (Tübingen: Mohr Siebeck).

Jestaedt, Matthias (2002), 'Verfassungsgerichtspositivismus: Die Ohnmacht des Verfassungsgesetzgebers im verfassungsgerichtlichen Jurisdiktionsstaat', in O. Depenheurer, M. Heintzen, M. Jestaedt, and P. Axer (eds), *Nomos und Ethos: Hommage an Josef Isensee zum* 65. *Geburtstag von seinen Schülern* (*Schriften zum Öffentlichen Recht*, vol. 886 (Berlin: Duncker und Humblot)), 183–228.

Jestaedt, Matthias (2007), 'Die Abwägungslehre – ihre Stärken und ihre Schwächen', in O. Depenheurer, M. Heintzen, M. Jestaedt, and P. Axer (eds), *Staat im Wort: Festschrift für Josef Isensee* (Heidelberg: Müller), 253–75 (Engl. trans. (2012): 'The Doctrine of Balancing—its Strengths and Weaknesses', in M. Klatt (ed.), *Institutionalized Reason: The Jurisprudence of Robert Alexy* (Oxford: Oxford University Press), 152–72).

Kahl, Wolfgang (2004), 'Vom weiten Schutzbereich zum engen Gewährleistungsgehalt. Kritik einer neuen Richtung der deutschen Grundrechtsdogmatik', 43 *Der Staat*, 167–202.

Kahn, Paul (1987), 'The Court, the Community and the Judicial Balance: The Jurisprudence of Justice Powell', 97 *The Yale Law Journal*, 1–60.

Kant, Immanuel (1965), *Grundlegung zur Metaphysik der Sitten* [1785], reprint of 3rd edn (Hamburg: Meiner) (Engl. trans. (2012): *Groundwork of the Metaphysics of Morals*, revised edn (Cambridge: Cambridge University Press)).

Kant, Immanuel (1990), *Kritik der reinen Vernunft [1781A/1787B]* 11th edn (Frankfurt am Main: Suhrkamp), 2 vols, W. Weischedel (ed.) (Engl. trans. (1998): *Critique of Pure Reason* (Cambridge: Cambridge University Press)).

Kasprzik, Brigitta (1985), 'Ist die Rechtspositivismusdebatte beendbar? Zur Rechtstheorie Niklas Luhmanns', 16 *Rechtstheorie*, 367–81.

Kellog, Frederic (2010), 'The Abuse of Principle: Analytical Jurisprudence and the Doubtful Case', *Social Science Research Network*, available at: http://papers.ssrn.com/sol3/papers.cfm?abstract_id=1549331 (accessed on 20 July 2010).

Kelsen, Hans (1945), *General Theory of Law and State* (Cambridge, MA: Harvard University Press) (Engl. trans. A. Wedberg).

Kelsen, Hans (1960), *Reine Rechtslehre*, 2nd edn (Vienna: Franz Deuticke) (Engl. trans. (1967): *Pure Theory of Law* (Berkeley, CA: University of California Press).

Klatt, Matthias (ed.) (2012), *Institutionalized Reason: The Jurisprudence of Robert Alexy* (Oxford: Oxford University Press).

Klatt, Mathias and Meister, Moritz (2012a), *The Constitutional Structure of Proportionality* (Oxford: Oxford University Press).

Klatt, Mathias and Meister, Moritz (2012b), 'Verhältnismässigkeit als Universelles Verfassungsprinzip', 51 *Der Staat*, 159–88.

Köbler, Gerhard (2003), *Juristisches Wörterbuch: Für Studium und Ausbildung*, 12th edn (Munich: Franz Vahlen).

Koch, Hans-Joachim (1977), 'Einleitung: Über juristisch-dogmatisches Argumentieren im Staatsrecht', in H.-J. Koch (ed.), *Seminar 'Die juristische Methode im Staatsrecht': Über Grenzen von Verfassungs- und Gesetzesbindung* (Frankfurt am Main: Suhrkamp), 13–157.

Kohlberg, Lawrence (1976), 'Moral Stages and Moralization: The Cognitive-Developmental Approach', in T. Lickona (ed.), *Moral Development and Behavior: Theory, Research, and Social Issues* (New York, NY: Holt, Rinehart and Winston), 31–53.

Kohlberg, Lawrence (1981), 'Appendix. The Six Stages of Moral Judgment', in L. Kohlberg, *The Philosophy of Moral Development: Moral Stages and the Idea of Justice* (*Essays on Moral Development*, vol. I) (New York, NY: Harper & Row), 409–12.

Koskenniemi, Martti (2002), *The Gentle Civilizer of Nations: The Rise and Fall of International Law 1870–1960* (Cambridge: Cambridge University Press).

Kremnitzer, Mordechai, Steiner, Talya, and Lang, Andrej (eds) (2020), *Proportionality in Action: Comparative and Empirical Perspectives on the Judicial Practice* (Cambridge: Cambridge University Press).

Kuhn, Thomas S. (1982), 'Commensurability, Comparability, Communicability', in *Proceeding of the Biennial Meeting of the Philosophy of Science Association*, vol. 2: *Symposia and Invited Papers*, 660–88.

Kuhn, Thomas S. (1996), *The Structure of Scientific Revolutions*, 3rd edn (Chicago, IL: The University of Chicago Press) (first published 1962).

Kumm, Mattias (2007), 'Political Liberalism and the Structure of Rights: On the Place and Limits of the Proportionality Requirement', in G. Pavlakos (ed.), *Law, Rights and Discourse: The Legal Philosophy of Robert Alexy* (Portland, OR: Hart), 131–66.

Kumm, Mattias and Walen Alec D. (2014), 'Human Dignity and Proportionality: Deontic Pluralism in Balancing', in G. Huscrof, B.W. Miller, and G. Webber (eds), *Proportionality and the Rule of Law: Rights, Justification, Reasoning* (Cambridge: Cambridge University Press), 67–89.

Kury, Mário da Gama (2003), *Dicionário de mitologia grega e romana*, 7th edn (Rio de Janeiro: Zahar).

Lacan, Jacques (1966), *Écrits* (Paris: Éditions du Seuil).

Ladeur, Karl-Heinz (1986). '"Prozedurale Rationalität"—Steigerung der Legitimationsfähigkeit oder der Leistungsfähigkeit des Rechtssystems?', 7 *Zeitschrift für Rechtssoziologie*, 265–74.

Ladeur, Karl-Heinz (2004), *Kritik der Abwägung in der Grundrechtsdogmatik* (Tübingen: Mohr).

Ladeur, Karl-Heinz (2007a), 'Schutz von Prominenz als Eigentum—Zur Kritik der *Caroline*-Rechtsprechung des Bundesverfassungsgerichts', in K.-H. Ladeur, *Das Medienrecht und die Ökonomie der Aufmerksamkeit* (Cologne: Halem), 113–46.

Ladeur, Karl-Heinz (2007b), *Der Staat gegen die Gesellschaft: Zur Verteidigung der Rationalität der 'Privatrechtsgesellschaft'* (Tübingen: Mohr).

Ladeur, Karl-Heinz (2014), 'Die transsubjektive Dimension der Grundrechte', in T. Vesting, S. Korioth, and I. Augsberg (eds), *Grundrechte als Phänomene kollektiver Ordnung* (Tübingen: Mohr), 17–38.

Ladeur, Karl-Heinz (2016), *Die Textualität des Rechts: Zur poststrukturalistischen Kritik des Rechts* (Weilerswist: Velbrück).

Ladeur, Karl-Heinz and Augsberg, Ino (2005), 'Auslegungsparadoxien: Zur Theorie und Praxis juristischer Interpretation', 36 *Rechtstheorie*, 143–84.

Lalande, André (ed.) (1968), *Vocabulaire technique et critique de la Philosophie, 12th edn* (Paris: Presses Universitaires de France).

Laporta, Francisco J. (1999), '*Legal Principles: Some Conjectures for Discussion*', in G. Meggle (assisted by Andreas Wojcik) (ed.), *Actions, Norms, Values* (Berlin: Walter de Gruyter), 279–84.

Larenz, Karl (1938), 'Volksgeist und Recht', I *Zeitschrift für deutsche Kulturphilosophie* 34, 39–60.

Larenz, Karl (1969), *Methodenlehre der Rechtswissenschaft*, 2nd edn (Berlin: Springer-Verlag).

Larenz, Karl (1983), *Methodenlehre der Rechtswissenschaft*, 4th edn (Berlin: Springer-Verlag).

Leisner, Walter (1997), *Der Abwägungsstaat – Verhältnismäßigkeit als Gerechtigkeit?* (Berlin: Duncker und Humblot).

Lerche, Peter (1961), *Übermass und Verfassungsrecht: Zur Bindung des Gesetzgebers an die Grundsätze der Verhältnismäßigkeit und der Erforderlichkeit* (Cologne: Carl Heymanns Verlag).

Lerche, Peter (1997), 'Die Verfassung als Quelle von Optimierungsgeboten', in J. Burmeister (ed.), *Verfassungsstaatlichkeit: Festschrift für Klaus Stern zum 65. Geburtstag* (Munich: Beck), 197–209.

Lévi-Strauss, Claude (1973), 'Introduction a l'œuvre de Marcel Mauss', in M. Mauss, *Sociologie et Anthropologie*, 5th edn (Paris: Presses Universitaires de France), vol. I, IX–LII (1st edn 1950).

Locke, John (1980), *Second Treatise of Government*, C.B. Macpherson (ed.) (Indianapolis, IN: Hackett Publishing Company (1st edn 1690).

Loewenstein, Karl (1942), *Brazil under Vargas* (New York, NY: Macmillan).

Loewenstein, Karl (1957), *Political Power and the Governmental Process* (Chicago, IIL: University of Chicago Press).

Luhmann, Niklas (1965), *Grundrechte als Institution: Ein Beitrag zur politischen Soziologie* (Berlin: Duncker und Humblot).

Luhmann, Niklas (1973), *Zweckbegriff und Systemrationalität: Über die Funktion von Zwecken in sozialen Systemen* (Frankfurt am Main: Suhrkamp).

Luhmann, Niklas (1974), *Rechtssystem und Rechtsdogmatik* (Stuttgart: Kohlhammer).

Luhmann, Niklas (1981), *Ausdifferenzierung des Rechts: Beiträge zur Rechtssoziologie und Rechtstheorie* (Frankfurt am Main: Suhrkamp).

Luhmann, Niklas (1983a), 'Die Einheit des Rechtssystems', 14 *Rechtstheorie*, 129–54 (Engl. trans. (1987): 'The Unity of the Legal System', in Gunther Teubner (ed.), *Autopoietic Law: A New Approach to Law and Society* (Berlin: Walter de Gruyter), 12–35).

Luhmann, Niklas (1983b), *Legitimation durch Verfahren* (Frankfurt am Main: Suhrkamp) (1st edn Neuwied: Luchterhand, 1969).

Luhmann, Niklas (1984), 'Reflexive Mechanismen', in N. Luhmann, *Soziologische Aufklärung* 1: *Aufsätze zur Theorie sozialer Systeme*, 5th edn (Opladen: Westdeutscher Verlag), 92–112 (first in 17 *Soziale Welt*, 1966, 1–23).

Luhmann, Niklas (1986a), *Ökologische Kommunikation: Kann die moderne Gesellschaft sich auf ökologische Gefährdungen einstellen?* (Opladen: Westdeutscher Verlag).

Luhmann, Niklas (1986b), 'Die Codierung des Rechtssystems', 17 *Rechtstheorie*, 171–203.

Luhmann, Niklas (1986c), *Die soziologische Beobachtung des Rechts* (Frankfurt am Main: Metzner).

Luhmann, Niklas (1987a), *Soziale Systeme: Grundriß einer allgemeinen Theorie* (Frankfurt am Main: Suhrkamp) (Engl. trans. (2004): *Social Systems* (Standford, CA: Standford University Press)).

Luhmann, Niklas (1987b), *Rechtssoziologie*, 3nd edn (Opladen: Westdeutscher Verlag) (Engl. trans. (2014): *A Sociological Theory of Law*, 2nd edn (Abingdon: Routledge)).

Luhmann, Niklas (1988), 'Positivität als Selbstbestimmtheit des Rechts', 19 *Rechtstheorie*, 11–27.

Luhmann, Niklas (1990a), 'Verfassung als evolutionäre Errungenschaft', 9 *Rechtshistorisches Journal*, 176–220.

Luhmann, Niklas (1990b), 'Interesse und Interessenjurisprudenz im Spannungsfeld von Gesetzgebung und Rechtsprechung', 12 *Zeitschrift für Neuere Rechtsgeschichte*, 1–13.

Luhmann, Niklas (1991), 'Der Gleichheitssatz als Form und als Norm', 77 *Archiv für Rechts- und Sozialphilosophie* (*ARSP*), 435–45.

Luhmann, Niklas (1993), *Das Recht der Gesellschaft* (Frankfurt am Main: Suhrkamp) (Engl. trans. (2004): *Law as a Social System* (Oxford: Oxford University Press)).

Luhmann, Niklas (1997), *Die Gesellschaft der Gesellschaft* (Frankfurt am Main: Suhrkamp), 2 vols (Engl. trans. (2012–2013): *Theory of Society* (Stanford, CA: Stanford University Press, vol. 1, 2012; vol. 2, 2013)).

Luhmann, Niklas (2000a), *Organisation und Entscheidung* (Frankfurt am Main: Suhrkamp).

Luhmann, Niklas (2000b), *Die Politik der Gesellschaft* (Frankfurt am Main: Suhrkamp).

Luhmann, Niklas (2002), *Einführung in die Systemtheorie*, D. Baecker (ed.) (Heidelberg: Carl-Auer-Systeme).

Luhmann, Niklas (2013), *Kontingenz und Recht: Rechtstheorie im interdisziplinären Zusammenhang*, J.F.K. Schmidt (ed.) (Frankfurt am Main: Suhrkamp).

Lyotard, Jean-François (1979), *La condition postmoderne* (Paris: Minuit).

Lyotard, Jean-François (1983), *Le différend* (Paris: Minuit) (Engl. trans. (1988): *The Differend: Phrases in Dispute* (Minneapolis, MN: University of Minnesota Press)).

MacCormick, Neil (1974), '"Principles" of Law', 19 *The Juridical Review: The Law Journal of Scottish Universities* 1, 217–26.

MacCormick, Neil (1995), *Legal Reasoning and Legal Theory* (Oxford: Clarendon Press) (1st edn 1978).

MacCormick, Neil (2005), *Rhetoric and the Rule of Law: A Theory of Legal Reasoning* (Oxford: Oxford University Press).

Maia, Antônio Cavalcanti (2007), 'As transformações dos sistemas jurídicos contemporâneos: apontamentos acerca do neoconstitucionalismo', 2 *Revista do Direito do Estado*, (Rio de Janeiro) 5, 243–65.

Maia, Antônio Cavalcanti (2009), 'Nos vinte anos da carta cidadã: do pós-positivismo ao neoconstitucionalismo', in C.P. Souza Neto, D. Sarmento, and G. Binenbojm (eds), *Vinte anos da Constituição Federal de* 1988 (Rio de Janeiro: Lumen Juris), 117–68.

Mainwaring, Scott, O'Donnell, Guillermo, and Valenzuela, J. Samuel (eds) (1992), *Issues in Democratic Consolidation: The New South American Democracies in Comparative Perspective* (Notre Dame, IN: University of Notre Dame Press).

Martins, Leonardo (2003), 'Proporcionalidade como critério do controle de constitucionalidade: problemas de sua recepção pelo direito e jurisdição constitucional brasileiros', 3 *Cadernos de Direito* (Piracicaba) 5, 15–45.

Mathieu, Betrand and Verpeaux, Michel (eds) (1998), *La constitutionalisation des branches du droit* (Paris: Economica/Aix-en-Provence: Presses Universitaires D'Aix-Marseille).

Maunz, Theodor (1959), *Deutsches Staatsrecht*, 9th edn (Munich: Beck).

Medeiros, Rui (1999), *A decisão de inconstitucionalidade: os autores, o conteúdo e os efeitos da decisão de inconstitucionalidade da lei* (Lisboa: Universidade Católica Editora).

Mendes, Gilmar Ferreira (1999), 'A proporcionalidade na jurisprudência do Supremo Tribunal', in G.F. Mendes, *Direitos fundamentais e controle de constitucionalidade: estudos de direito constitucional*, 2nd edn (São Paulo: Saraiva), 71–87.

Mendes, Gilmar Ferreira (2000), 'O princípio da proporcionalidade na jurisprudência do Supremo Tribunal Federal', 14 *Repertório IOB de jurisprudência: tributário, constitucional e administrativo*, 361–72.

Mendes, Gilmar Ferreira (2011), 'O princípio da proporcionalidade', in G.F. Mendes and P.G.G. Branco, *Curso de direito constitucional*, 6th edn (São Paulo: Saraiva), 246–64.

Métall, Rudolf Aladár (1969), *Hans Kelsen* (Vienna: Deuticke).

Michelman, Frank I. (1986), 'The Supreme Court, 1985 Term—Foreword: Traces of Self-Government', 100 *Harvard Law Review*, 4–77.

Möller, Kai (2007), 'Balancing and the Structure of Constitutional Rights', 5 *International Journal of Constitutional Law*, 453–68.

Möllers, Christoph (2003), 'Verfassunggebende Gewalt—Verfassung—Konstitutionalisierung: Begriff der Verfassung in Europa', in A. von Bogdandy (ed.), *Europäisches Verfassungsrecht: Theoretische und dogmatische Grundzüge* (Berlin: Springer), 1–57.

Möllers, Christoph (2015), *Die Möglichkeit der Normen* (Berlin: Suhrkamp).

Moreira, Eduardo Ribeiro (2008), *Neoconstitucionalismo: a invasão da Constituição* (São Paulo: Método).

Müller, Friedrich (1975), *Recht—Sprache—Gewalt: Elemente einer Verfassungstheorie I* (Berlin: Duncker und Humblot).

Müller, Friedrich (1990a), *Die Positivität der Grundrechte: Fragen einer praktischen Grundrechtsdogmatik*, 2nd edn (Berlin: Duncker und Humblot).

Müller, Friedrich (1990b), *Essais zur Theorie von Recht und Verfassung*, R. Christensen (ed.) (Berlin: Duncker und Humblot).

Müller, Friedrich (1994), *Strukturierende Rechtslehre*, 2nd edn (Berlin: Duncker und Humblot).

Müller, Friedrich (1995), *Juristische Methodik*, 6th edn (Berlin: Duncker und Humblot).

Müller, Jörg Paul (1993), *Demokratische Gerechtigkeit: Eine Studie zur Legitimität rechtlicher und politischer Ordnung* (Munich: Deutscher Taschenbuch Verlag).

Müller, Jörg Paul (1999), *Der politische Mensch—menschliche Politik: Demokratie und Menschenrechte im staatlichen und globalen Kontext* (Basel: Helbing & Lichtenhahn/C.H. Beck).

Neves, Marcelo (1992), *Verfassung und Positivität des Rechts in der peripheren Moderne: Eine theoretische Betrachtung und eine Interpretation des Falls Brasilien* (Berlin: Duncker und Humblot).

Neves, Marcelo (1998), *Symbolische Konstitutionalisierung* (Berlin: Duncker und Humblot).

Neves, Marcelo (2000), *Zwischen Themis und Leviathan: Eine Schwierige Beziehung—Eine Rekonstruktion des demokratischen Rechtsstaates in Auseinandersetzung mit Luhmann und Habermas* (Baden-Baden: Nomos).

Neves, Marcelo (2002), 'Gerechtigkeit und Differenz in einer komplexen Weltgesellschaft', 88 *Archiv für Rechts- und Sozialphilosophie* (ARSP), 323–48.

Neves, Marcelo (2007), 'The symbolic force of human rights', 33 *Philosophy & Social Criticism*, 411–44.

Neves, Marcelo (2009), *Transconstitucionalismo* (São Paulo: WMF Martins Fontes) (Engl. trans. (2013): *Transconstitutionalism* (Oxford: Hart, 2013)).

Neves, Marcelo (2011), 'From Consent to Dissent: The Democratic Constitutional State Beyond Habermas', in C. Ungureanu, K. Günther, and C. Joerges (eds), *Jürgen Habermas* (Aldershot: Ashgate), vol. 1, 99–132.

Neves, Marcelo (2015), 'Ideas in Another Place? Liberal Constitution and the Codification of Private Law at the Turn of the 19th century in Brazil', in T. Duve, T. Keiser, and M.R. Polotto (eds), *Derecho Privado y Modernización: América Latina y Europa en la Primera Mitad del Siglo XX* (Frankfurt am Main: Max Planck Institute for European Legal History), 47–81.

Neves, Marcelo (2018), 'Posfácio à edição brasileira (2018): constitucionalismo periférico 26 anos depois', in Marcelo Neves, *Constituição e direito na modernidade periférica: uma abordagem teórica e uma intepretação do caso brasileiro* (São Paulo: WMF Martins Fontes), 367–435.

Neves, Marcelo (2019), 'O profeta, os discípulos e o "enviado": Comentários a Virgílio Afonso da Silva', 5(1) *Revista de Estudos Institucionais* (Rio de Janeiro), 269–316.

Nozick, Robert (1990), *Anarchy, State, and Utopia* [1974] (Oxford: Blackwell).

O'Donnell, Guillermo (1996), 'Illusions About Consolidation', 7 *Journal of Democracy*, 34–51.

O'Donnell, G., Schmitter, P.C., and Whitehead, L. (eds) (1986), *Transitions from Authoritarian Rule: Latin America* (Baltimore, MD: The Woodrow Wilson International Center for Scholars).

Pareto, Vilfredo (1965), *Manuale di Economia Politica* (Roma: Edizioni Bizzari) (1st edn 1906).

Parsons, Talcott (1968), 'Interaction: Social Interaction, 7 *International Encyclopedia of the Social Sciences* [reimpression 1972], 429–41.

Parsons, Talcott et al. (1951), 'Some Fundamental Categories of the Theory of Action: A General Statement', in T. Parsons and E.A. Shils (eds), *Toward a General Theory of Action* (Cambridge, MA: Harvard University Press) (6th impression 1967), 3–29.

Pascua, José Antonio Ramos (1996), 'Die Grundlage rechtlicher Geltung von Prinzipien – eine Gegenüberstellung von Dworkin und Esser', in G. Orsi K. Seelmann, Stefan Smid, and U. Steinvorth (eds), *Prinzipien des Rechts* (Frankfurt am Main: Lang), 7–33.

Pavlakos, George (ed.) (2007), *Law, Rights and Discourse: The Legal Philosophy of Robert Alexy* (Portland, OR: Hart).

Peczenik, Aleksander (1971), 'Principles of Law. The Search for Legal Theory', 2 *Rechtstheorie*, 17–35.

Peczenik, Aleksander (1989), *On Law and Reason* (Dordrecht: Kluwer).

Perelman, Chaïm (1979), *Logique juridique: nouvelle rhétorique*, 2nd edn (Paris: Dalloz).

Perelman, Chaïm and Olbrechts-Tyteca, Lucie (1988), *Traité de l'Argumentation* (Brussels: Editions de l'Université de Bruxelles).

Piaget, Jean (1972), *Problèmes de Psychologie Génétique* (Paris: Denöel) (Engl. trans. (1973): *The Child and Reality: Problems of Genetic Psychology* (New York, NY: Grossman)).

Piaget, Jean (1995), *Le jugement moral chez l'enfant*, 8th edn (Paris: Presses Universitaires de France) (1st edn 1932) (Engl. trans. (1965): *The Moral Judgment of the Child* (New York, NY: The Free Press)).

Pimenta Bueno, José Antonio (1857), *Direito publico brazileiro e analyse da Constituição do Império* (Rio de Janeiro: Villeneuve).

Pinto Ferreira, Luiz (1971), *Princípios gerais do direito constitucional moderno*. 5th edn (São Paulo: Revista dos Tribunais), vol. 1.

Poincaré, Henri (1905), *La valeur de la Science* (Paris: Flammarion).

Pontes de Miranda, Francisco Cavalcanti (1974), *Tratado de direito privado*, 4th edn (São Paulo: Revista dos Tribunais), vols. I and V.

Poscher, Ralf (2003), *Grundrechte als Abwehrrechte* (Tübingen: Mohr Siebeck).

Pozzolo, Susanna (1998), 'Neoconstitucionalismo y la especificidad de la interpretación constitucional', 21 *Doxa—Cuardernos de Filosofía del Derecho*, 339–53.

Pozzolo, Susanna (2001), *Neocostituzionalismo e positivismo giuridico* (Turin: Giappichelli).

Prakken, Henry and Sartor, Giovanni (2004), 'The Three Faces of Defeasibility in Law', 17 *Ratio Juris*, 118–39.

Quaresma, Regina, Oliveira, Maria Lúcia de Paula, and Riccio de Oliveira, Farlei Martins (eds) (2009), *Neoconstitucionalismo* (Rio de Janeiro: Forense).

Rawls, John (1971), *A Theory of Justice* (Cambridge, MA: Harvard University Press).

Rawls, John (1993), *Political Liberalism* (New York, NY: Columbia University Press).
Raz, Joseph (1972), 'Legal Principles and the Limits of Law', 81 *Yale Law Journal*, 823–54.
Raz, Joseph (1999), *Practical Reason and Norms* (Oxford: Oxford University Press).
Reale, Miguel (1965), *Imperativos da revolução de março* (São Paulo: Martins).
Reale, Miguel (1979), *Teoria tridimensional do direito*, 2nd edn (São Paulo: Saraiva).
Reale, Miguel (1983), 'Momentos decisivos do constitucionalismo brasileiro, 20 *Revista de Informação Legislativa* 77, 57–68.
Rehbinder, Manfred (2000), *Rechtssoziologie*, 4th edn (Munich: Beck).
Reimer, Philip (2013), '"... Und machet zu Jüngern alle Völker"? Von "universellen Verfassungsprinzipien" und der Weltdimension der Prinzipientheorie der Grundrechte', 52 *Der Staat*, 27–57.
Rorty, Richard (1991), 'The Priority of Democracy to Philosophy', in R. Rorty, *Objectivity, Relativism, and Truth: Philosophical Papers I* (Cambridge: Cambridge University Press), 175–96.
Rosenfeld, Michel (1998), 'The Identity of the Constitutional Subject', in P. Goodrich and D.G. Carlson (eds), *Law and the Postmodern Mind: Essays on Psychoanalysis and Jurisprudence* (Ann Arbor, MI: The University of Michigan Press), 143–74.
Ross, W.D. (1930), *The Right and the Good* (Oxford: Oxford University Press).
Rudolf, Beate (2006), 'Council of Europe: Von Hannover *v.* Germany', 4 *International Journal of Constitutional Law*, 533–9.
Russell, Bertrand (1956), *An Inquiry into Meaning and Truth* (London: George Allen and Unwin) (1st edn 1940).
Russell, Bertrand (1994), 'Mathematical Logic as based on the Theory of Types' [1908], B. Russell, *Logic and Knowledge—Essays* 1901–1950 (London: Routledge), 59–102 (1st edn 1956).
Sajó, András and Uitz, Renáta (eds) (2005), *The Constitution in Private Relations: Expanding Constitutionalism* (Utrecht: Eleven International Publishing).
Sampaio Dória, A. de (1926), *Princípios constitucionais* (São Paulo: São Paulo Editora).
Sanchís Pietro, Luís (2000), *Justicia constitucional y derechos fundamentales* (Madrid: Trotta).
Sarlet, Ingo Wolfgang (2000), 'Direitos fundamentais e direito privado: algumas considerações em torno da vinculação dos particulares aos direitos fundamentais', in I.W. Sarlet (ed.), *A constituição concretizada: construindo pontes com o público e o privado* (Porto Alegre: Livraria do Advogado), 107–63.
Sarlet, Ingo Wolfgang (2004), *Dignidade da pessoa humana e direitos fundamentais* (Porto Alegre: Livraria do Advogado).
Sarmento, Daniel (2000), *A ponderação de interesses na Constituição Federal* (Rio de Janeiro: Lumen Juris).
Sarmento, Daniel (2001), 'Os princípios constitucionais e a ponderação de bens', in R.L. Torres (ed.), *Teoria dos direitos fundamentais*, 2nd edn (Rio de Janeiro: Renovar), 35–98.
Sarmento, Daniel (2004), *Direitos fundamentais e relações privadas* (Rio de Janeiro: Lumen Juris).
Sarmento, Daniel (2009), 'O neoconstitucionalismo no Brasil: riscos e possibilidades', in D. Sarmento (ed.), *Filosofia e teoria constitucional contemporânea* (Rio de Janeiro: Lumen Juris), 113–46.
Sartor, Giovanni (1994), 'A Formal Model of Legal Argumentation', 7 *Ratio Juris*, 177–211.
Sartor, Giovanni (2008), 'Syllogism and Defeasibility: a Comment on Neil MacCormick's Rhetoric and the Rule of Law', 59 *Northern Ireland Legal Quarterly*, 21–32.
Saussure, Ferdinand de (1922), *Cours de linguistique générale* (Paris: Payot).

Schauer, Frederick (1991), *Playing by Rules: A Philosophical Examination of Rule-Based Decision-Making in Law and in Life* (Oxford: Clarendon Press).

Schauer, Frederick (1998a), 'On the Supposed Defeasibility of Legal Rules', 51 *Current Legal Problems*, 223–40.

Schauer, Frederick (1998b), 'Formalism', 97 *Yale Law Journal*, 509–48.

Schauer, Frederick (2005), 'The Exceptional First Amendment', in M. Ignatieff (ed.), *American Exceptionalism and Human Rights* (Princeton, NJ: Princeton University Press), 29–56.

Schier, Paulo Ricardo (2007), 'Novos desafios da filtragem constitucional no momento do neoconstitucionalismo', in C.P. Souza Neto and D. Sarmento (eds), *A constitucionalização do direito: fundamentos teóricos e aplicações específicas* (Rio de Janeiro: Lumen Juris), 251–69.

Schlink, Bernhard (1976), *Abwägung im Verfassungsrecht* (Berlin: Duncker und Humblot).

Schlink, Bernhard (2001), 'Der Grundsatz der Verhältnismäßigkeit', in P. Badura and H. Dreier (eds), *Festschrift 50 Jahre Bundesverfassungsgericht*, vol. 2: *Klärung und Fortbildung des Verfassungsrechts* (Tübingen: Mohr Siebeck), 445–65.

Schlink, Bernhard (2012), 'Proportionality (1)', in M. Rosenfeld and A. Sajó (eds), *The Oxford Handbook of Comparative Constitutional Law* (Oxford: Oxford University Press), 718–37.

Schluchter, Wolfgang (1979), *Die Entwicklung des Okzidentalen Rationalismus* (Tübingen: Mohr).

Schmitt, Carl (2014), 'Neue Leitsätze für die Rechtspraxis (1933)', in P.-S. Herlinde and J. Fink (eds), *Rechtfertigung des Unrechts: Das Rechtsdenken im Nationalsozialismus in Originaltexten* (Berlin: Suhrkamp), 513–16.

Schuartz, Luis Fernando (2005), 'Nos limites do possível: "balanceamento" entre princípios jurídicos e o controle de sua adequação na teoria de Robert Alexy', in L.F. Schuartz, *Norma, contingência e racionalidade: estudos preparatórios para uma teoria da decisão jurídica* (Rio de Janeiro: Renovar), 179–228.

Schuartz, Luis Fernando (2009), 'A desconstitucionalização do direito de defesa da concorrência', in C.P. Souza Neto, D. Sarmento, and G. Binenbojm (eds), *Vinte anos da Constituição Federal de 1988* (Rio de Janeiro: Lumen Juris), 761–80.

Schuppert, Gunnar Folke (1998), 'The Constitutionalisation of the Legal Order', in E. Riedel (ed.), *German Reports on Public Law: Presented to the XV International Congress on Comparative Law, Bristol, 26 July to 1 August 1998* (Baden-Baden: Nomos), 18–39.

Schuppert, Gunnar Folke and Bumke, Christian (2000), *Die Konstitutionalisierung der Rechtsordnung: Überlegungen zum Verhältnis von verfassungsrechtlicher Ausstrahlungswirkung und Eigenständigkeit des 'einfachen' Rechts* (Baden-Baden: Nomos).

Schwarz, Roberto (2000), 'As ideias fora do lugar', in R. Schwarz, *Ao vencedor as batatas: forma literária e processo social nos inícios do romance brasileiro*, 4th edn (São Paulo: Duas Cidades/Editora 34), 9–31 (1st edn 1977) (Engl. transl. (1992): 'Misplaced Ideas: Literature and Society in Late-Nineteenth-Century Brazil', in R. Schwarz, *Misplaced Ideas: Essays on Brazilian Culture* (London: Verso), 19–32).

Schwarz, Roberto (2012), 'Por que "ideias fora do lugar"?', in R. Schwarz, *Martinha versus Lucrécia: ensaios e entrevistas* (São Paulo: Companhia das Letras), 165–72.

Searle, John R. (1978), 'Prima Facie Obligations', in J. Raz (ed.), *Practical Reasoning* (Oxford: Oxford University Press), 80–90.

Segato, Rita Laura (2006), 'Antropologia e direitos humanos: *alteridade* e ética no movimento de expansão dos direitos universais', 12 *Mana: Estudos de Antropologia Social* (Rio de Janeiro) 1, 207–36.

Segato, Rita Laura (2011), 'Que cada pueblo teja los hilos de su historia: el pluralismo jurídico en diálogo didáctico con legisladores', in V. Chenaut, M. Gómez, H. Ortiz, and M.T. Sierra (eds), *Justicia y Diversidad en América Latina. Pueblos indígenas ante la globalización* (México, DF: CIESAS), 357–83.

Sevcenko, Nicolau (1984), *A revolta da vacina: mentes insanas em corpos rebeldes* (São Paulo: Brasiliense).

Shapiro, Scott J. (2007), 'The "Hart–Dworkin" Debate: A Short Guide for the Perplexed', in A. Ripstein (ed.), *Ronald Dworkin* (Cambridge: Cambridge University Press), 22–55.

Shapiro, Scott J. (2011), *Legality* (Cambridge, MA: Harvard University Press).

Sieckmann, Jan-Reinhard (1990), *Regelmodelle und Prinzipienmodelle des Rechtssystems* (Baden-Baden: Nomos).

Sieckmann, Jan-Reinhard (1994a), 'Zur Abwägungsfähigkeit von Prinzipien', Supplement (*Beiheft*) 53 *Archiv für Rechts- und Sozialphilosophie*, 203–13.

Sieckmann, Jan-Reinhard (1994b), 'Logische Eigenschaften von Prinzipien', 23 *Rechtstheorie*, 163–89.

Sieckmann, Jan-Reinhard (1997), 'Zur Analyse von Normkonflikten und Normabwägungen', in G. Meggle and A. Mundt (eds) *Analyomen 2: Proceedings of the 2nd Conference 'Perspectives in Analytical Philosophy'* (Berlin: Walter de Gruyter), vol. 3, 349–56.

Sieckmann, Jan-Reinhard (2000), 'Begriff und Struktur von Regeln, Prinzipien und Elementen im Recht', in B. Schilcher, P. Koller, and B.-C. Funk (eds), *Regeln, Prinzipien und Elemente im System des Rechts* (Vienna: Verlag Österreich), 69–82.

Sieckmann, Jan-Reinhard (2006), *El modelo de los principios del derecho* (Bogotá: Universidad Externado de Colombia).

Sieckmann, Jan-Reinhard (ed.) (2007), *Die Prinzipientheorie der Grundrechte: Studien zur Grundrechtstheorie Robert Alexys* (Baden-Baden: Nomos).

Sieckmann, Jan-Reinhard (2009), *Recht als normatives System: Die Prinzipientheorie des Rechts* (Baden-Baden: Nomos).

Silva, José Afonso da (2008), *Aplicabilidade das normas constitucionais*, 7th edn, 2nd impression (São Paulo: Malheiros).

Silva, Virgílio Afonso da (2002a), *Grundrechte und gesetzgeberische Spielräume* (Baden-Baden: Nomos).

Silva, Virgílio Afonso da (2002b), 'O proporcional e o razoável', 798 *Revista dos Tribunais* (São Paulo), 23–50.

Silva, Virgílio Afonso da (2003), 'Princípios e regras: mitos e equívocos acerca de uma distinção', 1 *Revista Latino-Americana de Estudos Constitucionais* (Belo Horizonte), 607–30.

Silva, Virgílio Afonso da (2005), 'Interpretação constitucional e sincretismo metodológico', in V.A. da Silva (ed.), *Interpretação constitucional* (São Paulo: Malheiros), 115–43.

Silva, Virgílio Afonso da (2006), 'O conteúdo essencial dos direitos fundamentais e a eficácia das normas constitucionais', 4 *Revista de Direito do Estado* (Rio de Janeiro), 23–51.

Silva, Virgílio Afonso da (2007), 'Prinzipientheorie, Abwägungskompetenz und Gewaltenteilung', in J.-R. Sieckmann (ed.), *Die Prinzipientheorie der Grundrechte: Studien zur Grundrechtstheorie Robert Alexys* (Baden-Baden: Nomos), 215–30.

Silva, Virgílio Afonso da (2008), *A Constitucionalização do direito: os direitos fundamentais nas relações entre particulares* (São Paulo: Malheiros).

Silva, Virgílio Afonso da (2009), *Direitos fundamentais: conteúdo essencial, restrições e eficácia* (São Paulo: Malheiros).

Silva, Virgílio Afonso da (2010), 'Colisões de direitos fundamentais entre ordem nacional e ordem transnacional', in M. Neves (ed.), *Transnacionalidade do direito: novas perspectivas dos conflitos entre ordens jurídicas* (São Paulo: Quartier Latin), 101–12.

Silva, Virgílio Afonso da (2011), 'Comparing the Incommensurable: Constitutional Principles, Balancing and Rational Decision', 31 *Oxford Journal of Legal Studies*, 273–301.

Silva, Virgílio Afonso da (2016), 'The Brazilian Supreme Court Needs Iolaus: A Reply to Marcelo Neves' Objections to Balancing and Optimization', 2 *Direito.UnB: University of Brasília Law Journal* 1, 96–117.

Simon, Herbert (1955), 'A Behavioral Model of Rational Choice, 69 *The Quarterly Journal of Economics* 1, 99–118.

Simon, Herbert (1956a), 'Rational Choice and the Structure of the Environment', 63 *Psychological Review* 2, 129–38.

Simon, Herbert (1956b), 'A Comparison of Game Theory and Learning Theory', 21 *Psychometrika: a Journal of Quantitative Psychology* 3, 267–72.

Souza Neto, Cláudio Pereira de and Sarmento, Daniel (eds) (2007), *A constitucionalização do direito: fundamentos teóricos e aplicações específicas* (Rio de Janeiro: Lumen Juris).

Spencer Brown, G. (1971), *Laws of Form* (London: George Allen and Unwin) (re-impression of the 1st edn 1969).

Starck, Christian (1992), 'Die Verfassungsauslegung', in J. Isensee and P. Kirchhof (eds), *Handbuch des Staatsrechts der Bundesrepublik Deutschland*, vol. VII (Heidelberg: Müller), 189–229.

Steinmetz, Wilson (2001), *Colisão de direitos fundamentais e princípio da proporcionalidade* (Porto Alegre: Livraria do Advogado).

Steinmetz, Wilson (2004), *A vinculação dos particulares a direitos fundamentais* (São Paulo: Malheiros).

Steinmetz, Wilson (2005), 'Princípio da proporcionalidade e atos de autonomia privada restritivos de direitos fundamentais', in V.A. da Silva (ed.), *Interpretação constitucional* (São Paulo: Malheiros), 11–53.

Streck, Lenio Luiz (2009), 'A crise paradigmática do direito no contexto da resistência positivista ao (neo)constitucionalismo', in C.P. Souza Neto, D. Sarmento, and Gustavo Binenbojm (eds), *Vinte anos da Constituição Federal de* 1988 (Rio de Janeiro: Lumen Juris), 203–28.

Struck, Gerhard (1971), *Topische Jurisprudenz* (Frankfurt am Main: Athenäum).

Summers, Robert S. (1992), 'Form and Substance in Legal Reasoning', in R.S. Summers, *Essays on the Nature of Law and Legal Reasoning* (Berlin: Duncker und Humblot), 138–53.

Sunstein, Cass R. (1994), 'Incommensurability and Valuation in Law', 92 *Michigan Law Review*, 779–861.

Sunstein, Cass R. (1998), 'Practical Reason and Incompletely Theorized Agreements', 51 *Current Legal Problems*, 267–98.

Sunstein, Cass R. (2003), *Why Societies Need Dissent* (Cambridge, MA: Harvard University Press).

Sunstein, Cass R. (2009), *A Constitution of Many Minds: Why the Founding Document Doesn't Mean What It Meant Before* (Princeton, NJ: Princeton University Press).

Sweet Stone, Alec and Mathews, Jud (2008), 'Proportionality Balancing and Global Constitutionalism', 47 *Columbia Journal of Transnational Law*, 72–164.

Sweet Stone, Alec and Mathews, Jud (2019), *Proportionality, Balancing and Constitutional Governance: A Comparative and Global Approach* (Oxford: Oxford University Press).

Tarello, Giovanni (1980), *Interpretazione della legge* (Milan: Giuffrè).

Tarski, Alfred (1935), 'Der Wahrheitsbegriff in den formalisierten Sprachen', 1 *Studia Philosophica*, 261–405.

Teubner, Gunther (1989), *Recht als autopoietisches System* (Frankfurt am Main: Suhrkamp) (Engl. trans. (1993): *Law as an Autopoietic System* (Cambridge, MA: Blackwell)).

Teubner, Gunther (1996a), 'Altera Pars Audiatur: Das Recht in der Kollision anderer Universalitätsansprüche', Supplement (*Beiheft*) 65 *Archiv für Rechts- und Sozialphilosophie*, 199–220.

Teubner, Gunther (1996b), 'De Collisione Discursuum: Communicative Rationalities in Law, Morality, and Politics', 17 *Cardozo Law Review* 4–5, 901–18.

Teubner, Gunther (2008), 'Selbstsubversive Gerechtigkeit: Kontingenz- oder Transzendenzformel des Rechts', 29 *Zeitschrift für Rechtssoziologie*, 9–36. (Engl. transl. (2009): 'Self-subversive Justice: Contingency or Transcendence Formula of Law?', 72 *Modern Law Review*, 1–23).

Teubner, Gunther (2012), *Verfassungsfragmente: gesellschaftlicher Konstitutionalismus in der Globalisierung* (Berlin: Suhrkamp) (Engl trans (2012): *Constitutional Fragments: Societal Constitutionalism and Globalization* (Oxford: Oxford University Press)).

Thomas, Tracy (2007), 'Proportionality and the Supreme Court's Jurisprudence of Remedies', 59 *Hastings Law Journal*, 73–135.

Tönnies, Ferdinand (1979), *Gemeinschaft und Gesellschaft: Grundbegriffe der reinen Soziologie* (Darmstadt: Wissenschaftliche Buchgesellschaft) (re-impression of the 8th edn 1935).

Torres, Ricardo Lobo (2000), 'Da ponderação de interesses ao princípio da ponderação', in Urbano Zilles (ed.), *Miguel Reale: estudos em homenagem a seus* 90 *anos* (Porto Alegre: Edipucrs), 643–51.

Tur, Richard H.S. (2001), 'Defeasibilism', 21 *Oxford Journal of Legal Studies*, 355–68.

Tushnet, Mark (2008), *Weak Courts, Strong Rights: Judicial Review and Social Welfare Rights in Comparative Constitutional Law* (Princeton, NJ: Princeton University Press).

Vale, André Rufino do (2009), *Estrutura das normas de direitos fundamentais: Repensando a distinção entre regras, princípios e valores* (São Paulo: Saraiva/Brasília: IDP).

Venit, Marjorie Susan (1989), 'Heracles and the Hydra in Athens in the First Half of the Sixth Century B.C.', 58 *Hesperia: The Journal of the American School of Classical Studies at Athens* 1, 99–113.

Von Wright, Georg Henrik (1963), *Norm and Action: A Logical Enquiry* (London: Routledge & Kegan Paul).

Von Wright, Georg Henrik (1994a), 'Sein und Sollen', in G.H. von Wright, *Normen, Werte und Handlungen* (Frankfurt am Main: Suhrkamp), 19–43.

Von Wright, Georg Henrik (1994b), 'Rationalität: Mittel und Zwecke', in G.H. von Wright, *Normen, Werte und Handlungen* (Frankfurt am Main: Suhrkamp), 123–38.

Wahl, Rainer (1981), 'Der Vorrang der Verfassung', 20 *Der Staat*, 485–516.

Wahl, Rainer (2007), 'Das Verhältnis des EMRK zum nationalen Recht—Die Relevanz unterschiedlicher Entwicklungsphase', in S. Breitenmoser, B. Ehrenzeller, and M. Sassòli (eds) *Human Rights, Democracy and the Rule of Law: Liber amicorum Luzius Wildhaber* (Zurich: Dike/Baden-Baden: Nomos), 865–94.

Waldron, Jeremy (1994), 'Fake Incommensurability: A Response to Professor Schauer', 45 *Hastings Law Journal*, 813–24.

Waldron, Jeremy (2005), 'Foreign Law and the Modern *Ius Gentium*', 119 *Harvard Law Review*, 129–47.

Walzer, Michael (1983), *Spheres of Justice: A Defense of Pluralism and Equality* (New York, NY: Basic Books).

Walzer, Michael (1998), 'Vorwort zur deutschen Ausgabe', in M. Walzer, *Sphären der Gerechtigkeit: Ein Plädoyer für Pluralität und Gleichheit* (Frankfurt am Main: Suhrkamp), 11–4 (German trans. by C. Offe).

Warat, Luis Alberto (1972), *Semiótica y derecho* (Buenos Aires: Eikón).

Warat, Luis Alberto (1979), *Mitos e teorias na interpretação da lei* (Porto Alegre: Síntese).

Warat, Luis Alberto (1984), *O direito e sua linguagem*, assisted by L.S. Rocha and G.G. Cittadino (Porto Alegre: Fabris).

Webber, Grégoire C.N. (2010), 'Proportionality, Balancing, and the Cult of Constitutional Rights Scholarship', 23 *Canadian Journal of Law and Jurisprudence*, 179–202.

Weber, Max (1924), *Wirtschaftsgeschichte: Abriss der universalen Sozial- und Wirtschaftsgeschichte*, 2nd edn (Munich/Leipzig: Duncker und Humblot) (Engl. trans. (1961): *General Economic History* (New York, NY: Collier Books)).

Weber, Max (1968a), 'Idealtypus, Handlungsstruktur und Verhaltensinterpretation (Auszüge)', in M. Weber, *Methodologische Schriften*, J. Winckelmann (ed.) (Frankfurt am Main: Fischer), 65–167.

Weber, Max (1968b), 'Die drei reinen Typen der legitimen Herrschaft', in M. Weber, *Methodologische Schriften*, J. Winckelmann (ed.) (Frankfurt am Main: Fischer), 215–28 (first published in *Preußische Jahrbücher*, vol. 187, 1922).

Weber, Max (1973), 'Die "Objektivität" sozialwissenschaftlicher und sozialpolitischer Erkenntnis', in M. Weber, *Gesammelte Aufsätze zur Wissenschaftslehre*, J. Winckelmann (ed.), 4th edn (Tübingen: Mohr), 146–214 (first published in *Archiv für Sozialwissenschaft und Sozialpolitik*, vol. 19, 1904) (Engl. trans. (1949): '"Objectivity" in Social Science and Social Policy', in M. Weber, *The Methodology of the Social Sciences* (New York, NY: The Free Press), 50–112.

Weber, Max (1985), *Wirtschaft und Gesellschaft: Grundriß der verstehenden Soziologie*, J. Winckelmann (ed.), 5th edn (Tübingen: Mohr) (1st edn 1922) (Engl. trans. (1968): *Economy and Society: Outline of Interpretive Sociology* (New York, NY: Bedminster Press), 3 vols).

Weinberger, Ota (1999), '*Prima Facie* Ought: A Logical and Methodological Enquiry', 12 *Ratio Juris*, 239–51.

Welsch, Wolfgang (1996), *Vernunft: Die zeitgenössische Vernunftkritik und das Konzept der transversalen Vernunft*, 2nd edn (Frankfurt am Main: Suhrkamp).

Yowell, Paul (2014), 'Proportionality in United States Constitutional Law', in L. Lazarus, C. McCrudden, and N. Bowles (eds), *Reasoning Rights: Comparative Judicial Engagement* (Portland, OR: Hart), 87–114.

Zoller, Elisabeth (2003), 'Congruence and Proportionality for Congressional Enforcement Powers: Cosmetic Change or Velvet Revolution?', 78 *Indiana Law Journal*, 567–86.

Zucca, Lorenzo (2008), Conflicts of Fundamental Rights as Constitutional Dilemmas, in E. Brems (ed.), *Conflicts between Fundamental Rights* (Antwerp: Intersentia), 19–37.

Index

For the benefit of digital users, indexed terms that span two pages (e.g., 52–53) may, on occasion, appear on only one of those pages.